תכונה טובה
ואוהב חסד ולכן
מוגדר

A CHASSIDIC JOURNEY

A CHASSIDIC JOURNEY

The Polish Chassidic Dynasties of Lublin, Lelov, Nikolsburg and Boston

FELDHEIM PUBLISHERS
JERUSALEM NEW YORK

Based on *Shalsheles Boston*
by Meir Valach, published in Hebrew
by Mosdos Boston (Jerusalem 1994),
as translated by Eliezer Shore.

ISBN 1-58330-568-8
First published 2002
Copyright © 2002 by R. Levi Yitzchok Horowitz

All rights reserved.
No part of this publication may be translated,
reproduced, stored in a retrieval system or transmitted,
in any form or by any means, electronic, mechanical,
photocopying, recording, or otherwise,
without permission in writing from the publishers.

FELDHEIM PUBLISHERS
POB 35002 / Jerusalem, Israel
202 Airport Executive Park, Nanuet, NY 10954

www.feldheim.com

Printed in Israel

This book is dedicated to
Martin Roth
(Elimelech ben Zvi Hirsh ע״ה)

who altered the world with simple acts of kindness.

*When visiting the sick, helping the elderly,
even greeting strangers, he demonstrated an
understanding of human dignity.
This sensitivity, coupled with humility and a
wholehearted love of people, was a powerful* תיקון עולם.

אי״ה, his recognition of the צלם א-לוקים *in every person
and his* גמילות חסדים *that naturally followed,
will continue to better Hashem's world
through his children and grandchildren,
who were privileged to learn from his example.*

*Dedicated by his children,
friends of the Bostoner Rebbe, shlita,*
Robert (Reuven) and Joan (Esther) Roth

In loving memory of

The Bostoner Rebbetzin
Raichel Horowitz, A"H

whose passing on 16 Tammuz 5762 (16 June 2002) was mourned by the many hundreds of families, from all walks of life, whose lives were transformed by her warm smile, parental concern, sage advice and enduring kindness.

A woman of inconceivable strength, selflessness and self-sacrifice, she unhesitatingly dedicated her entire life to helping others.

Combining rare nobility, unfeigned friendliness and super-human effort, she modestly gave new meaning to the lives of future generations of Jews, both within and outside of the Bostoner Chassidic community.

The descendant of great Rebbeim and the devoted wife and dedicated partner of the Bostoner Rebbe,

R. Levi Yitzchok Horowitz, shlita,
she left her many children, grandchildren, great-grandchildren, Chassidim and friends an inspiring legacy of service and love.
May her memory be a blessing.

Dedicated by Robert and Joan Roth

Foreword

by the Bostoner Rebbe, shlita

FIRE GIVES BOTH WARMTH and light. The same is true of the spiritual fire of Chassidus that began with the Ba'al Shem Tov and has — in our own family — been passed down by our holy ancestors from the Chassidic dynasties of Lelov, Nikolsburg and Boston. It is thus with great joy that we commend this book to our dear friends.

What can we say about such tzaddikim as my holy father, the first Bostoner Rebbe, *zt"l*? They concealed their spiritual achievements with all their might. How can we fully appreciate their greatness, when only their outermost aspects were ever revealed?

As a boy, I heard many Chassidic stories from both my parents, stories which have inspired me throughout my life. Many are included here; and I hope they will inspire you as well. "A son honors his father, and a servant his master" (*Malachi* 1:6). That is, if a son honors his father, a tzaddik, by relating stories of his life, then the servants of Hashem, who read the stories, will be inspired to honor their Master.

In the case of my father, the few quoted examples of his Torah thoughts are but a drop from the ocean of his creativity. He had a large book filled with complex insightful *chiddushim*, which he refused to publish during his life and which Hashem saw fit to hide after his passing. A man of two worlds, much of my father's life was spent in the study-halls of Jerusalem; but he also played a leading role in establishing Torah Judaism in America in the early part of the last century. Although he never successfully returned to Jerusalem, he did bring something of Jerusalem to his Boston home. All that we have accomplished since his passing is merely a continuation of his endeavors.

In our family, Chassidus has journeyed from Poland to Eretz Yisrael to America and back again. But it has always remained, at its core, the same: a unique way of binding all Jews together, to each other and to our Father in Heaven.

With gratitude we welcome the publication of these stories about the great Chassidic leaders of the past. It is an obligation to make known their holy ways, that our fellow Jews may "hear and learn, and fear Hashem your G-d, and observe to do all the words of this Torah" (*Devarim* 31:12).

Jerusalem 5762

Contents

One:
The Seer of Lublin 1

Two:
Reb Dovid of Lelov 19

Three:
Love of Israel 27

Four:
Torah and Avodah 47

Five:
The End of an Era 63

Six:
Reb Moshe of Lelov 75

Seven:
The Journey to the Holy Land 85

Eight:
Reb Elazar Menachem Mendel 103

Nine:
Reb Dovid'l Biderman 119

Ten:
The Family Horowitz 131

Eleven:
Reb Shmuel Shmelke of Nikolsburg 141

Twelve:
Rabbi Pinchas Dovid haLevi Horowitz 159

Thirteen:
Boston 181

Fourteen:
A Passion for Mitzvos 201

Fifteen:
Journeys 219

Sixteen:
Boston in New York 235

Seventeen:
The Chain Continues 245

Genealogy 257

Selected Sources 259

Glossary 261

A CHASSIDIC JOURNEY

ONE
The Seer of Lublin

The Origins of Polish Chassidus

First there was the darkness. The poverty and persecution of ordinary Jews in the small towns of 16th to 18th century Poland often defies description. The false Messianic movements of the Sabbatians and Frankists only increased the depression of a dispersed nation near despair. Then rumors spread of a new light being lit in the Carpathian Mountains to the south.

The holy Ba'al Shem Tov had revealed himself; and under his successor, Reb Dov Baer, the holy Maggid of Mezritch, the Chassidic brotherhood soon became a Chassidic movement. Chassidus quickly spread throughout Eastern Europe. Greeted with both suspicion and zeal, it unleashed the holy fire in every Jew and brought him closer to his Maker. In short, it was a force to be reckoned with.

On the soil of Poland, the intense inner life of Chassidism found a unique outward expression for over 200 years, a period roughly extending from the American Revolution to World War II. Characterized by fiery enthusiasm, simplicity, humility and communal warmth, the tightly knit Chassidic brotherhoods were held together by a chain of outstanding spiritual leaders, or Rebbes.

A CHASSIDIC JOURNEY

The Ba'al Shem Tov, zt"l, founded the Chassidic movement about 275 years ago. Here, Reb Levi Yitzchok Horowitz, shlita, the Bostoner Rebbe, prays at his kever (grave) in Mezhibuzh.

The first major Polish Rebbe, the Rebbe Reb Elimelech of Lyzhansk (1717–1787), was a disciple of the Maggid of Mezritch. His main disciple, Reb Yaakov Yitzchok Horowitz, the Seer (*Chozeh*) of Lublin, in turn, raised a whole generation of Rebbes who spread out, often in dazzling variety, to serve the far-flung, rapidly growing Chassidic communities of Poland, and beyond. Each of these began their own chain of spiritual giants whose dynasties and influence continue to this day.

The stories in this book, culled from many sources, focus on just one such chain, beginning with the Seer and his disciple, Reb Dovid of Lelov, and continuing generation after generation, intertwining again and again with other chains, to form important Chassidic dynasties in Europe, America and Eretz Yisrael.

The title page of the first edition of the Noam Elimelech, written by the Rebbe Reb Elimelech of Lyzhansk, zt"l, the leader of Polish Chassidus in his generation.

The Seer and the Maggid

Although quite young, Reb Yaakov Yitzchok did have an opportunity to personally study under the Maggid of Mezritch, who was well aware of the Seer's exceptional spiritual talents.

On his first Shabbos visit, so one story goes, the young Reb Yaakov Yitzchok walked into the busy kitchen of the Maggid's court on Friday afternoon. Picking up a piece of raw fish, he salted it and put it back on the table, to be tossed into the huge steaming cauldron with hundreds of similar servings. "I always help make the piece of fish I am served on Shabbos," he said with utter seriousness.

Reb Shneur Zalman of Liadi, one of the Maggid's senior disciples and later the first Lubavitcher Rebbe, was present at the time. He was shocked by the young man's impudence. How could he be so sure that he would get that particular piece of fish out of the hundreds of pieces served? Before the piece of fish went into the pot, Reb Zalman secretly tied a small piece of red thread through it. In it went and, hours later, the pot was emptied onto platters, to be served at the Maggid's *tisch*.

Reb Shneur Zalman watched in amazement as the platter with the marked fish slowly made its way to the young visitor's side of the room, then to his corner, then to his table, and then...the piece of fish went not to Reb Yaakov Yitzchok, but to another Chassid sitting beside him. So close, but yet so far!

The Chassid lifted the marked piece of fish on his fork, and opened his mouth in anticipation; but suddenly his hand began to tremble. He put the fish down and then tried again. Again his hand trembled too violently for him to eat. Finally, he put the fish back on his plate and, with a gesture of rejection, pushed it aside with his hand...right in front of Reb Yaakov Yitzchok, who proceeded to eat it calmly, as if he had been expecting it all along!

The Maggid himself once said, "There has not been a soul like the Seer's since the days of the prophets." As his appellation implied, the Seer was, indeed, capable of seeing great, hidden things both in Heaven and on Earth.

The story is told that once, when the Chassidim assembled a *minyan* in the Maggid's study to pray, the Maggid ordered the young Yaakov Yitzchok to leave the room. Only because they lacked a tenth man did the Maggid finally allow him back in. However, once the Maggid reached the words, *Ein k'Elokeinu*, "There is none like our G-d," the Seer fainted.

"Didn't I warn you about letting that young man pray with us?" the Maggid complained. "He actually saw the Heavenly Hosts fill the room, and he saw that there really is none like our G-d. That's why he fainted — whereas you saw nothing!"

The Humility of the Seer

Later, the Seer's disciples maintained that they could not grasp even a fraction of his true spiritual greatness — not merely because of his high level, but because he hid his true identity even from those closest to him. Reb Simcha Bunim of Pshischah once commented that the Seer's prophetic ability and wonder-working were just a smoke screen that concealed who he truly was. Yet, the Seer actually considered himself "the least of all men, of all creation." He considered everyone to be better than him, even his servants.

Reb Levi Yitzchok of Berditchev once planned a trip to Lublin, when the Seer was already a Rebbe with thousands of Chassidim. Still, on the day before the visit, the Seer paced nervously in his room. "Master of the Universe," he prayed, "What can I do? When this tzaddik looks me in the face, he will immediately recognize that I am not a tzaddik myself, and I will be so ashamed." Suddenly he stopped. "But what about You, Master of the Universe? Why am I not even more embarrassed before You?" He thought for a moment and answered his own question, "That is because I am accustomed to You; but how dare I look that tzaddik in the face?"

How could the Seer think of himself in this way? Certainly he was aware of his unique spiritual level. Perhaps it was precisely because he was on such a high level that he was worried. Even the slightest transgression might include him in the category of "those who recognize their Creator, but rebel against Him." This was also the way of the Seer's Rebbe, the Rebbe Reb Elimelech of Lyzhansk, who also referred to himself as the lowliest of men. "I'm sure that the Rebbe is sincere," said his disciple, Reb Moshe of Kozhnitz, on one such occasion, "but how could that really be?" "Consider," the Rebbe replied, "if you strike someone with a thick stick, the damage may not be that severe. But if you slash him with a sharp knife, it cuts to the core. Likewise, an ordinary person who commits serious transgressions may not damage himself as much as a tzaddik who commits even the slightest one."

"My only comfort," the Seer once told his *mechutan*, Reb Mordechai of Chernobyl, "is that when I finally return to dust, I will stop angering my Creator." And on another occasion, he cried out, "Woe to the generation that has me for its leader!"

Two Types of Criticism

The Seer's soul-searching was more than mere self-denigration. The Seer actually attributed all of his spiritual accomplishments to his humility. "I decided in my heart to be always lowly in my own eyes, because Hashem takes pity on a person who is embarrassed by his sins, and brings him closer than a perfect tzaddik, which I certainly am not." Or again: "There are those who doubt that there can be miracles in our days, for we lack the integrity and the brilliance of previous generations. But if a person holds himself in low esteem, Hashem does not reject his prayers.... It is not as easy for a great person to consider himself low, as it is for a person who is truly nothing at all...[but] be lowly in your own eyes and you will perform miracles and strengthen everyone's faith."

The Seer found a hint to this in the verse, "And Avraham returned to his young men, and they rose and went together" (*Bereshis* 22:19). He lowered himself to the level of the young men, that is, those who were new to the way of Torah and, since he considered himself one of them, they could go together.

Conversely, once, when the Seer's disciples repeated some of the slanderous statements his opponents spread about him, the Seer's face turned white.

The Seer of Lublin

"Why is the Rebbe so upset?" they asked. "The Rebbe often says the same things about himself!"

"True," the Seer replied, "but I criticize myself with a contrite heart and a desire to fix what is wrong. My enemies, however, make such statements with mockery and derision. That does not lead to improvement."

In one oft-retold story, the Rav of Lublin, an accomplished scholar but an opponent of the Chassidic way, once asked the Seer how he could allow Chassidim to come to him, since he was not as learned or pious — in the Rav's opinion — as the other great men in the city. In his humility, the Seer asked, "What then should I do?"

"Call your Chassidim together and tell them that they are mistaken, that you are neither a tzaddik nor a Rebbe, and they will stop coming to you." The Seer readily agreed and, on the next Shabbos, he publicly confessed his total "unworthiness." News of his incredible self-effacement and humility rapidly spread, and soon the Seer had far more Chassidim than before.

At their next meeting, the Rav told the Seer, "Since your Chassidim are such great admirers of humility, you had best take the opposite tack. Call them together and tell them how great and deserving you are. Then they will hate your boasting and leave you."

"No," said the Seer, "that I cannot do. I may not be a tzaddik, but I am not a liar either!"

The Talmud states, "Even if the entire world calls you a tzaddik, consider yourself wicked in your own eyes" (*Niddah* 30b). How is this possible, asked the Seer. Certainly, if the entire world calls a person a tzaddik, he must be one. However, a person who sees how truly great and awesome Hashem is, realizes that he will never be able to fulfill even a fraction of his obligations to Him and in that sense, he considers himself wicked. "This is especially true of a person like myself," the Seer concluded, "who has already sinned."

Joy and Trembling

The Seer's great humility never made him depressed or bitter. Indeed, he held that, "If a person's humility leads him to depression, it is a sign of pride. A truly humble person is happy to find his faults, for Hashem loves truth and will cling to him."

The Seer's joy in serving Hashem was legendary. Reb Chaim of Sanz once commented, "A person who has not heard the prayers in Lublin, has never heard prayer in his life. When his Chassidim begin their prayers with the words 'Sing to the L-rd, call on His Name,' the very walls dance with joy!"

Shortly before his wedding, Reb Aryeh Leib Lipshutz asked the Seer if he could join him for the upcoming High Holidays, despite the usual prohibition of leaving one's wife during the first year of marriage. "It is permissible to travel to Lublin," the Seer replied. Reb Aryeh Leib was perplexed. Legally, what was the difference between visiting the Lubliner or any other tzaddik?

After returning home, he saw the *Sefer haChinuch*'s ruling that one can leave home and rejoice for several days with one's friends, even during his first year of marriage. Then he understood. In Lublin the Seer's emphasis was on joy; so he could go there to join his friends for the holidays.

Joy yes; but Lubliner Chassidus epitomized "Serve the L-rd with fear, rejoice with trembling" (*Tehillim* 2:13). Delight at serving the Creator was tempered by the constant recognition of His awesome Presence. Reb Meir'l of Premishlan once said, "If you want to understand the verse, 'And Yitzchok trembled exceedingly greatly' (*Bereshis* 27:33), just look at the Holy Seer of Lublin."

The Seer of Lublin

Reb Yehudah Leib of Zhilkov once spent Sukkos in Lublin. Before reciting *Hallel*, the Seer entered his *sukkah* to recite the blessing over the *lulav*. "We all followed behind him. Before pronouncing the blessing, the Seer started shaking and trembling in fear, and continued to do so for about an hour. The others thought this was the main thing, and they also started to tremble and shake, each according to his understanding. I, however, sat down on a bench and waited until the outer fear passed. I realized that all this was only his preparation. Then I stood and closely watched how the Rebbe recited the blessing. There is no way to describe the awesome level he was on at that moment."

Devotion to Torah

The Seer's love of G-d was matched by his love of Torah. In his youth, he studied at the rigorous yeshiva of Reb Shmuel Shmelke of Nikolsburg, in the town of Shinov. Reb Shmelke appreciated the saintliness of his young student, and would stand beside him every morning to answer "Amen" to his blessings. "When Yaakov Yitzchok makes a blessing," Reb Shmelke used to say, "all the Heavenly Hosts answer 'Amen'." Reb Simcha Bunim similarly called him "an overflowing treasure-house of the Torah and its secrets."

The Seer learned Torah *li'shmah*, without any ulterior motives. In his youth, he had wanted to write a commentary on *Seder Kodashim*, one of the most difficult areas of the Talmud.

Later, after he was already Rebbe to thousands of Chassidim, he considered sending all of them away, so that he could lock himself in his room and devote all of his time to study. When word of this plan reached Reb Dovid of Lelov, Reb Dovid rushed to Lublin to dissuade him. "The Torah says, 'And Moshe descended from the mountain to the people' (*Shemos* 19:34). Rashi comments that Moshe went straight to the people, without first attending to his own business. What business could Moshe possibly have had in the desert? Only the study of Torah. Nevertheless, he laid that aside to lead the nation." When the Seer heard these words, he abandoned his plan.

The Seer also demanded that his students devote their utmost in time and energy to learning Torah. "When the Torah says, 'And you shall eat your bread to the full' (*Vayikra* 26:5), this refers to the bread of Torah," said the Seer. "That is the true sustenance of man." Conversely, when a person abandons Torah study, he incurs Hashem's anger, as the verse says, 'And Yaakov left Be'er Sheva and went towards Charan' (*Bereshis* 28:11). When Yaakov left Be'er Sheva, where he studied Torah, he encountered Hashem's anger (*charan af*)."

The Seer was once talking with his friend, Reb Menachem Mendel of Rimanov.

"Do you have Chassidim?" the Seer asked.

"Some of them may be Chassidim," Reb Menachem Mendel replied.

"In what way are they Chassidim?"

"They sit day and night learning Gemara, Tosafos and halachah."

"Then they are most certainly Chassidim!" the Seer exclaimed.

On at least one occasion, the Seer signed his name with the following appellation: "He who longs and hopes to magnify the glory of Hashem, and to increase the desire for the constant study of Torah, for the sake of His Name alone."

The Seer even attributed his *ruach hakodesh* (a lower degree of prophecy) to his Torah study. While still a child, the Divrei Chaim of Sanz became a student of the Seer. One day, as the Seer was receiving a long line of Chassidim, giving them advice and helping them with their problems, he suddenly stopped and asked everyone except the Divrei Chaim to leave the room. He locked the door and then spent several minutes reciting *mishnayos* by heart. Then he turned to the Divrei Chaim and explained.

"Years ago, when a Jew needed advice, he would go to the *Kohen Gadol*, who would inquire of the *Urim v'Tumim*. But today a Jew goes to a Torah scholar for guidance. To those scholars who learn Torah for its own sake the hidden light of the Torah is revealed. Then they can see answers to all problems. But, sometimes, dealing with their congregation weakens their connection to the Torah and they lose this inner light. Thus, I closed the door and studied some *mishnayos* to renew my attachment to the Torah. Why am I telling you this? Because, one day, you too will be a leader of Israel. Therefore, you must know that *ruach hakodesh* is drawn only from the Torah."

The Seer found a hint to this in the verse, "And [Avraham] sat in the door of his tent in the heat of the day" (*Bereshis* 18:1). When one learns Torah with burning desire, one opens the door to Divine illumination.

Love of Israel

The Seer taught that "Torah study leads to the love of Hashem, and the love of Hashem leads to love of the Jewish People, because a person who loves the father will also love the son." He even gave Kabbalistic reasons for this love. Since the tzaddik is the root soul of all Israel, his soul embraces all Jewish souls. He therefore loves them all and is willing to devote himself entirely to their welfare. A tzaddik's humility also leads to *ahavas Yisrael*, for "when a person sees only the good in himself, he will end up seeing the flaws in others; however, if he is low in his own eyes, he will love all Israel."

Furthermore, "he must see the strengths of Israel, but not their weaknesses...and even those few undeniable sins that Israel commits, he must judge favorably, for a tzaddik does not want to see Jews in a lowly state."

Although the Seer saw everything from one end of the earth to the other, he would not look at the flaws of the Jewish People. He always tried to emulate his Creator, Who "beholds no iniquity in Yaakov" (*Bemidbar* 25:21).

"When the Seer received the *kvitel* (written request) of a good Jew," Reb Sar Shalom of Belz would say, "he looked at it, meditated on it, gazed into the root of the person's soul, saw how many times he had been reincarnated, what damages he had caused in previous lives, which particular sins he was caught in, which mitzvah was his strong point, under which celestial influences he was born, and whether he would succeed in his deeds or not. But when he received the *kvitel* of a sinner, he would immediately cast it away, so as not to look upon the disgrace of a fellow Jew."

The Chassidim say that the Seer's gaze originally encompassed the entire world. However, in order not to see the bad in the people of Israel, he asked Hashem to take back his holy power. Hashem answered only half his prayer. He drastically reduced the Seer's ability so that he could only see clearly for a distance of 1,600 miles; beyond that, his vision became dim. Seeing that his prayer was not fully answered, he begged Reb Mordechai of Neschiz to pray that Hashem should remove the rest; but Reb Mordechai refused. Hashem had given the Seer this power, and he was obligated to use it. Still he treated every Jew he met, righteous or not, as if he were a tzaddik, as if he truly saw only good.

"How beautiful are the Jews," the Seer would say. "According to our Sages, even Jewish sinners are as full of mitzvos as a pomegranate is full of seeds. Why a pomegranate? Because one drinks only its inner nectar and discards the peel. So too, with a Jewish transgressor: his sins are only external, whereas his essence is wondrous indeed."

Upon hearing a person's problems, the Seer would never be judgmental; and he would seek to lessen the punishment of the Heavenly Court: "When a Jew is crushed by suffering you must never say that he deserves it. Instead, you must pray for him and save him. Do not justify Divine decrees; instead, beg Hashem to annul them and send only goodness and kindness to Israel."

Body and Soul The Seer's concern was not limited to his followers' spiritual well-being, he saw to their material needs as well. "Wealth can draw down the light of holiness," explained the Seer, "as *Chazal* have said, 'If there is no bread, there is no Torah.' Conversely, poverty can lead to transgression.... Thus, the role of tzaddik is to bring blessings to the Jewish People." He regarded it as a privilege to help others in every way possible. Once, a Jew arrived in Lublin late at night to ask the Seer to pray for a woman in childbirth. Not knowing exactly where the Seer lived, the messenger wandered aimlessly through the dark streets, until he saw lights still burning in one house. He knocked and the Seer himself opened the door. "Why are you out so late, my friend?" The man told him all about his mission, and without revealing his identity, the Seer invited him in. He fed him supper, made his bed and then wished him a good-night. There was plenty of time to go to the Seer tomorrow. The man woke up the next morning distraught. How could he have slept while that poor woman suffered?

"Don't worry," the Seer comforted him. "I took care of your mission for you. The Seer wishes you a *mazal tov* on the birth of a boy, and on the improving health of the mother."

On another occasion, a beggar knocked on the Seer's door. Again the Seer personally invited him in, fed him, and even cleaned up the table after him. That was too much for the Seer's students. "We can understand that our Rebbe wants the mitzvah of feeding the poor, but does he also have to clean the table? He has attendants for that." The Seer overheard them and commented, "When the *Kohen Gadol* finished with his holy service on Yom Kippur, he still went back into the Holy of Holies to retrieve the incense spoon he had left there. That too was an *avodah*; and he didn't send his attendant to do it for him!"

The Seer's Passing

Napoleon Bonaparte had begun his great march across Eastern Europe towards Russia. Three of the greatest tzaddikim of that generation — the Seer of Lublin, the Maggid of Kozhnitz and Reb Menachem Mendel of Rimanov — had joined together to try to use the invasion to hasten the Redemption. Using their great spiritual powers, they sought to convert the Napoleonic wars into the battle of Gog and Magog that precedes the coming of the Messiah. It was a path fraught with danger, and success was far from assured. "If we have a joyful Simchas Torah," the Seer told his Chassidim, "we will have a joyful Tishah b'Av."

That Simchas Torah eve, he commanded his followers to dance with all their strength. He called a small group aside and warned them, "Do not take your eyes off me for a moment; the forces of evil are out to stop our holy work." He went into his room on the second floor of the shul for a moment and then, suddenly, the door slammed shut by itself. When the Chassidim pried it open, they found the room empty! Only a small window was open.

The Chassidim ran out into the snow to search for their

Rebbe. After many hours, Reb Eliezer of Chelmnik heard someone groaning. "Who is there?" he shouted. "Reb Yaakov Yitzchok ben Matil," came the reply. Reb Eliezer gave a shout and the other Chassidim came running. The Seer had been thrown a great distance from the shul. The Chassidim carried him back. Reb Shmuel of Karov held the Seer's head. The Seer was murmuring something...*Tikun Chatzos*, dirges bemoaning the destruction of the Holy Temple!

Afterwards, the Seer complained, "Why didn't you tell me that the Kozhnitzer Maggid had passed away? Had I known that, I would never have attempted what I did. All the forces of evil rose up against me. Had the Kozhnitzer Maggid not descended from the Upper Worlds and spread his tallis under me to cushion my fall, I would have been dead by now."

The Chassidim did not have a joyful Simchas Torah; and their Tishah b'Av was worse. The Redemption did not come; and the Seer passed away that very Tishah b'Av.

The kever of the Seer of Lublin, zt"l, disciple and successor of the Rebbe Reb Elimelech, and the Rebbe of Reb Dovid of Lelov.

From the Seer's Circle: Rabbi Tzvi Hirsh

The Seer's son, Reb Tzvi Hirsh, was deeply loved by all the tzaddikim of his generation. Like his father, he was exceptionally humble and he possessed great spiritual gifts. Once, the Maggid of Kozhnitz "opened" Reb Tzvi Hirsh's eyes and Reb Tzvi was able to see the three Patriarchs themselves.

Reb Tzvi's self-effacement knew no bounds. When Reb Tzvi Hirsh Hakohen of Rimanov, one of the great tzaddikim of the generation, became seriously ill, the Seer's son prayed, "Master of the Universe! This generation can get along without Reb Tzvi Hirsh of Lublin [himself], but it can't survive without Reb Tzvi Hirsh of Rimanov. Take this Tzvi Hirsh in place of that one." A short time later, he suddenly passed away.

Rabbi Nota of Chelm

Reb Tzvi Hirsh was the son-in-law of Reb Nota of Chelm, author of *Neta Sha'ashuim*. Reb Nota had been a student of the Rebbe Reb Elimelech of Lyzhansk, the Seer of Lublin, Reb Boruch of Mezhibuzh and Reb Mordechai of Neschiz. Once, on Yom Kippur in Lyzhansk, he stood in prayer the entire day, without once moving. "Reb Nota's fear of Hashem is so great," the Rebbe Reb Elimelech explained, "that he is simply unable to move his limbs, while surrounded by the glory of the King!"

Reb Nota was known for his good advice and miraculous powers. "A tzaddik cannot answer questions," he taught, "until he divests himself of his physicality, and clings to the Holy One. Then the *Shechinah* speaks through him." In this introduction to *Neta Sha'ashuim*, his grandson wrote, "I will not mention here all the miracles I heard that my grandfather performed, for there is not enough paper to record them." Reb Nota himself wrote, "When a tzaddik serves Hashem perfectly, he transcends the realm of time and space. Thus he is able to influence the physical world, which is under the influence of time."

Countless Chassidim traveled to Chelm to ask Reb Nota for blessings of all kinds. Reb Nota himself, however, stressed the importance of spiritual blessings, for only then can one ask for material ones.

"Every person must believe that the tzaddik is able to help him," wrote Reb Nota. "It is this very faith that enables the tzaddik to help. Thus the verse says, 'And he called his name Noach, saying, This one shall comfort (*yinachamenu*) us' (*Bereshis* 5:29). That is, by saying it, so it came to pass." Reb Nota also emphasized the role of the tzaddik. "It is impossible for a person to love and cling to Hashem solely through his own efforts; but he can do so fully through the influence of the tzaddik. Thus, the verse says, 'And they believed in Hashem and in Moshe His servant' (*Shemos* 14:31)."

Like the Seer, Reb Nota's humility was legendary. "The greatest sin of a Jewish leader is pride," he wrote. "This is hinted at in the words of the Hebrew verse, 'When a leader has sinned.' The first letter of each Hebrew word spells out the word *ani*, I. That is the greatest sin!" He was famous for his great love of the Jewish People, helping them see everything in a positive light. For example, one of his rich Chassidim once came to him with a strange complaint. "Rebbe, I have everything I want in life: children, health and livelihood."

"So what is wrong?"

"This is precisely the problem. I know I am not a tzaddik. So why should I deserve all this? I must be receiving my future reward now. Perhaps, *chas v'shalom*, Hashem does not want to reward me in the World to Come!"

"But don't you wear eyeglasses?" Reb Nota reassured him. "Don't they cause you suffering? Sometimes you forget them. Sometimes they break. You are not living your World to Come; your glasses cause you suffering enough!"

Rebbetzin Matil Feigeh

Reb Nota's daughter, Malchah, and the Seer's son, Reb Tzvi Hirsh, were blessed with a daughter, Matil Feigeh, named for the Seer's saintly mother. She later married Reb Elazar Menachem Mendel of Lelov, the grandson of Reb Dovid of Lelov, one of the Seer's most important disciples. The cord of love and humility which characterized Lelov and Lublin thus grew thicker as new strands were added in every generation.

Rebbetzin Matil Feigeh moved to the Old Yishuv of Jerusalem with Reb Elazar Menachem Mendel and his father, Reb Moshe Lelover. There, in a city known for its many righteous people, she was regarded as a special *tzadekes*. When Reb Yechezkel Shraga Shinover, the son of the Sanzer Rav, visited Jerusalem, he made sure to visit her home on Shabbos to personally wish her a *Gut Shabbos*.

Rebbetzin Matil Feigeh had grown up in Lublin. She once told her grandson, Reb Pinchas Dovid, the first Bostoner Rebbe, that as a child she had once visited the study of the Seer in Lublin. There she saw the window through which he had been hurled. Even though she was a little girl at the time, the window was so narrow that even she was unable to pass through it!

TWO
Reb Dovid of Lelov

Destined for Greatness

The Seer of Lublin had a great influence on most of the great Polish Rebbes of the next generation, including Reb Dovid of Lelov and his younger contemporary the Yehudi haKodesh of Pshischah. As with many early Chassidic leaders, Reb Dovid Lelover's life is shrouded in legends and mystery. His family's lineage stretched back to King David himself and, at one point, they had a family tree that listed every generation. Reb Dovid's father, Reb Shlomo, was a respected householder, known for his modesty and honesty. He once tried to sell his merchandise to a shopkeeper for fifteen rubles, but the shopkeeper declined. Later that day, Reb Shlomo decided that he could reduce his price to thirteen rubles and still make a profit. Meanwhile, the shopkeeper had also reconsidered. When the two men met again, the shopkeeper was prepared to pay fifteen, but Reb Shlomo refused to take more than thirteen. This act of honesty was one reason, said the tzaddikim of his generation, that he merited such a holy son.

Reb Dovid was born in 1745 in the town of Bialeh, near Lelov. The two holy brothers, Reb Elimelech of Lyzhansk and Reb Zusya of Hanipoli, often traveled across the Polish countryside dressed as paupers, to share the exile of the *Shechinah* and hasten the Redemption. Once, when Reb Dovid was a boy, they followed their holy intuition to Reb Dovid's house in Bialeh. There they found the boy at home alone. When his mother returned, they asked her how she had merited such a special son.

"As for me," she said, "I am a simple Jew, as is my husband. However, every Shabbos, during the *Seudah Shelishis*, he sings '*Y'tzaveh tzur chasdo*' with great intensity. When he reaches the words, 'May we merit to see our children and our children's children immersed in Torah and mitzvos,' he presses his head against the wall and begs Hashem for such a son — so intensely that he faints. Every week I have to revive him." The two tzaddikim blessed her and departed.

One morning, when Reb Dovid was still a small child of five or six, he went to the local baker and asked for a favor. He needed a roll on credit, because his family was very poor. The baker gave him the roll, and no sooner had Dovid left the shop than the dough in the baker's oven started rising over the edges of the baking pans and pouring down the sides. The baker couldn't bring enough pans to catch it all, so powerful was the blessing that had permeated the dough.

Hidden and Revealed

Such miracles would have been more frequent had Reb Dovid not tried to hide his holiness his entire life. Once when Rav Shlomo of Zalshin was leaving for Lelov, a neighbor asked him to take a block of cheese to Reb Dovid. "I know the Rebbe," he said. "Please, tell him this gift is from me." When Rav Shlomo relayed the man's words, Reb Dovid replied, "He only thinks he knows me. By the time I was nine years old, even the angels in Heaven knew nothing of me!"

Even the penetrating eyes of his Rebbe, the Seer of Lublin, could not fathom who he was. A few hours before Reb Dovid passed away, his Chassidim noticed that he was laughing. "I've hidden myself so well," he explained, "that even the Seer doesn't realize what I am." Later, the Seer beheld him in a dream, burning like fire and shining with a great light. "I never knew he was so great," the Seer later told his followers.

Although Reb Dovid's spiritual attainments may have been hidden, his kindness and humility were apparent from his youth. His family was so poor that his father had to struggle greatly just to buy him a winter coat. Reb Dovid was very excited to receive it. Then the very next day, on his way to school, he saw a small boy in torn clothes standing in the cold and crying. Reb Dovid immediately took off his new coat and gave it to the boy. When he returned home, his mother asked him, "Dovid, what happened? Where is your new coat?"

"I gave it to a poor boy who needed it," he replied.

"What? Quick, eat your lunch and run back to school before your father comes home. If he catches you without that coat, he will give you quite a beating."

"That's all right Mother," young Dovid replied. "If beating me would make Father feel better, then let him."

Afflictions of Love Even when Reb Dovid grew up and married, he continued to follow his own way of Divine service. As a young man living in his father-in-law's house, he practiced a severe regimen of self-affliction. His father-in-law, a simple man, could not understand such strange behavior. When he heard how Reb Dovid would immerse himself in frozen lakes, or roll naked in the snow as penance, he became enraged. Once, he even threw Reb

Dovid out of the house, and one of the servants had to let him back in through a back door. Yet the servant also was bewildered by Reb Dovid's actions. "Have you really sinned so much that you must afflict yourself so?" he asked. "What can I do?" replied Reb Dovid. "I still have not reached the level of complete love for all Jews."

During the early years of Reb Dovid's marriage, he spent all week studying in an out-of-town *beis midrash*, returning to his father-in-law's house only for Shabbos. On one such trip home, he accepted a lift from a Jewish wagon driver. In the middle of the journey, the horse suddenly stood still. The wagon driver hit the horse with his whip, but it refused to budge. Reb Dovid told the driver, "Tie the reins to the wagon, and come down into the carriage with me. Let the horse go where it wants, Hashem will help us reach our destination." The wagon driver did as he was told; and the horse took off like lightning, only to stop a few moments later. They were already home!

The wagon driver went inside and excitedly told the whole family about their miraculous journey. Only then did Reb Dovid's father-in-law finally begin to appreciate him.

With the Rebbe Reb Elimelech of Lyzhansk

As Reb Dovid matured, he slowly found himself drawn to Chassidus, and longed to travel to the holy Rebbe Reb Elimelech of Lyzhansk (then the leader of his generation in Poland). Unsure that he was a fit vessel to receive such great light, he first accepted a lengthy and rigorous program of fasting and self-discipline, as prescribed in *Sefer haKaneh*, completing it twice!

The path of Chassidus, however, is not one of self-affliction, for it is better to serve Hashem with joy. "When a person fasts," said the Ba'al Shem Tov, "he inevitably feels

Reb Dovid of Lelov

some tinge of pride on account of his efforts. And that pride ruins everything." In fact, according to the first Rebbe of Gur, the *Chidushei haRim*, the Rebbe Reb Elimelech said that he "split apart the Heavens to eliminate the need for such behavior." Thus, when the Rebbe Reb Elimelech first met Reb Dovid, he immediately recognized where the young man's practices could lead, and began by teaching him a lesson in true humility.

When Reb Dovid arrived at the *beis midrash*, he found a long line of Chassidim waiting for a chance to greet the tzaddik. He took his place in line, and eventually his turn arrived.

"Where are you from?" the Rebbe asked.

"From Bialeh, a small town."

"And what do you do?"

"I am the Rav of the town."

"And who is the lowliest Jew in the town?"

Reb Dovid was stunned by the unexpected question but, before he could answer, the Rebbe had already turned to the next person in line. Reb Dovid was confused. Was all his elaborate preparation for naught? It must be a mistake. He would try again tomorrow.

The next day, he again waited in line and, when his turn came, the Rebbe asked him the same question: "Who is the lowliest Jew in your town?"

Reb Dovid was ready and started to explain: "As Rav of the city, most of my time is spent with the learned Jews in the synagogue. I am not familiar with every Jew in town, especially the lower elements..." But the Rebbe had already turned to the next person in line.

"Perhaps the Rebbe is simply testing my *ahavas Yisrael*, my love of all Jews," Reb Dovid concluded. The next day, Friday, Reb Dovid once more stood in line, and once more was asked the same question: "Who is the lowliest Jew in your town?"

"Rebbe, I cannot know what is in the heart of every Jew, nor am I fit to pass judgment. I don't..." But the Rebbe was already giving a hearty *Shalom* to the next person in line.

Reb Dovid sadly returned to his room. What could he do, where could he go? There wasn't enough time to return home; but, if he prayed in the *beis midrash*, he knew what to expect. Everyone would file past the Rebbe to receive a *Gut Shabbos*, while he would get the same embarrassing question. He decided to pray in his room.

Brokenhearted, he began to *daven Minchah*. Towards the end of his prayers, he suddenly thought: "Who is the lowliest Jew in my town? It's me! I'm the lowliest Jew in my town. All the others Jews are happily welcoming the Shabbos in shul, while I pray alone here in this tiny hotel room, far away from home. Surely I must be the worst of all!

Just then he heard a loud knock at the door. The Rebbe's attendant had come to invite him to pray in the *beis midrash*. When he arrived the Rebbe turned to him with a smile, "Now that you know — *Shalom Aleichem!*" From then on, Reb Dovid became one of the Rebbe Reb Elimelech's closest disciples.

Reb Dovid's father, however, was a vigorous opponent of the Chassidic movement, and considered his son's journey to Lyzhansk a waste of time (*bitul Torah*). When Reb Dovid returned home, his enraged father began rummaging around the house trying to find his walking stick to give his son a sound beating. Reb Dovid quickly ran and got it. "Here, Father," he said. "Now you can beat me as much as you like!"

With the Seer of Lublin

As Reb Dovid's relationship with the Rebbe Reb Elimelech developed, he became acquainted with the Rebbe's other great disciples, including Reb Yaakov Yitzchok Horowitz,

Reb Dovid of Lelov

the Seer of Lublin, who already headed his own Chassidic court in Lanzhut. Reb Dovid's respect and admiration for the Seer was boundless. Once, while in Lyzhansk, he heard that the Seer had arrived. He ran to his inn to greet him. Then, since Shabbos was fast approaching, Reb Dovid quickly turned to leave. The Seer stopped him. "You seem very worried about the Shabbos. Do you really know so precisely when it arrives?"

"Of course," said Reb Dovid. "When Shabbos draws near, the veins in my hand start to throb with fear." He pulled up his sleeve and showed them to the Seer. "Then what do you think of this story?" the Seer said, telling Reb Dovid a seemingly meaningless parable about a farmer and a king's daughter. "It seems to be an allegory for the following Kabbalistic teaching of the Arizal..." The Seer was so pleased with Reb Dovid's answer that he hugged him and said, "From now on, you are one of my men." Thus, even while remaining a disciple of the Rebbe Reb Elimelech, Reb Dovid visited the Seer in Lanzhut.

After the Rebbe Reb Elimelech's death, Reb Dovid became one of the Seer's chief disciples, although they were about the same age. He considered the Seer the leader of his generation and constantly sought to introduce the other great souls of his time to the Seer.

During the Napoleonic wars, when the roads were closed and travel to Lublin became difficult, many Chassidim gathered in Lelov to hear Torah from Reb Dovid. On one such Shabbos, Reb Dovid sat at the head of his table and cheerfully announced, "Now I am sitting at the table of the Seer of Lublin." What did he mean? "If the world really knew the greatness of my Rebbe, so many people would flock to him that his table would stretch all the way from Lublin to Lelov. So right now I am sitting at the far end of the Rebbe's table, only the tables in between are missing."

Indeed, on that Shabbos, so they say, Reb Dovid delivered the exact same *dvar Torah* at *Seudah Shelishis* that the Seer delivered at his Shabbos table in Lublin.

Many years later, when the Seer would recite *Ein k'Elokeinu* to the special melody of the Maggid of Mezritch, Reb Dovid would walk back and forth in the adjacent shul, snapping his fingers in delight. "Don't you hear?" he would explain. "The Rebbe is teaching us the language of the birds!"

Reb Dovid's love and respect for the Seer was reciprocated. Once Reb Dovid and his son, Moshe, came to Lublin for a visit and, inadvertently, took the usual lodgings of Reb Kalonymous Kalman, author of the *Me'or v'Shemesh*. When Reb Kalonymous arrived, he was upset that his place was taken. As soon as Reb Dovid heard this, he told his son to hire a wagon to take them back to Lelov.

Reb Kalonymous became panicky; this had certainly not been his intention. He quickly went to see Reb Dovid and urged him to stay wherever he pleased; but Reb Dovid and his son returned home.

When Reb Kalonymous shared his distress with the Seer, the latter commented, "Don't you understand? Reb Dovid merely has to visit us, and all the Heavenly gates swing open to accept our prayers. Once this has been accomplished, he can return home. He was only looking for an excuse, and you gave it to him!"

Since most of the many stories about Reb Dovid cannot be dated, the next two chapters group together stories which help illuminate some of his outstanding character traits: his Torah, *avodah* and love of all Israel.

THREE
Love of Israel

The Store

Reb Dovid successfully concealed his high spiritual level from the eyes of his companions; but he was unable to conceal his burning love for the Jewish People.

Reb Dovid supported himself with a small grocery store. Once a customer entered the shop and asked him where he could buy salt. Reb Dovid first listed all the other stores in town, and only then concluded, "And you can also buy it here, if you like." Another morning, when he arrived at work, he noticed that his competitor's store was still closed. He ran to wake him. "Get up quickly!" he urged. "Customers are already coming!"

Reb Dovid never became rich from his business, nor did he want to. Once, when a large group of Chassidim visited him in Lelov for Shabbos, his wife, Rebbetzin Chana, complained, "Where will we get enough silverware for the guests?" Reb Dovid answered, "You should know that we could have golden spoons if we wanted — but it is better not to want."

Reb Dovid saw his store as an opportunity to serve Hashem. One morning, when he was sitting at home, wrapped in tallis and tefillin, a non-Jew knocked on his door.

He wanted to buy salt, and Reb Dovid went to his shop and weighed the man's order. "Add on a little more," the gentile whispered slyly. Reb Dovid immediately did the opposite. He took the entire order, poured it back into the sack, and returned home. "When that fellow came to buy salt," he later told his students, "I went only to fulfill the mitzvah, 'You shall have a just measure' (*Vayikra* 19:35). But when I saw that he wanted to cheat the scale, I turned around and came home." According to Reb Yitzchok of Vorki, Reb Dovid never did anything that was not the fulfillment of a halachah.

Once, Reb Dovid and Reb Yitzchok of Vorki were traveling on the road. In the middle of the night, they reached the town of Alkosh. The only light came from the shop of Reb Beirish, the baker, and they headed in that direction. There they found Reb Beirish busy with his work, preparing for the next day's orders.

When he looked up and saw the two tzaddikim at his door, Reb Beirish was embarrassed to be seen involved in such mundane activities. Reb Dovid consoled him. "I wish that I could support myself like you do. You give bread to the hungry. Likewise, the tailor provides men with warm clothes, and the cobbler fixes their shoes. Can we imagine the reward that awaits them? So what if they get paid; they have to support themselves so they can continue their good work. Every Jew knows that the only real work is to show kindness to other Jews."

One morning, Reb Dovid went to his store and gave away all of his merchandise to the Jews in the marketplace. When his wife arrived at the shop, she surveyed the empty shelves with satisfaction. Then she looked in the cash box, which was just as empty! She turned to her husband in dismay. He answered her look: "Every day I see you selling your wares to the non-Jews; so I said to myself, why should the Jews deserve any less?"

Love of Israel

One day Reb Dovid closed his little shop for good. He explained the matter simply. "When I see a customer go to my competitor's store, I'm delighted that he is making a living. But I recently realized that not everyone feels this way. Whenever a customer comes into my store, I may actually be causing my competitor anguish! So I had to close my shop. How could I cause another Jew pain?"

His son, Reb Moshe, also had a shop. Once he complained about a competitor across the street, who was stealing his customers. "True, you may lose money," Reb Dovid replied. "But isn't it wonderful to see your neighbor making such a good living?"

Good for Others

Shortly before his death, Reb Dovid told the story of the Talmudic sage Rabbi Chanina ben Dosa, (*Ta'anis* 24a). When he would travel on the road and get caught in the rain, he would say, "The whole world is at ease, and Chanina is suffering!" and the rain would immediately stop. "How could Rabbi Chanina weigh his personal comfort against the good of the entire world?" Reb Dovid asked. "The answer is that the entire world was sustained by the merit of Rabbi Chanina ben Dosa (*Berachos* 17b). He was the channel through which all blessings flowed into creation. Therefore, a downpour that caused him discomfort was not beneficial to the world as a whole. That was why he prayed that it stop. I'm sure that was his intention, and if I reach his chamber in Heaven, I will ask him!" In a sense, Reb Dovid was also talking about himself. His personal joy or distress was always in response to what he perceived was good for the world.

Reb Dovid's stepbrother, Reb Yitzchok Isaac Visoker, once approached him for a blessing. Reb Yitzchok lived in the countryside and wanted to move to the city where he could be among Jews and pray with a *minyan*. Reb Dovid answered him, "My dear brother, when a poor man asks for charity, what does he usually get? A few coins at best. But when he comes to your farm, you invite him in, you give him a meal and a hot drink, you let him sit by the fire and revive his soul. When you get to the Next World, which mitzvah would you rather have? I think you should stay on your farm."

Reb Dovid constantly worked on his concern for others. Reb Shlomo of Radomsk wrote: "This is the way of all true tzaddikim, to love other Jews more than they love their own children, as it says about Mordechai the Tzaddik: 'He sought peace on behalf of his people, and peace on behalf of his descendants' (*Esther* 10:3). First for his people, then for his descendants. Thus, I heard Reb Dovid of Lelov once say: 'Why do people think of me as a tzaddik? I still love my own family more than the rest of the Jewish people'."

When Reb Dovid's young son became sick, the Chassidim gathered to pray on his behalf. Reb Dovid heard them and started to cry. "Why are you crying?" they asked. "Your son will get better." "I'm crying," he said, "because we don't pray so intensely when someone else's son gets sick!"

Endless Love

Reb Dovid once went to spend the High Holidays with the Seer of Lublin. On Yom Kippur eve, the congregation was about to begin *Kol Nidre* when they noticed that Reb Dovid was missing. No one knew where to find him. The congregation waited as long as they could, and finally had to pray without him. He had been on his way from the *mikveh* to the shul, when he heard a child crying in one of the nearby houses. The parents had gone to shul and left the baby sleeping. Reb Dovid went into the house and rocked the baby back to sleep!

Once, an unexpected guest showed up at Reb Dovid's house, and he had no food to offer him. Reb Dovid quickly took the very special *shemurah matzos* he had been saving for Pesach, cooked them in milk and gave them to his guest. To his shocked family, he explained, "We learn the mitzvah of *shemurah matzah* from the verse, 'You shall guard the matzos' (*Shemos* 12:17). But from these same words, *Chazal* learn, by reading mitzvos instead of matzos, 'When you have the opportunity to do a mitzvah, don't let it get stale!' With these matzos, I fulfilled the second explanation of the verse. When Pesach comes, I will fulfill, G-d willing, the first explanation with other matzos."

Reb Dovid particularly loved the Jews of the small, isolated communities that dotted the Polish countryside. He shared their loneliness and the difficulties they faced, living far from the larger Jewish communities. Once he passed through a small village with only one Jew. When the Jew saw Reb Dovid's carriage roll by, he came running after it crying, "Rebbe, Rebbe, please stop!"

Reb Dovid stopped his wagon. The village Jew asked him, "Your Jewish brother is living here, all alone, among *goyim*. How can you pass right through without stopping to see how he is doing?"

From then on, Reb Dovid stopped whenever he passed through a town with Jews; thus it always took him at least twice as long to travel anywhere. Even a journey of a few miles could take him a week or more. Whenever Reb Dovid dozed off in his carriage, his attendants would speed from town to town because, when awake, he would insist on stopping at every Jewish home.

Once, Reb Dovid gave them strict orders to stop at a certain town, where a Jew lay bedridden. Before they arrived,

Reb Dovid fell asleep and his attendants sped past the town. When Reb Dovid awoke, he demanded that they turn around and return to the town. When they arrived at the invalid's home, they found that he had passed away only moments before.

"Oh, Yaakov," cried Reb Dovid to his driver, "just look what you have done! If we had been here, he might have lived a little longer; and, if not, with our help he could have gone straight to Heaven."

Once Reb Dovid and his friend, Reb Lipa of Nevapeleh, were walking across the Polish countryside. They came to a small village in which there lived a Jewish family. They went to visit them, but only a young man was at home. They wished him good morning, he responded, and then they continued on their way.

A short while later, they heard someone calling them, "Stop! Stop!" The young man and his father were running after them at full speed. Startled, Reb Dovid and Reb Lipa also started running. They were afraid that they were victims of mistaken identity. Something was probably missing from the farmer's house, and he probably suspected that these two wanderers were the thieves.

"Stop! Stop!" the father and son cried, running even faster. "We're not going to hurt you!" Reb Dovid and Reb Lipa finally stopped, and the father and son caught up to them.

"Why did you run away?" asked the father. "I only want to give you a gift."

"But why?" they asked.

"My son has been mute his whole life. His 'good morning' to you were the first words he ever spoke! Please come back with us and let us honor you."

"You see," Reb Dovid said to his friend, "Hashem has shown us great kindness and we didn't even know it. If that young man had not answered our greeting, we might have assumed that he considered it beneath his dignity, since we seemed to be vagrants. Then we would have been terribly upset to see such *midos* in a Jew. Heaven granted him speech just to save us from such a terrible mistake!"

Similarly, Reb Dovid once delivered a package to the house of the Maggid of Vidislov. He handed it to one of the daughters, who happened to be sick. As he left, he casually remarked, "Good-bye and be well." The girl immediately recovered!

Once Reb Dovid was traveling by foot from Lelov to Zarnovitza to attend the wedding of the Seer's daughter. As he passed near the town of Vidislov, a nobleman's carriage drove by. Tied to it by ropes, and stumbling along behind, was an old Jewish couple.

"Stop! Stop!" Reb Dovid cried. "Why are you torturing these poor old people?"

"This couple leases an inn from me and they haven't paid the rent. They already owe me 150 teller!"

"But what do you gain by punishing them?" Reb Dovid argued. "Let them go free and I will pay their debt. I have no money with me now, but I will write you a promissory note. I am the Rabbi of Lelov."

The nobleman agreed and he released the two Jews.

At that same time, the Seer himself was in Vidislov, also on the way to the wedding. His attendants brought him his carriage, he put one leg on the footstep, and then he froze in place. He stood there motionless for two hours! Finally, Reb Dovid came walking down the street of the town. The Seer immediately entered the carriage and motioned to Reb Dovid to join him. "Don't worry about the promissory note," he told him. "We'll see that it gets paid." And they continued on to the wedding together.

That nobleman had several flocks of sheep. Later that year, two gentile merchants came to him and offered to buy his wool for 150 tellers more than the normal price. Suddenly he realized that this was the exact amount that the old couple had owed him. Surely the business deal had somehow come about through the intervention of the Rabbi of Lelov.

This nobleman had a son who could not speak. "If the Lelover Rabbi's power is so great," he reasoned, "surely he can help my son." So he prepared a gift for Reb Dovid and traveled with his son to Lelov. "I am canceling the debt the Rabbi owes me," he told Reb Dovid, "and I also ask him to heal my son."

Reb Dovid lifted his eyes to Heaven. "Master of the Universe! This man may be a dog, but there are a lot of barking dogs in the world too!" Immediately the boy regained his speech.

Fire from Sinai   Reb Dovid was once traveling in a wagon with a number of young scholars. He did not tell the wagon driver his final destination but, at every crossroad, pointed out the direction in which to turn. At nightfall they arrived in the city of Tchenstekov and found lodgings. In the morning, Reb Dovid went to the local schoolhouse and called one young boy, Yisroel Yitzchok from Zalshin, aside and tested him on his studies. Later, as Reb Dovid left the city, he told his traveling companions, "He was the one I had in mind."

Thereafter, a holy fire began to burn in Yisroel Yitzchok's heart, a deep desire to travel to Lelov and to study with Reb Dovid. Short of funds, he convinced another young man to travel to Lelov and take him along. After several weeks with Reb Dovid, Yisroel Yitzchok told his companion,

"You can return to Tchenstekov, I'm staying here." Reb Dovid directed the boy in the path of Torah and *avodas Hashem*, and eventually brought him to the Seer of Lublin. On Reb Dovid's recommendation, the boy joined the *minyan* of the Seer and eventually became renowned as Reb Yitzchok of Vorki. He used to say, "In one meeting, Reb Dovid, like Elisha, can completely change a person's life."

Both the Yehudi haKodesh and Reb Yeshaya of Pshadburz, became Chassidim of the Seer through Reb Dovid's influence. He met them when they were studying in a local *beis midrash*, sitting concealed by the large stove, so that no one would interrupt them. Reb Dovid went over to them and spoke about the greatness of the Seer of Lublin, until the two men felt a desire to visit him.

"You cannot visit him until I tell you the root of the Seer's soul, and you understand how it relates to yours," said Reb Dovid. "I'm traveling now but, when I return, I will tell you, and take you with me." Reb Dovid kept his word and, eventually, they became leading disciples of the Seer.

Sometime later, a Chassid name Reb Shmaryahu visited Reb Yeshaya in Pshadburz. In the middle of a meal, Reb Yeshaya began muttering to himself, "I'm not going to forgive him. No one can make me forgive him!" The Chassid expressed his amazement, and Reb Yeshaya explained: "Before I became a Chassid, I would sit and study with the Yehudi haKodesh day and night, without interruption. One day, Reb Dovid of Lelov came and took us to a private room and began to teach us Chassidus with such fire and enthusiasm that we didn't know where we were. We seemed to be at Mount Sinai. It was as if Reb Dovid were Moshe Rabbeinu, and his words were like those of the Living G-d, heard from out of the fire. We weren't in this world at all!

"Suddenly, a man came in and told us it was time to join them for the *Minchah* prayers. The Holy Lights went out, and I've never been able to forget that pain. The man who interrupted us eventually passed away; and, just now, his soul came to me to be healed, but how can I forgive him?"

One Good Deed Leads to Another

Reb Dovid always repaid one good deed with another. One cold winter night, a local non-Jew was passing a frozen river near Lelov when he noticed someone dunking in the water. He went to investigate, and found Reb Dovid using the icy water as a *mikveh*! After Reb Dovid came out, half frozen, the man covered him with his warm fur coat. Grateful, Reb Dovid blessed him with a long life, "until 120," and the blessing was fulfilled!

Reb Dovid's gratitude extended beyond his earthly life. Once, in the early hours of the morning, a passing Jew noticed a man lying unconscious on the frozen riverbank. Reb Dovid had passed out from the cold as he had left the frigid water. The man wrapped Reb Dovid in his coat and carried him home. He lay him in his bed and cared for him until he revived.

"You saved my life," Reb Dovid said. "What should I bless you with? Wealth or the World to Come?"

"The World to Come."

"If so, I will appear to you before you die," Reb Dovid promised.

Years went by, and Reb Dovid of Lelov passed from this world to the next. His rescuer grew old, and eventually his condition deteriorated until, one Shabbos day, he seemed to be on the verge of death. The Chevrah Kaddisha, the local burial society, came to attend to him in his last moments but, when they arrived, he told them, "Go away, my time has not yet come." Immediately after Shabbos, however, he sent for them again. "Now my time has come," he said. With his last breaths, he told them the story of the Rebbe's promise.

"When you came to me earlier, I turned my face to the wall and prayed to see Reb Dovid. The holy ministering angels went to call him, but he refused to come during Shabbos. But just now he came, so I must say my final confession..."

Jewish Money

Reb Dovid was not only ready to endanger his life for the sake of a Jewish soul; he would even put himself at risk to save a Jew's money.

A poor man once came to Reb Dovid crying about his misfortune. His house had been broken into and his meager possessions — his wallet, his tallis and tefillin, and a few other items — had all been stolen. Reb Dovid calmed the man down and asked him to wait a few minutes. He then went out in the bitter winter cold and broke a hole in the ice. He immersed himself again and again in the frozen water, until his attendant became worried. "Rebbe, please come out of there. You'll get sick!" But Reb Dovid refused to listen. "I'm not coming out until my prayers are accepted and that poor man's belongings are restored!"

A few minutes later, Reb Dovid left the water, and went home with his attendant. The poor man was still sitting there. After a short while, there was a loud knock at the door. "Open up! Open up!" shouted a rough voice. They opened the door slightly and someone — they couldn't see who — threw in a package containing all of the poor man's belongings and ran away.

Even Animals All his life Reb Dovid fulfilled the verse: "His compassion is on all His works" (*Tehillim* 145:9). Many times during the summer, at the big county fairs, while the wagon drivers were busy selling their wares, Reb Dovid would carry pails of water out to the thirsty horses, those of Jews and gentiles alike.

One Friday afternoon Reb Dovid was returning to Lelov by carriage. Suddenly the horse stopped in the middle of the road and refused to move. The wagon driver struck it with his whip. "How can you do that?" Reb Dovid exclaimed, "How can you cause such pain to an animal?"

"Rebbe, its almost Shabbos!"

"True," Reb Dovid replied, "but, when you reach the Next World and stand before the Heavenly Court, this horse will call you to trial. Even if you are vindicated, you'll feel awfully embarrassed to be standing in judgment with a horse."

Whenever Reb Dovid traveled to the Seer in Lublin, he would invite every Jew he passed on the road to join him in the carriage. But if the men and their valises weighed down the wagon, he would ask them, "Please, leave your baggage with me and continue on to Lublin by foot. Let's not torture this poor horse!"

One Rosh Hashanah morning in Lublin, just before shofar blowing, the congregation noticed that Reb Dovid was missing. The Seer waited as Reb Yitzchok of Vorki ran to the inn to search for him. There he found Reb Dovid, wrapped in his tallis, holding his hat filled with grain, feeding the horses. The wagon driver had run to shul and had forgotten to give them food, but Reb Dovid did not forget. Once the horses had finished eating, Reb Dovid returned to shul. The congregation was still waiting for him. When the Seer saw him, he remarked with a broad smile, "Reb Dovid has prepared us to blow shofar!"

Love of Israel

Indeed, we learn that if a person is kind to animals, who have no good deeds, Hashem is kind to him when he has none either (see *Tzivos haRivash* 13a). On the other hand, Reb Dovid's horses had plenty of good deeds! Whenever he would come into a town, he would gather together all the Jewish children, give them pennywhistles, and ride them around town on his carriage as they piped merrily away, just to make them happy. Often he would comment, "I'm jealous of these horses which give joy to so many Jewish children."

See No Evil The Me'or v'Shemesh, Reb Kalonymous Kalman, once wrote, "A person beholds the world according to his inner character. A tzaddik cannot see evil in others, because the light and goodness of Hashem shines in him. Wherever he looks, he sees only good." Reb Dovid's love of Israel was so intense that he simply couldn't believe that a Jew could sin, and would try with all his might to judge each person favorably.

Reb Dovid and Reb Yitzchok of Vorki were once staying in a small village, and decided to visit the Jewish families there. When they reached the house of a certain unscrupulous, public sinner, Reb Yitzchok tried to keep Reb Dovid from entering. "Rebbe," he told him, "That man is truly wicked!" Reb Dovid paid no attention and pointed to the *mezuzah* on the door. "How can you say he is wicked? See, he has a *mezuzah*."

Reb Dovid's *mechutan*, the Yehudi haKodesh, once visited him for three months in an effort to learn his special way of Divine service, but still couldn't grasp it. At the end of the visit, Reb Dovid escorted the Yehudi home. As usual, he stopped to visit every Jewish family in every town they passed. He would encourage each family and address their father respectfully as "Rav of the City." All this time, the Yehudi would wait outside, with growing impatience that his trip home was taking so long.

In one particular house, Reb Dovid spent half an hour talking. When he finally emerged, the Yehudi asked him in exasperation, "What took you so long there?"

Reb Dovid answered, "In this house there is a rather coarse fellow, a butcher by trade, who lives with his elderly parents. When I came in, he was busy at work. He gave his father a knife to cut up a side of beef, and when the old man proved too weak for the job, his son became so angry he bellowed, 'If I didn't fear G-d, I would beat you!' When I heard that he feared G-d, I couldn't bring myself to leave him."

"Really," Reb Dovid used to say, "every Jew has a core of complete goodness, even if he himself is unaware of it. The bad is only external, not intrinsic to his soul at all." The inner Jewish soul is simply not inclined to sin.

Reb Dovid once saw a Jew sinning, with no possible excuse.

"What can he do, the poor man," explained Reb Dovid. "He's weak!"

"Why, that man is in the best of health!" retorted the outraged onlookers.

"No," explained Reb Dovid. "The Mishnah states, 'Who is strong? One who conquers his evil inclination' (*Avos* 4:1). This man is definitely weak."

"It is impossible to find bad in a Jew," said the Chidushei haRim in Reb Dovid's name. "And if you think that you have, that's only the non-Jewish part of him." The Chidushei haRim himself added, "Since a non-Jew is forbidden to keep the Shabbos, a person must be particularly careful to eliminate that non-Jewish part of himself every week before the Shabbos arrives."

Love of Israel

I Think the Opposite!

Reb Dovid's compassion often led him to see things differently than others. Once, in the middle of the winter, when the snow was piled high and the cold cut to the bone, a poor Jew, with peeling shoes and threadbare coat came knocking at Reb Dovid's door. Reb Dovid didn't have a coin to give him but, looking at the poor man's feet, said to himself, "I can always stay at home, but this Jew must walk around in the snow almost barefoot." So he gave his own shoes to the beggar.

When his wife returned home and found him barefoot, she was horrified. She quickly borrowed some money from the neighbors and ran to the market to buy Reb Dovid some used shoes. She was directed to a non-Jewish butcher who had a pair to sell. To her amazement, he offered her husband's own shoes to her. The Jewish beggar had traded them in for a cut of *treif* meat! The Rebbetzin bought the shoes and returned home.

"Look what you did," she complained. "You gave your shoes to a sinner who poisoned his soul with *treif* meat."

"Calm down," Reb Dovid told her. "Do you think that poor Jew, who had to trudge through the snow in bare feet, would trade in his new shoes just to fill his appetite?

"Obviously, he was hungry to the point of death. He was probably already sick. Of course, it's permissible to feed a dying person *treif* food to save his life. It was right for him to trade in those shoes. And as for us, not only did we get the mitzvah of *tzedakah*, we even got the mitzvah of saving a Jewish life!"

Another time, the townspeople of Lelov caught a wayward Jew transgressing the Shabbos. They started chasing him with sticks. The man ran for his life — and, in his confusion, ran straight into the home of Reb Dovid. The townspeople stood angrily outside, while inside, Reb Dovid received the man warmly, sat him at his table and brought him bread and fish. The man ate until he was full.

The Rebbetzin came in and complained. "Who are you feeding? Look out the window. The entire town is waiting to grab this man and teach him a lesson." Reb Dovid replied calmly, "If a Jew who is already ensnared by the evil inclination can hold himself back from sin for even one minute, he deserves reward!"

On the eve of every Yom Kippur, the Seer of Lublin would review all his deeds of the previous year to be sure that he never once became angry. As for Reb Dovid of Lelov, it was said that he never even reached the point of being annoyed. He would interpret the verse: "Do not hate your friend in your heart" as meaning "because of your heart." If you see your friend stumble in a matter in which you are strong, do not hate him because his heart is not as strong as yours.

In this vein, Reb Dovid explained the epithet in the *motza'ei Shabbos* song, "Eliyahu haNavi": "A man who saw twelve generations." What's so praiseworthy about seeing twelve generations? Reb Dovid suggested that, although older generations generally have no patience for the younger ones, Eliyahu haNavi had such love and tolerance that he thought kindly of people twelve generations after his own.

Know Your Friend

Before the butchers of Lelov would buy a cow, they would often first ask Reb Dovid to examine it and advise whether or not it was kosher. Reb Dovid was once sitting with the Yehudi haKodesh to conclude a marriage agreement between their two children. A local butcher came in and asked Reb Dovid to come with him to the market and look at a cow. Reb Dovid immediately arose and left. When he returned, his wife asked, "You were arranging your son's marriage. How could you leave to go look at a cow?"

Reb Dovid answered, "I knew that the Yehudi haKodesh wouldn't get upset if I went; but I was worried that the butcher might get upset if I stayed!"

Reb Dovid once heard a simple Jew praying. Between every verse the man would say Hashem's Name. When Reb Dovid asked him why, the man explained, "I've heard that two *yud*s printed together are an abbreviation for Hashem's Name(״) See, they are printed between every sentence in my prayerbook(:)."

"No, sometimes two dots are just the end of a sentence, and sometimes they are Hashem's Name," explained Reb Dovid. "Whenever you have two *yuddin* or two *Yiddin* (Jews) standing one beside the other, treating each other equally, the *Shechinah* rests between them, and they form Hashem's Name. But whenever one *Yid* thinks he is higher than the next, they don't form Hashem's Name!"

Making Peace

Division between Jews pushes away the *Shechinah*, explained Reb Dovid. Haman accused the Jews of being "a nation scattered and divided," because they were sunk in strife. Thus, Esther's first command to Mordechai was to "gather together all the Jews." That alone helped bring their redemption. Indeed, "If all Jews were truly able to join together," Reb Dovid once said, "they could reach all the way to the Throne of Glory and draw down such blessing and goodness that there would never be any lack." Thus, Reb Dovid worked his entire life to make peace between individuals and communities.

As a young man on his way to visit the Rebbe Reb Elimelech of Lyzhansk, Reb Dovid once became thoroughly lost in a thick forest. Tired and confused, he turned his eyes to Heaven and wept. Suddenly, he saw a man standing in front of him.

"Why are you crying?" asked the man.

"I'm lost, night is falling, and I'm scared of the wild beasts in the woods."

"Don't worry," said the stranger. "Come with me." Reb Dovid followed the man through the woods, until they finally emerged on the outskirts of Lyzhansk.

Before they parted, the man said Reb Dovid, "I will teach you two things that you must remember your entire life. First, when a person wants to graft two trees together, he first must remove all the knots and rough spots in the wood; and second, rather than searching after the faults in another, it is better to search for the faults in oneself." Only many years later did Reb Dovid understand those words of Eliyahu haNavi to their core.

Often, the rough spots we find in others are merely imaginary. Reb Dovid and Reb Yitzchok of Vorki were once walking across the countryside. As they entered a small village, a strange woman came running after them and started beating and cursing Reb Yitzchok. "This is what you deserve, you scoundrel, for abandoning your wife and children!"

Reb Dovid quickly intervened and proved to the woman that Reb Yitzchok was not her long lost husband. She was extremely embarrassed and begged for forgiveness. "There is nothing to forgive," said Reb Dovid. "You thought you were hitting your absconding husband, who deserves to be hit!"

Afterward, Reb Dovid told Reb Yitzchok, "During most arguments, both sides think that the other person is unworthy and to blame. You just have to show them that it is a case of mistaken identity, and then the difficulty will resolve itself."

Love of Israel

The other essential road to peace is prayer. Once Reb Dovid and Reb Yitzchok traveled to a certain town to make peace between its warring factions. They first prayed *Minchah* at the local shul. Immediately afterwards, Reb Dovid told his disciple, "Hitch up the horses. We're leaving."

"But Rebbe," Reb Yitzchok objected, "we came here to make peace. Why are we leaving so soon?"

"Peace has already been made. When I prayed in the *Shemoneh Esreh*, 'Let He Who makes peace in His Heavens, make peace for us and for all Israel,' my prayers were accepted, so now we can go home!"

FOUR
Torah and Avodah

A Place Apart

"A Jew must have three things," Reb Dovid once said. "Even if he has many worries, he must still have a composed mind. In a tavern full of drunkards, he must still be able to meditate on Hashem; and in a city full of strife, he must still find a place to rest."

Reb Dovid's "house" was a single small room, in which his family lived, in which he entertained guests, and in which he received his Chassidim. "If a piece of string is considered a wall for a making an *eruv* for Shabbos," he said serenely, "it can create a private room for me as well." Whenever he needed privacy, he simply cordoned off one corner of the room with a piece of string.

Whenever Reb Dovid attended the Shabbos *tisch* of the Seer of Lublin, he always sat at the far end, away from the limelight. "If Korach had only known," he maintained, "that a person can serve Hashem quietly, in some unnoticed corner, and still accomplish as much as the *Kohen Gadol* in the Holy of Holies, he would never have fought with Aharon over the priesthood, and he would never have been lost from the congregation."

Reb Dovid, the Yehudi haKodesh and Rav Fishel, the Strikover Rav, once visited the Kozhnitzer Maggid. The Maggid, who was extremely frail, lay on his bed, near which a table with food and drink was prepared for his guests. The Yehudi pulled his chair up close to the Maggid and began discussing deep secrets of Torah, while Reb Dovid and the Strikover Rav sat at the table. The Strikover Rav leaned over to try and catch scraps of their holy conversation, while Reb Dovid sat quietly buttering his toast. The Kozhnitzer Maggid turned to the Strikover Rav and asked him, "Why don't you act like this other young man? He sits there eating a piece of toast, and his every bite is another offering to Hashem!"

True Humility Reb Dovid's great humility reflected his insight. Of what could he be proud? Of knowledge? A person who knows something, realizes that he knows nothing! Of righteousness? The sons of Yaakov were judged strictly until they admitted, "We are to blame!" Of longing to serve Hashem? The Talmud says: "A person who comes to purify himself is helped from Heaven," to which Reb Dovid added, "He is even helped to come and seek purification." Of being free of sin? In Reb Dovid's eyes, so was everyone else! What was there to be proud of? Even towards the end of his life, when thousands of Chassidim flocked to him, Reb Dovid would comment, "All the rivers descend to the sea, because it is lower than them all."

Humility leads to love of Israel. King Solomon said, "As water reflects face to face, so is the heart of a man to his fellow" (*Mishlei* 27:19). "Why," asked Reb Dovid, "use the image of water, rather than a mirror? Because to look into a mirror a person looks upward; to look into the water, he

Torah and Avodah

looks downward. Indeed, the more he lowers himself, the larger the reflection becomes. So too, between friends, the lower a person makes himself, the greater his friend becomes in his eyes, and the more love can exist between them."

Nevertheless, both pride and humility can serve Hashem. "A person must have two pockets," Reb Dovid said. "One should contain the maxim, 'The world was created for me,' and the other, 'I am but dust and ashes.' Unfortunately, many people confuse these two pockets. When it comes to doing a mitzvah, they say, 'Who am I to do such a great thing?' Yet in matters concerning their responsibility to society, they are quite sure that the world was created for them alone."

The Power of Faith

Chazal ask in *Midrash Bemidbar Rabbah* 18:7: "Korach was a smart man, so why did he get involved in such foolishness?" Reb Dovid explained, "*Chazal* wanted to know why Korach got involved in the foolishness of being so smart." Simple faith is a better approach, and Reb Dovid never worried about the future. *Parashas Va'eschanan* begins, "And [Moshe] beseeched Hashem at that time." All of Moshe's prayers were only directed toward the present, "that time," not tomorrow.

Reb Dovid once arrived in a certain town in the wee hours of the morning. Only one shop was open. "Certainly," Reb Dovid thought, "the owner has risen early to study a little before daybreak." When Reb Dovid entered, he was surprised to see the owner standing idly behind the counter.

"Why open your shop so early?" Reb Dovid asked. The man explained that his livelihood was suffering from his competitors and that he had decided to open his store before them to attract early customers. Reb Dovid was appalled by the man's lack of faith. He lifted his hands in disbelief and quoted the Psalmist, "In vain do you rise early, sit up late, and eat the bread of toil, for to His beloved [Hashem] gives tranquility" (*Tehillim* 127:2). The man later testified that during that entire day, not one customer entered his store.

Reb Dovid often told the story of a man who was destitute. To strengthen his faith in Hashem, he decided not to ask anyone for food. His condition got worse and worse until, one day, too weak to stand, he collapsed from hunger on the outskirts of town. As he lay helpless on the ground, he heard the rumble of an approaching carriage. He cried out, the carriage stopped, and several Jews descended and, without his asking, gave him food. "What a pity that he gave up at the last moment," Reb Dovid concluded. The passing carriage was only a test. If he hadn't cried out, manna would surely have rained down upon him from Heaven!"

Similarly, Reb Dovid was once traveling near the town of Bialeh. He was extremely thirsty, but couldn't find water. "Master of the Universe," he said, "Moshe Rabbeinu hit a rock and water flowed out. I fully believe it can happen again." He stuck the end of his walking stick into the ground, and when he removed it, water flowed from the hole. He drank and was satisfied.

Lelov — Lo Lev

Even among the holy students of the Seer of Lublin, Reb Dovid was renowned for his fear of G-d and for his pure and simple faith. His emphasis on the service of the heart, over that of the mind, led the Divrei Chaim of Sanz to point out that "Lelov" has the same letters as the words *lo lev* (he has heart).

Torah and Avodah

At the great wedding of the grandson of the Seer, the Seer sat the Me'or v'Shemesh and Reb Dovid of Lelov on one side of him, and the Yehudi haKodesh and Reb Yeshaya of Pshadburz on the other. He explained, "Reb Dovid and the Me'or v'Shemesh are both outstanding in their fear of Hashem. So they should sit together. The Yehudi haKodesh and Reb Yeshaya are both giants in Torah. So they should sit together."

Reb Dovid worked hard to maintain this simplicity, to seem like one of those "clever men who make themselves like beasts" (*Chullin* 5b). Once when his friend, Reb Reuven haKohen of Zavnah, told him a piece of Torah, Reb Dovid replied, "I'm sure when the *Mashiach* comes he will learn this bit of Torah with us, and then we will understand it!"

The Secret Scholar

Reb Dovid always tried to hide his true greatness in Torah. No one ever saw him studying. He would hide in the attic to be undisturbed. In the depths of winter, he would wrap his feet with pillows and continue learning; but whenever he heard someone coming up the stairs, he would hurriedly put away his book.

Once, Reb Dovid's brother-in-law, Rabbi Chaim Beldechovitz, came visiting, and Reb Dovid prepared a bed for him in the attic. Reb Chaim, anxious to watch his brother-in-law study, only pretended to fall asleep. Later, Reb Dovid came up to the attic and opened a *Tikunei Zohar*. Suddenly he rose and approached the bed. "Chaim, aren't you asleep yet?" A heavy slumber fell over the young man, who saw nothing of Reb Dovid's nighttime activities.

Reb Dovid once undertook a week-long fast — from Shabbos to Shabbos. On Friday afternoon, a guest suddenly appeared at his house. Reb Dovid treated the man cordially, offering him something to eat and drink; but the guest refused to partake of the food unless his host joined him. Although only a few hours remained to complete the fast and reap its spiritual benefits, Reb Dovid released himself from his vow and joined the man in the meal, just so no one would suspect that he was fasting.

Once the Seer of Lublin was studying a particularly difficult comment of the Maharsha on the Gemara, and he asked Reb Dovid to explain it.

"How could I know?" Reb Dovid responded.

"Nevertheless, give me an answer," the Seer pressed.

"Please, don't make fun of me."

"Reb Dovid," said the Seer, "I insist on hearing your opinion."

Reb Dovid nodded his head in submission and proceeded to give the most brilliant and clear answer imaginable.

On another occasion, the Maggid of Kozhnitz visited the Seer in Lublin and asked him to explain a difficult section of the Zohar. "Only Reb Dovid of Lelov could understand that," replied the Seer.

Later, when Reb Dovid visited Lublin, the Seer ordered him to visit the Maggid in Kozhnitz. There the Maggid asked him to explain the difficult Zohar. Once again, Reb Dovid claimed ignorance. The Maggid pressed him, until Reb Dovid gave an answer, with remarkable clarity. "All the sick people who need help come to me for a blessing," said the Maggid, "but Jews like you, who could help me, all go to Lublin instead!"

According to the Chidushei haRim, when Reb Dovid was only twenty-five years old, he had already learned the entire Talmud twenty-four times. And yet, even Reb Dovid's close friend and *mechutan*, the Yehudi haKodesh, initially knew nothing of his brilliance. The Yehudi haKodesh agreed to the marriage of their children based only on Reb Dovid's holiness and *avodas Hashem*. When, quite by accident, he

Torah and Avodah

learned of Reb Dovid's brilliance in Torah, he jumped on the table and started dancing with joy. Afterwards, he bought everyone drinks to make a *l'chaim*.

A Simple Story

The Maggid of Kozhnitz was once visiting the Seer in Lublin, and the two tzaddikim began discussing their disciples. "Send me two of your better students with whom I can discuss concepts in Torah and Chassidus," the Maggid asked. The Seer agreed and sent for Reb Dovid and the Yehudi haKodesh.

"Do you know how to learn?" the Maggid first asked the Yehudi haKodesh.

"I do," the Yehudi replied, and he began a complex explanation of a deep *sugyah* (topic), much to the Maggid's delight. When the Yehudi concluded, the Maggid turned to Reb Dovid.

"And you, do you also know how to learn?"

Reb Dovid gave a smile. "Why should the Maggid think that I know how to learn!"

"Certainly you know how to learn Gemara," the Maggid said.

"Gemara!" Reb Dovid answered with surprise.

"How about Midrash?" the Maggid continued.

"Midrash!" said Reb Dovid.

"Well," said the Maggid, "can you at least tell me a story?"

"A story I know!" announced Reb Dovid, and began to relate a simple tale. When he concluded, the Maggid was beaming.

"Thank you," the Maggid responded. "For a long time I have been trying to understand that Kabbalistic teaching in the *Tikunei Zohar*. Your story provided me the explanation!"

"What is the difference between me and Reb Dovid?" the Yehudi haKodesh commented. "My work in Torah has brought me to the fear of Hashem, while Reb Dovid's fear of Hashem has brought him to a deep understanding of Torah."

Nothing More to Say

Once, while in the city of Piltz, Reb Dovid went to visit the local rabbi, Rav Avraham Tzvi Hirsh, the author of *Bris Avraham*. The Rav greeted Reb Dovid warmly and asked him for a favor. "I am about to give a lecture to my students in the yeshiva. Could I review it with you first?"

"You know I am not a *talmid chacham*," replied Reb Dovid. "At least give me a few minutes to look at the Gemara." So Reb Dovid began to read aloud from the Gemara pages on which the Rav had built his lesson. As he read, he explained the words to himself. Rav Avraham Tzvi overhead his explanations and was amazed. "Now I have nothing more to say!" he declared. "I had built my lesson on a number of questions which you have answered so thoroughly that they have all been solved!"

Once, when the Yehudi haKodesh was visiting Reb Dovid in Lelov, he met another great scholar, Rabbi Dov Beirish, head of the rabbinical court of Bendin. A question of halachah came before them, and the Yehudi asked Rabbi Dov Beirish to decide it.

"Why does the master not answer himself?" the Rav of Bendin asked.

"To do so would be like a student answering in front of his teacher, since Reb Dovid of Lelov is here," answered the Yehudi.

The Rav of Bendin smiled. "And why aren't I worried about the same thing?"

"You're not worried because you do not know him as I do!"

The Rav of Bendin stopped smiling.

Greater than Both

The Yehudi haKodesh once traveled for two weeks across the Polish countryside with Reb Yeshaya of Pshadburz, to a wedding in Zarnovitza. They spent their time engrossed in Torah study, reviewing most of the Talmud, *Rishonim* and *Acharonim* by heart.

At one point, they entered into a vigorous debate, in which each of them produced brilliant proofs for his own position, but neither could disprove the other's. "We will ask someone greater than both of us to give us the answer," said the Yehudi.

Reb Yeshaya was skeptical. "If we can't agree with each other, why would we concede to a third party?"

"You'll see," replied the Yehudi. "We will readily agree to his opinion."

"Which great scholar are you referring to?" Reb Yeshaya asked.

"Reb Dovid of Lelov," said the Yehudi. Reb Yeshaya was amazed; since when was he a *gaon*? When they reached Zarnovitza, they asked Reb Dovid their questions. He solved their problem on the spot using a vast array of Talmudic commentaries.

Reb Yeshaya was stunned. "When the *Mashiach* comes," he declared, "Reb Dovid will be his judge! In Talmud and halachah, Reb Dovid is as great as Rabbi Yonason Eibeshitz; and in Kabbalah...I have absolutely no idea!"

On another occasion, Reb Dovid and the Yehudi haKodesh stopped to visit the learned local Rabbi of a small town. The Yehudi engaged the Rav in a deep, complex Talmudic debate. Each brought proofs to disprove the other's position, to no avail.

"Let's ask Reb Dovid which of us is right," the Yehudi suggested.

The Rabbi laughed. "How can a person who is never seen learning solve the dilemma of two scholars?"

The Yehudi haKodesh asked Reb Dovid, nonetheless, and immediately received a clear, brilliant answer. When the local Rabbi heard his words, he removed his shoes and went to receive Reb Dovid's reproach, as the halachah mandates for one who belittles a qualified Torah scholar.

True Learning

Reb Dovid learned Torah differently from others. He once found his son, Reb Moshe, in the *beis midrash* learning Gemara on a purely intellectual level. He went over to him and closed the Gemara. "This is not how one learns," he said.

How then does one learn? Reb Dovid would test his grandson, Reb Yosef Hirsh, every Shabbos. Once, Reb Dovid was dissatisfied with his grandson's learning. Reb Yosef reviewed the material a second time; but Reb Dovid was still displeased. Reb Yosef reviewed the text once more, until his understanding was absolutely clear. But Reb Dovid was still not satisfied.

Reb Yosef Hirsh began to cry. "If I don't know it by now, I will never know it!"

"You understand the material fine," said Reb Dovid, "But you lack something else. When you learn the Gemara and mention the name of a sage, it's not enough to know what he said. You must see him standing in front of you as if he were still alive."

Once, Reb Dovid was traveling to Pshischah to visit the Yehudi haKodesh. Along the way he became tired,

Torah and Avodah

removed his shoes, and took a nap in the carriage. When the Yehudi heard that Reb Dovid was coming, he ran out to meet the wagon. Climbing onto the outside step, he hung onto the carriage until it pulled up in front of his house. Then he entered the carriage and greeted Reb Dovid warmly. To show his love, he even began putting on Reb Dovid's shoes. He put on one shoe and, when he began searching for the next, Reb Dovid gestured to it with his walking stick.

Once in the house, the Yehudi treated Reb Dovid with so much respect that his own students were amazed. "Don't be surprised," he told them. "I've been trying to understand a certain teaching of the Arizal for twenty-two years; and Reb Dovid pointed to his shoe with his stick in such a way that he clarified it completely!"

Once, an old man came to the Chidushei haRim and wanted to tell him a thought he had heard from Reb Dovid. "How can we understand what he said?" exclaimed the Chidushei haRim. "He spoke in a language that is incomprehensible to us!" Likewise, the Yehudi haKodesh once said, "I can give 400 explanations of every word of my *mechutan*, and still not penetrate its depths!"

If Reb Dovid's Torah knowledge was so well concealed, how much more hidden was the depth of his everyday speech. Regarding the verse, "And Dovid blessed Hashem in the eyes of the people, and Dovid said..." (I *Divrei ha-Yamim* 29:10), he commented: In truth, Dovid was blessing Hashem, but in the eyes of the people, it seemed as if he was saying something quite else.

He also concealed how he brought his fellow Jews closer to Hashem. Some tzaddikim move through the world, mixing with people to influence them directly, while others more discreetly use their great personal holiness to uplift their generation. Reb Dovid was a tzaddik of the latter type.

He once found Reb Simcha Bunim of Pshischah speaking directly to a young scholar about Chassidus. Reb Dovid interrupted him, "If you want to fill him with fear of Hashem, you would do better to pray for him."

Reb Dovid once visited the scholar Reb Yaakov Blum of Tchenstekov. Since Reb Yaakov was in the middle of delivering a *shiur*, he greeted his guest briefly and then returned to his students. Reb Dovid sat quietly in the corner of the room and listened, leaving about a quarter of an hour later. As soon as Reb Dovid had left, Reb Yaakov felt a burning desire to speak to him. He quickly sent one of his students to look for him, but Reb Dovid had already left for home. Reb Yaakov immediately set off for Lelov. He stayed there several days and became one of Reb Dovid's closest students.

In order to draw great souls to Chassidus, Reb Dovid was willing to do anything, even to reveal his most precious secret, his mastery of Torah. Once Reb Dovid tried to attract the Rav of Tshakshin, the author of *Chosen Yeshuos*, to Chassidus; but the latter replied sharply, "How can you teach me? 'A boor cannot be a Chassid'" (*Avos* 2:5). Reb Dovid took him to his house and they discussed the depths of Torah the entire night. By morning, the Rav readily admitted that it was quite fitting for Reb Dovid to draw people to Chassidus.

Nor was his influence limited to the famous and educated. In Pshadburz there lived a simple, unlearned man, who possessed a tremendous fear of Heaven. "When I was a child," he explained, "Reb Dovid of Lelov passed through our town, dressed in rags like a wandering beggar. All of the children ran after him and teased him. Suddenly, he turned to me and declared, 'My child, you should fear G-d!' From that moment on, a pure spirit entered me and has never left!"

The Holy Rabbi Chaim Dovid

A certain Jew contracted a serious intestinal disease, for which his doctors had no cure. It seemed as though his days were numbered. Several of his friends suggested that he visit the great hot spring baths of Europe; perhaps they would provide a cure. Before setting out, the man consulted his physician, Dr. Chaim Dovid Bernhard, one of the leading physicians in Poland. An assimilated Jew, he had studied at the Institute of Medicine in Breslau, Germany. Returning to his homeland, he had moved to Piatrikov to become the personal physician of Prince Zeinshtik.

Dr. Bernhard strongly warned the man against traveling. His condition was so serious that he might not make it home. Feeling that he had no other choice, the sick man traveled to the baths anyway, but even there found no relief. The resident doctors were so worried by his condition that they urged him to return home rather than die in a foreign land. Totally brokenhearted the man began his long trip home.

Traveling across Poland, he passed through Lelov. "Let me visit the holy Rabbi who lives here," he thought. "Perhaps he will pray for my recovery." Reb Dovid told the man: "Pay no attention to those doctors; they don't know what they are talking about." He gave him some strong brandy and old, salted cheese. "Here, make a *l'chaim* and get some sleep!" The man ate, drank, and then slept all night. In the morning he woke up...totally healed!

The man took leave of Reb Dovid and returned home to Piatrikov. When Dr. Bernhard saw him, he turned white, as if he had seen a ghost. The man should have been dead, but here he was, alive and well! He examined him and found that the disease had completely disappeared. The man then told Dr. Bernhard the story of his meeting with Reb Dovid of Lelov.

The doctor was stunned. "He healed you with poison!" he explained. "There is nothing worse for your disease than brandy and salted cheese. I must travel to Lelov to meet this man!"

Shortly thereafter, a local nobleman near Lelov fell sick. He asked a baron in Warsaw to send him an expert doctor, and the baron quickly sent Dr. Bernhard. By the time he arrived, the nobleman had already died, but Dr. Bernhard took the opportunity to visit the mysterious tzaddik.

Reb Dovid welcomed him. "When Shaul went in search of his lost donkeys, his attendant told him, 'Behold the G-dly man, Shmuel haNavi, lives in the city. Let us go there. Perhaps he can tell us about the way we have come' (I *Shmuel* 9:6). This seems odd. They were looking for their donkeys, not the way they had come — that they already knew! But they wanted to know why Hashem had led them on such a futile search, what their path truly led to. So Shmuel told them where they had really been: Hashem had arranged it so Shmuel could anoint Shaul as king over Israel."

"Here too, you have traveled all the way from Piatrikov to Lelov, apparently for no reason. But that was not the real reason for your journey. We have something much more important to talk about." Reb Dovid then began to talk with the doctor about Hashem, Torah and *teshuvah*. During their discussion, Dr. Bernhard asked the tzaddik twenty-four difficult questions. Reb Dovid answered twenty of them. "For the remaining four, we will have to ask the Seer in Lublin."

The two men set off. As soon as they entered the house of the Seer, even before opening their mouths, the Seer said to them, "If a Jew is troubled by such-and-such a question, here is the answer! If he is troubled by this other question here is its answer!" And he answered all four remaining questions.

Torah and Avodah

Dr. Bernhard did complete *teshuvah* and became a very special Jew, known as "the holy Rabbi Chaim Dovid of Piatrikov." He rose, level after level, until the Seer commented that his *teshuvah* had reached even higher than that of Dr. Gordon, the Czar's doctor, who was among the inner circle of the Maggid of Mezritch. "He is like our heart," said the Seer; and, one Shavuos, the Seer showed him a vision of the Giving of the Torah.

Rabbi Chaim Dovid was often visited by the great Chassidic Rebbes of his time, who would come to learn from his holy ways; but he himself always clung to Reb Dovid of Lelov. Whenever he spoke about all the tzaddikim he had met, he would place Reb Dovid in an entirely different category: "There is none like him!"

Even after Reb Dovid had passed away, his soul would appear to Rabbi Chaim Dovid and teach him. Once, Rabbi Chaim Dovid was sleeping on a couch. Reb Dovid appeared to him in a dream, saying, "There is *sha'atnez* in this couch! Get up quickly and check it!" He checked it, and indeed found *sha'atnez* there.

On his last Rosh Hashanah, Rabbi Chaim Dovid told his family, "Every year, on this day, Reb Dovid has appeared to me and said, 'My son, go home; I will do *Tashlich* for you.' But this year he did not come, so I know that my end is near."

Many years after Rabbi Chaim Dovid's death, his son, Rabbi Yaakov Yitzchok of Piatrikov, came to the Sefas Emes of Gur. "Please, Rebbe, pray that I should fear Hashem," he begged. "My father had been in much lower places than I, and yet in the end, he became very great." The Sefas Emes replied, "True, but who can compare himself to his mentor, the holy Reb Dovid of Lelov!"

Towards the end of his days, when Reb Dovid of Lelov had already contracted the illness that would take his life, he commented, "I don't need to live any longer. I came into this world only to make Rabbi Chaim Dovid a *ba'al teshuvah*. Now that the job is done, I need no longer stay."

An additional factor in Reb Dovid's passing seems to be related to the tension that arose between the Seer of Lublin and the Yehudi haKodesh. Although we can never fully comprehend the underlying motivations of these great tzaddikim, knowing that "both opinions are the words of the Living G-d," let us now turn to one of the most enigmatic and painful incidents in the history of Chassidus, one that almost tore apart Polish Jewry.

FIVE
The End of an Era

The Yehudi haKodesh in Lublin

Yaakov Yitzchok of Pshischah, the Yehudi haKodesh, a great tzaddik and a brilliant scholar, was a younger friend and contemporary of Reb Dovid of Lelov. A week before Reb Dovid first brought the Yehudi to Lublin, the Seer was told, "Your successor will have the same name as you, Yaakov Yitzchok." A few days later, a Chassid by that name arrived in Lublin, but the Seer rejected him. When the Yehudi haKodesh arrived, however, the Seer rejoiced greatly and soon began sending his finest students to Pshischah to study.

In Pshischah, the Yehudi gathered a group of young scholars from whom he demanded the utmost commitment to Torah study and *avodas Hashem*. Just as the Children of Israel had to leave civilization to receive the Torah "in an unsown land" (*Yirmeyahu* 2:2), a Chassid had to abandon all his worldly desires in order to become a student of the Yehudi. The approach of the Yehudi was so intense that only a few special individuals could successfully follow it. As Reb Uri of Strelisk once commented, "The Seer resembles Rashi's tefillin; the Yehudi haKodesh, Rabbeinu Tam's. True, according to Kabbalah, Rabbeinu Tam's tefillin are more holy, but the accepted halachah follows Rashi. Rabbeinu Tam's tefillin are only for unique individuals, outstanding in their service of Hashem."

Sources of Controversy

The Yehudi's insistence on intense concentration in prayer often delayed prayers in Pshischah past their halachic limits. The Yehudi also sought to vault his followers up to a very high level of spirituality immediately, without all the usual, more gradual preparations. "The Yehudi haKodesh wants to institute a new approach to serving Hashem," said Reb Uri of Strelisk. "He wants to draw down Heaven before lifting up the earth; but this approach has never been attempted before."

The resulting opposition from other Chassidic leaders was not directed against the Yehudi and his closest disciples, who were all tzaddikim, but against lesser individuals who sought to imitate their ways without being on the necessary high spiritual level. For example, Reb Naftali of Ropshitz used to say, "I am not concerned about the Tzaddik of Pshischah, but with his followers. One must work many years to arrive at such high levels. To try to jump to them immediately allows the side of impurity to intermingle with one's deeds."

The Yehudi's opponents could point to such authorities as Reb Yaakov Yosef of Polynoye, who wrote, "Each person must proceed according to his level rather than grasp for levels beyond his ability, for then nothing will remain. Many tried to imitate Rabbi Shimon bar Yochai, but they did not succeed, because they were not truly on his level. I heard this from the Ba'al Shem Tov himself." Similarly, the Seer taught that a person should serve Hashem simply, without becoming involved in complicated speculation. "Why do we blow the shofar on Rosh Hashanah?" the Seer once asked. "Because Hashem said, 'Blow!'" Reb Naftali of Ropshitz similarly wrote, "Moshe and Aharon never wanted more than what Hashem wanted for them. Nor did they ever seek out matters beyond their understanding."

Reb Dovid Supports the Yehudi haKodesh Despite the cogent arguments on both sides, Reb Dovid of Lelov primarily supported the approach of the Yehudi haKodesh. This lent special weight to the Yehudi's position, since Reb Dovid was a senior disciple of the Seer and a former student of the Rebbe Reb Elimelech. Reb Dovid agreed that one must pray with great intensity, even if the prayers were delayed in the process. He used to say, "Just as smoke rises from burning wood, while the embers remain below, so too only the inner intentions of prayers rise above, while their words remain below like ashes." Still, Reb Dovid preferred proceeding slowly on the spiritual path. He interpreted the verse, "And Hashem said to Avram: Go for yourself" (*Bereshis* 12:1) as "'Go according to yourself,' slowly, according to your own ability. Just as a person picks a fruit while it is still green and lets it slowly ripen; so he must move gradually from level to level to reach true fear of G-d."

Some disciples of the Seer began claiming that the Yehudi had rejected his Rebbe's teachings, and that his frequent trips to Lublin were only "shopping trips" to find and draw away the best students. The Yehudi adamantly denied these claims and constantly deferred to his Rebbe. The Seer, for his part, proceeded cautiously, demanding that such claims be backed up by further proof.

Once, when the Yehudi haKodesh visited Lublin, the Seer sent several Chassidim to investigate these charges. When Reb Dovid heard about this, he ran to warn the Yehudi, who was indeed teaching Torah to several younger disciples. The Yehudi immediately disbanded the group, and the Seer's agents found nothing.

"How can I ever repay you?" the Yehudi haKodesh asked Reb Dovid.

"Before I decide what I want," he answered, "let me first take off my coat," a reference to his upcoming death, when he would remove the garments of this physical world.

The Gap Widens The relationship between the Seer and the Yehudi haKodesh continued to deteriorate. On one occasion, the Seer showed the Yehudi and Reb Dovid a slanderous letter written by one of the Yehudi's opponents. It accused the Yehudi of disparaging the Seer before his disciples.

"Does the Rebbe really believe this letter?" the Yehudi asked.

"Our Sages have stated that a pact has been made with slander that it will always be believed."

"What then should I do?"

"I faced the same problem when I was a student of the Rebbe Reb Elimelech," the Seer confided. "So I stopped traveling to Lyzhansk and moved to a different part of the country [from Lanzhut to Rozbedov]. Do the same. Stop coming to Lublin."

The Yehudi remained silent. After they left, Reb Dovid commented, "The Rebbe is right. Do what he says, and stop visiting him."

"But my case is not the same as his," sighed the Yehudi. "The Seer also learned Torah from the Maggid of Mezritch; but I have no other Rebbe."

The tension continued to grow. Finally, one Friday night, the Seer tried to cast the Yehudi down from his high spiritual level. The Seer sat at his *tisch*, swaying back and forth in the deepest meditation, oblivious to his surroundings. Suddenly Reb Dovid of Lelov knocked the table with his hand and a bottle of wine fell over and broke. The Seer immediately came back to himself.

"Who hit the table?" he demanded.

"I did," replied Reb Dovid. The Seer remained silent.

Afterwards, Reb Dovid explained to his companions, "I saw that the Rebbe's soul was soaring through the Heavens, searching for the root of the Yehudi haKodesh's soul. He wanted to uproot all his spiritual accomplishments. So I struck the table to interrupt his thoughts. Perhaps I shouldn't have indirectly broken a bottle on Shabbos, but robbing the Yehudi of his spiritual stature would have been like death for him, and saving a life overrides Shabbos."

The attacks on the Yehudi haKodesh continued. On Shavuos, Reb Dovid overheard the Seer comment, "Now we must uproot great mountains." Reb Dovid was terrified. On the second day of the festival, the Seer uttered these words again. Immediately after the holiday, Reb Dovid took his leave of the Seer and traveled to Pshischah. When he arrived, the Yehudi haKodesh greeted him. "Welcome, welcome, Reb Dovid of Lelov. Don't worry! I hid myself in the supernal worlds so well that even the Rebbe couldn't enter there."

Reb Dovid's Passing

Because Reb Dovid supported the Yehudi haKodesh, he too became an object of slander, and the Seer turned against him as well. In 1813, Reb Dovid bought a new house in Lelov. As he crossed the threshold for the first time, his hat fell off his head and he gestured that he was in great pain. A short time later, at the *bris* of the son of Rabbi Shmuel of Kaminsk, he instructed Reb Shmuel to name his son Dovid, hinting that his time in this world was near its end.

That Chanukah, Reb Dovid and Reb Yitzchok of Vorki traveled to the Yehudi haKodesh in Pshischah. "It would be proper to have something to drink," Reb Dovid commented. Reb Yitzchok ran out and returned with bottles of wine, liquor, beer and brandy. Why?

"The Rebbe said 'something to drink' but didn't specify what he wanted."

The Yehudi haKodesh closely examined Reb Yitzchok. "He will be one of my disciples," he said. "Send him to me for *Rosh Chodesh Shevat*." Several days before *Rosh Chodesh*, Reb Dovid became ill. Reb Yitzchok refused to leave his side; but Reb Dovid made him travel to Pshischah.

Reb Dovid's condition worsened. His family sent his attendant, Reb Shmuel Kopel, to Pshischah, to ask the Yehudi haKodesh to pray for his health; but the Yehudi only sighed deeply.

On the 7th of Shevat (5574/1814) on *erev Shabbos*, a Jewish doctor was called to Reb Dovid's bedside. When the doctor felt his pulse, Reb Dovid asked, "Please tell me which part of my body has sinned, so I will know how to do *teshuvah*."

The doctor called the family members aside to tell them that the patient's condition was critical. Reb Dovid overheard the conversation and corrected them. "Why do you say that my condition is 'bad'? You'll see. I will soon return home!"

When the Chassidim were allowed into the room, they found Reb Dovid chuckling. "I have hidden my achievements so well that even the Seer is not aware of them; only the Yehudi haKodesh has some idea." Then he added, "The true story of Reb Dovid ben Shlomo will not be known

The End of an Era

The ohel enclosing the kever of Reb Dovid Lelover, zt"l, the first Lelover Rebbe and a prominent follower of the Seer of Lublin

until the coming of the *Mashiach*." Reb Dovid then turned his face to the wall and passed away. He was 68 years old.

At that moment, in Pshischah, the Yehudi haKodesh told Reb Yitzchok of Vorki, "I see Reb Dovid in the Heavens, and he is illuminating all the worlds."

Reb Yitzchok immediately understood what had happened. He tore his clothes and pulled his hair in mourning. "Why did you bring me here, away from my Rebbe?" he demanded. "I was concerned for your life," the Yehudi replied. "I worried that, out of your attachment to Reb Dovid, your soul might depart with his."

At the same moment, in the town of Pintz, Reb Aharon, the *chavrusa* of Reb Dovid, called his son. "Did you see the trail of fire that fell from the sky? Reb Dovid of Lelov has passed away; and I must soon join him. We were studying together, and stopped in the middle of a *sugyah* (topic)." Within days, Reb Aharon also passed away.

Final Regret

Among his last requests, Reb Dovid asked that his *Kiddush* cup be sent to the Seer in Lublin, as a remembrance. That Friday night, the Seer picked up Reb Dovid's cup to make *Kiddush* (to increase his merit); but suddenly, his hand started to shake. He put the cup down, and then picked it up again, but had to put it down once more. "What a loss, what a loss," he groaned. "He will never be forgotten." After *Kiddush*, the Seer turned to one of the leaders of the opposition against Reb Dovid and the Yehudi. "You spoke lies!" he said with fury.

Shortly thereafter, the Seer saw Reb Dovid in a dream. His form was radiant and glowing like fire. "Had I only known that he was so great," the Seer said later, "I would never have opposed him."

The Yehudi haKodesh was deeply grieved over the loss of his friend and *mechutan* and, on the 19th of Tishrei (5575/1815), he too passed away. As for the Seer of Lublin, his soul was strongly attached to the Yehudi's, and he passed away on Tishah b'Av of that same year.

Greater in Their Deaths

"Tzaddikim are greater in their deaths than in their lives," says the Talmud (*Chullin* 7b), and thousands of Chassidim came to Reb Dovid's grave to pray for help and deliverance. One year on Reb Dovid's *yahrtzeit*, his son Reb Avigdor announced to the crowd, "I swear to you, that my father hears the prayers of all who come here." On another *yahrtzeit* his grandson, Reb Dovid ben Moshe, entered the mausoleum alone. He was shocked to see a man standing there, his face burning like fire. When he later carefully described the man to the elders of Lelov, they told him that he had seen his grandfather.

Reb Dovid promised his descendants that for ten generations he would hear their prayers at his grave and help them. Many years later, one of Reb Dovid's granddaughters, the wife of Reb Zev Wolf Naimon of Zarick, became paralyzed by a stroke. Unable to walk, she was carried to the mausoleum of her holy grandfather where, for several hours, she cried for Heaven's mercy. She began to feel miraculously better, tried to stand...and succeeded! A few moments later, she left the grave on her own.

Reb Dovid's merit also shielded others. The Rav of Kavil had a son who was about to be drafted into the Polish army, which meant years of separation from Judaism, with almost no chance of keeping Shabbos, *kashrus*, or other mitzvos. The Rav tried everything to get his son an exemption, but was unsuccessful. Finally, the Rav's father appeared to him in a dream. "The *yahrtzeit* of Reb Dovid Lelover is only a few days away," he said. "Travel to his grave and pray there. Remind him that we were friends and traveled many times together to Lublin. Tell him that I need help for my grandson." The Rav did as instructed and, a short while later, his son received his exemption.

Similarly, when a young Chassid of the Sochachover Gaon was about to be drafted into the army, the Gaon blessed him with a speedy release. When nothing happened, the Chassid returned several times begging for deliverance. One day the Sochachover Gaon dreamt he was at the Shabbos *tisch* of Reb Dovid Lelover. Suddenly, his young Chassid entered and asked Reb Dovid for his blessing. "Of course," he said to all the Chassidim, "This young man must be exempt from the army!" Later, the young man told the Sochachover Gaon that he had indeed received an exemption.

The boy had been praying at Reb Dovid's grave at the exact moment his Rebbe had experienced his vision.

In the Heavenly Court

Once, Reb Emmanuel, the son of Reb Dovid's disciple, Reb Yeshaya of Pshadburz, and Reb Yerachmiel, the son of the Yehudi haKodesh, were talking.

"Did you know that when Reb Dovid Lelover died, the supernal assembly appointed him to the Heavenly Court?" said Reb Yerachmiel. "For he loved Israel deeply, and knew how to judge each Jew favorably. He knew the power of the evil inclination, and the weakness of a person already caught in its snares.

"Unfortunately for us," he continued, "during the twenty years since then, Reb Dovid has ascended level after level in the Upper Worlds. Now he is no longer able to judge individuals on our low level."

The Line Continues

A memorial light was kept burning constantly in the cemetery vault of Reb Dovid, like the golden menorah in the Holy Temple that was never extinguished. Once the caretaker returned from a lengthy trip and realized that he had forgotten to arrange for someone to replenish the oil. When he entered the vault, he found the light still burning brightly — without oil! The same is true of the light of Reb Dovid himself. It will never be extinguished.

Reb Dovid's Tefillin

Before his death, Reb Dovid divided his property between his three holy sons: Reb Moshe of Lelov, Reb Nechemia and Reb Avigdor. The Yehudi haKodesh referred to them as "Amen," an acronym for the first letters of their names. Although all three were completely dedicated to serving Hashem, Reb Moshe primarily took his father's place as Rebbe.

It was, however, Reb Avigdor who inherited his father's tefillin. These were not ordinary tefillin, but especially written for Reb Dovid by the Ohr Pnei Moshe, Reb Moshe of Pshivorsk. It is said that when that tzaddik wrote tefillin, fire would flash from the letters.

Reb Dovid had once traveled to Pshivorsk on the recommendation of the Seer. When he arrived, the Ohr Pnei Moshe was engrossed in writing a pair of tefillin. He did not return Reb Dovid's greeting, for according to Kabbalah, one must not speak in the middle of writing. After he finished, he turned to Reb Dovid.

"*Shalom Aleichem.* Where are you from?"

"From Lelov," Reb Dovid replied.

"And your name?"

"Dovid."

"I see. Then you must be the Reb Dovid of Lelov that Eliyahu haNavi told me about. He told me to write two pairs of tefillin for you." Reb Moshe went to his cabinet, took out two pairs of tefillin (Rashi and Rabbeinu Tam) and handed them to Reb Dovid. They were wrapped in paper with the name "Reb Dovid of Lelov" already written on it!

These very special tefillin were passed on to Reb Avigdor, and from him to his son, Reb Dovid Yitzchok of Zarick. Once a fire broke out in Zarick and quickly consumed its flammable, wooden houses. Everyone ran for their lives. Reb Dovid Yitzchok grabbed his tallis bag containing his grandfather's tefillin and fled, with many of the townspeople, to a small cemetery on the outskirts of the town. Soon, however, the fire reached the cemetery as well, and everyone had to run once again for their lives. In his haste, Reb Dovid Yitzchok left his precious tallis bag behind. When he returned after the fire, he found the bag and its tallis completely burned, while the tefillin were unsinged in their cases!

Although the Ohr Pnei Moshe had promised that any tefillin he wrote would remain kosher forever, Reb Dovid Yitzchok feared that the heat may have damaged the parchment inside, so he sent the tefillin to his brother-in-law, Reb Chaim, the *Dayan* of Lelov, to be checked.

Reb Chaim had dreamt about using these tefillin for years. When he opened the cases, he found the parchments to be in perfect condition, but decided he would borrow them for awhile, putting them in his own tefillin. He substituted other kosher parchments in the now empty cases and returned them to Reb Dovid Yitzchok.

Sometime later, another fire broke out in Zarick and, this time, Reb Dovid Yitzchok's tefillin were totally consumed. He was devastated. What sins had he committed that now made him unworthy of wearing his holy tefillin? He worried himself sick, took to his bed, and his family feared for his life. When Reb Chaim heard what had happened, he immediately raced to his brother-in-law's side with the true parchments; and Reb Dovid's Yitzchok's health was completely restored.

SIX
Reb Moshe of Lelov

Reb Moshe's Youth

Reb Moshe of Lelov was born in 1777. He was a recognized *ilui* (genius) from his youth, and his father, Reb Dovid of Lelov, had spared no effort in developing his mind. "In the winter of my eighth year," Reb Moshe once said, "the entire house was freezing because we couldn't afford firewood and warm clothing. My father put me in a barrel of feathers up to my neck, and then taught me the Gemara with all the *Rishonim* and *Acharonim*."

When Reb Moshe was between the ages of eleven and thirteen years old, whenever he wanted to leave the house, his father would tie a cloth around his eyes and guide him to his destination to insure that he did not see anything indecent. At his bar mitzvah, his father told him, "Now you no longer need the cloth. Before, you had the soul of a genius; but I also wanted you to have the soul of a tzaddik. Today you received it." Then he added, "I was not worthy of traveling to the Land of Israel; but you, my son, will be worthy."

Reb Dovid reaffirmed these words years later when, before his death, he left two of his three houses to his other sons, Nechemia and Avigdor. "Don't worry," Reb Dovid told Reb Moshe, "you have a home waiting for you in Jerusalem."

Hidden Greatness Like his father, Reb Moshe concealed his spiritual accomplishments, and few individuals knew his true greatness. The Yehudi haKodesh, however, would often order the *shaliach tzibur* to wait until Reb Moshe finished his *Shemoneh Esreh* prayers, before beginning the reader's repetition, a sign of respect usually reserved for Torah leaders.

Once, Reb Yeshaya of Pshadburz, Reb Dovid's disciple, also delayed the reader's repetition for Reb Moshe. "Why did you wait?" Reb Moshe asked. "Are you making fun of me?"

"If the Rebbe is not silent, I will reveal to everyone who he truly is," said Reb Yeshaya. Reb Moshe remained quiet.

Like his father, Reb Moshe opened a small shop; indeed, he sought to emulate his father in every way.

His Growing Family Reb Moshe married Rivkah Rachel, the daughter of the Yehudi haKodesh of Pshischah. In 1814, Rivkah Rachel gave birth to their first son. Before the child was born, she traveled to her father to ask what to name the baby. "When the child is born, you will know," he replied. By the time the baby was born, both Reb Dovid Lelover and the Yehudi haKodesh had passed away; and the bereaved parents named him Yitzchok Dovid.

Rivkah once told her father the she was afraid of the pain of childbirth. The Yehudi handed her his walking stick. "Hold this in your hand when the time comes, and everything will be all right." Her subsequent labor pains were indeed eased and, at the end of her life, when she moved to Eretz Yisrael, she took the stick with her. Before her death, she asked that the stick be buried with her, to aid her on her long, final journey. The Chevrah Kaddisha fulfilled her unusual request, but had to cut the stick in two, since it was too long to fit in her grave.

Shortly before his wife gave birth to their second son, Reb Moshe fell asleep at the table. In his dream, three tzaddikim came to him and asked that the child be named after them. He gave his word to two of them: Rabbi Elazar, the son of the Rebbe Reb Elimelech of Lyzhansk, and Rabbi Menachem Mendel of Rimanov (he never revealed who the third tzaddik was). Reb Moshe awoke to cries of "*Mazal tov!* It's a boy!" As promised, he named the boy Elazar Menachem Mendel.

Finding a Rebbe After his father passed way, Reb Moshe turned to his father-in-law for guidance, but, within the year, the Yehudi haKodesh also passed away. The Yehudi's own Chassidim then turned to Rabbi Abala of Neishtat, who had taught the Yehudi Kabbalah (later they turned to Reb Simcha Bunim of Pshischah). Reb Moshe, however, and his friend, Reb Yitzchok of Vorki, decided to travel in search of their own Rebbe.

Their first stop was the home of Rabbi Moshe of Opte, the student and successor of the Seer of Lublin, and the author of *Ohr l'Shamayim*. Although he received them warmly, he advised them to keep searching for a Rebbe. They next set out for Russia, to visit Reb Mordechai of Chernobyl. On their way, they stopped to visit Reb Yeshaya of Pshadburz. Although Reb Yeshaya had been a close personal friend of the Yehudi haKodesh, he had remained a faithful follower of the Seer of Lublin, his *mechutan*. He tried to dissuade the two young men from traveling to Russia.

"You remind me of Reb Isaac ben Yekels of Krakow," he told them. "He dreamt repeatedly of a buried treasure under a bridge in Prague. He traveled all the way there to search for his treasure and found...nothing! A passing soldier asked him what he was doing; and he told the soldier about his dream. The soldier laughed. 'You believe in dreams! Why, every night I dream that there is a treasure buried under the stove in the house of a Jew named Isaac in Krakow, but do you think I bother traveling there?' Reb Isaac hurried home, found the treasure and built the synagogue in Krakow that is still named after him today. The same is true of you. You are traveling all the way to Russia to find a Rebbe; but you already have one right here: Reb Simcha Bunim of Pshischah."

Reb Mordechai of Chernobyl Despite Reb Yeshaya's advice, the two men continued on foot to Russia, a several months' journey. When they finally arrived, they agreed not to reveal their identities to anyone. That Friday, they went to introduce themselves to Reb Mordechai.

"Where are you from?" he asked Reb Yitzchok.

"From Zarick."

"I never heard of it," Reb Mordechai replied. "And you?" he asked Reb Moshe.

"From Lelov."

"Oh, I have certainly heard of Lelov," the tzaddik responded.

The two young men were amazed. Lelov was such a small town in a such a distant land, and travelers between the two countries were infrequent.

Reb Moshe of Lelov

"You want to know how I heard of Lelov?" Reb Mordechai smiled. "Although my holy father [Menachem Mendel of Chernobyl] has passed away, he still comes every day to learn with me. For several weeks this year he failed to appear. I was worried that I had done something wrong, so I fasted many days and repeatedly immersed myself in a *mikveh*, but still he did not appear. Finally, after thirty days, he appeared once more. 'My son, I know how upset you were when I did not come, but I had no choice. A great Polish tzaddik, Reb Dovid of Lelov, recently passed away, and they honored him in Heaven by allowing him to teach Torah. He taught a lesson for thirty days and all the souls went to hear him, myself included.'"

Reb Yitzchok pointed to Reb Moshe. "Rebbe, this young man is Reb Dovid's son, and I was his student!"

Reb Mordechai was delighted to receive them; but after Shabbos, he sent them on their way. "You do not have to travel so far to see me," he told them. "You yourselves are already fit to be leaders of Israel."

Even before Reb Mordechai Chernobyl's endorsement, the Seer of Lublin had also given his approbation. Whenever the Seer wanted to bestow the mantle of leadership on someone, he invited him to make *Kiddush* before the Chassidim at the Friday night *tisch*. One Shabbos, when Reb Moshe Lelover was in Lublin, the Seer honored him with *Kiddush*. The Seer himself poured the wine into a special glass cup and, after Shabbos, presented the cup to him as a gift.

Although Reb Moshe treasured the cup — he took it to Eretz Yisrael with him, promising to work miracles with it and hasten the Redemption — he postponed becoming a leader. He followed the verse, "Buy truth, and do not sell it" (*Mishlei* 23:23). As long as there is still truth to learn (buy), the time has not yet come to start teaching (selling). Reb Moshe continued to search for a Rebbe.

Reb Simcha Bunim

Finally, following Reb Yeshaya's advice, Reb Moshe and Reb Yitzchok traveled from Chernobyl back to Pshischah to visit Reb Simcha Bunim, the Yehudi haKodesh's successor. During their first meeting, Reb Simcha Bunim told Reb Yitzchok, "You had thirteen questions in your mind concerning Reb Mordechai of Chernobyl. I will answer them for you, so you can accept him as your Rebbe."

Reb Yitzchok was amazed. He had never voiced his private doubts to anyone. "Still," he thought, "*ruach hakodesh* alone is not enough to make Reb Bunim my Rebbe." Only after he and Reb Moshe had spent some time in Pshischah and had seen Reb Bunim's true greatness did they accept him as their new teacher. Soon thereafter, Reb Moshe returned to Lelov.

The Test of Poverty

Like his father, Reb Moshe was totally unconcerned with this world and, although great holiness filled his home, his family suffered terrible poverty. Reb Moshe's clothes were always torn with one patch on top of another. He had a belt of straw, and his tallis was made from a sheet with tzitzis attached to the corners; but he didn't care. "A person who cares the slightest bit for this world," he said, "hasn't even begun to serve Hashem."

It pained Reb Shmuel Kopel, Reb Dovid's old attendant, to see the family ravaged by cold and hunger. He suggested that Reb Moshe travel with him across Poland to visit wealthy followers to solicit their aid. At first, Reb Moshe refused, so great was his trust in Hashem, but as conditions worsened, he finally agreed.

Reb Moshe concealed his greatness so well that even Reb Shmuel Kopel did not fully appreciate the young tzaddik.

Reb Moshe of Lelov

During their travels, he often addressed him casually. One winter day, however, Reb Shmuel stopped the wagon in the middle of the woods to feed the horses. When he finished, Reb Moshe had disappeared. Reb Shmuel waited and waited, but Reb Moshe did not return. Reb Shmuel began following Reb Moshe's footsteps in the fresh snow, calling out his name. Receiving no answer, he became increasingly worried. Perhaps Reb Moshe had become lost; maybe he had collapsed from the cold. Finally, deep in the woods, Reb Shmuel heard distant cries. He quickened his pace — perhaps Reb Moshe had been hurt — but when he came to a small clearing in the woods, he froze in his tracks.

Reb Moshe stood there all alone, wrapped in his tallis and tefillin, his face drenched with sweat despite the freezing cold, pouring out his heart in prayer. Reb Shmuel was speechless. He had never realized that Reb Moshe was so great. He waited silently for the tzaddik to finish praying, and then led him silently back to the wagon. From then on, Reb Shmuel treated Reb Moshe with the highest respect, and proclaimed his greatness in every town they entered.

As Reb Moshe's fame spread, Chassidim from all over Poland came to Lelov to warm themselves by his fire. Rabbi Moshe of Kozhnitz, author of the *Be'er Moshe*, once said, "If a person wants to see a bit of the splendor of Moshe Rabbeinu, let him look at the face of Reb Moshe of Lelov."

Rabbi of Pshadburz

In the year 1843, Reb Moshe finally accepted the post of Rabbi and *Av Beis Din* in Pshadburz. The position had been previously held by such great men as Reb Yeshaya of Pshadburz and the Saba Kaddisha of Radoshitz; but, despite the prestigious appointment, Reb Moshe remained humble. His Rebbe, Reb Simcha Bunim, had once explained the verse, "You lift the humble to the heights," as: even when Hashem lifts the humble up, they remain humble.

"I once had a regular study period with Reb Moshe," said Rabbi Shmuel Zanvil Tzvi of Polovna. "For weeks, it seemed to me that he didn't know how to learn at all. Then he started to ask questions as difficult as those of the *Rishonim*, and I realized what a deep and penetrating mind he had."

Humble — To a Degree

Despite his humility, Reb Moshe also knew where to draw the line. He once visited his friend Reb Tzvi Hirsh Hidziler, a scholar who, in his humility, thought absolutely nothing of himself. Several foul-smelling animal hides were drying on the stove, and Reb Moshe could barely enter the house.

"What's this, Reb Tzvi Hirsh?" he asked. "I thought you studied Torah all day. Since when did you start tanning hides?"

"My children work as tanners," he answered, "and it is easier for them to dry their hides by me."

"It's true," Reb Moshe chided, "that *Chazal* say that Hashem gave the Torah on Mount Sinai because it was low and humble; but why didn't Hashem give the Torah in a valley, which is lower still? Because even humility has its limits. A person has to be a bit like a mountain, so other people can't trample on him."

Reb Moshe also applied this principle to himself. When one of the local scholars in Pshadburz tried to discredit a *shochet* whom Reb Moshe had appointed, Reb Moshe opposed the scholar with full force. Reb Moshe proved his mettle in many halachic controversies and soon became known as a brilliant legal authority. Although, like his father-in-law, the Yehudi haKodesh, Reb Moshe sought to use his brilliance to conceal his high spiritual level, he was unsuccessful. Thousands of Chassidim flocked to Pshadburz to learn from his ways, to seek his guidance, and to request his blessings.

SEVEN
The Journey to the Holy Land

Another World

As Reb Moshe Lelover's fame continued to grow, so did his holiness and detachment from this world. His deeds started to become mysterious even in the eyes of his own followers. "Three years before his journey to Eretz Yisrael," said Reb Chaim of Sanz, "Reb Moshe was already in another world. He could no longer bear the air of *galus* (exile)."

Once a poor scholar came to him, begging for relief from his poverty. Reb Moshe blessed him, "May Hashem grant you terror and save you from your debts!" Baffled, the young man returned home. That night, he awoke to see his Polish neighbor sharpening a large knife just outside his window. Panic gripped him — his end was near! Finally, he stammered out, "What are you doing?"

"Sorry," the neighbor replied. "My son is coming and I'm simply sharpening my knife to cut him some meat."

The young scholar's terror abated, but from that moment on his fortune changed, and he soon became quite wealthy. Reb Moshe's unusual blessing had been effective.

Safety and Success

A young man who wanted to travel to Germany on business once came to ask Reb Moshe for his blessing. Instead, Reb Moshe opened his desk drawer, handed him a small wooden shotglass and said, "For protection and success."

The surprised young man took the cup and packed it with his belongings. He borrowed money to buy merchandise, and set off on the road alone. En route, he was attacked by a fierce bandit. With a trembling heart, the young man handed over his purse.

"Now I have to kill you," said the bandit, brandishing his sword, "so you do not go running to the police." The young man begged for his life, but to no avail. Suddenly, he remembered Reb Moshe's wooden shotglass "for protection."

"What does one do with a shotglass?" he thought.

He turned to the highwayman. "Please, let me drink one last drop of whiskey before I die."

Himself addicted to liquor, the bandit agreed. The young man took a bottle of whiskey from his bag and filled the glass. The smell intoxicated the robber. He grabbed the shotglass and downed its contents in a single gulp. The young man quickly, with all his strength, rammed the shotglass deep into the robber's throat. It wedged there and the bandit began to gasp for air. He stumbled around helplessly, and finally fell lifeless to the ground.

Afraid that the rest of the gang would soon appear, the young man lifted the corpse onto his wagon and covered it with straw. Then he emptied the robber's bag into his own, regaining his stolen funds, and set off once more. "Once I get to a Jewish settlement, I will figure out what to do," he thought.

At the very next village, he found the townsmen standing around a large poster. It was a proclamation from the

The Journey to the Holy Land

king promising a rich reward to whoever helped to capture a dangerous highwayman, dead or alive. The young man immediately recognized the description, and headed for the local authorities. He showed them the dead highwayman in his wagon, and soon received the reward. In the blink of an eye, he had become a wealthy man, all through Reb Moshe's blessing and his little wooden shotglass.

When the Jews of the town heard of this miracle, they offered a tremendous sum for the shotglass — even the local authorities wanted to purchase it for their museum — but the young man refused. He drove his wagon to the local fair, purchased the highest quality goods, and returned to his town to make a hefty profit. As for the shotglass, he passed it down to his descendants as a family heirloom. (The tzaddik Rabbi Shimon Biderman later heard the story and was shown the shotglass by one of the man's descendants.)

The Move to Eretz Yisrael

Reb Moshe continued to ascend spiritually, rising to a level on which he could no longer benefit from life in *galus*. He longed to move to Eretz Yisrael, to the palace of the King, where even the air makes one wise (*Bava Basra* 158b). He also recalled what his father, Reb Dovid of Lelov, had told him on the day of his bar mitzvah, that he would one day move to the Holy Land. But, most of all, he longed for the final Redemption, to stand before the Western Wall, to raise his voice like a shofar, and to hasten the deliverance. He felt that if only he could pray there, the *Mashiach* would surely come. Thus, he made his journey not merely for personal spiritual gain, but on behalf of all Israel.

While Reb Moshe had always refused to take money from his followers, this case was different. "Whoever is able to donate money to this cause," he announced, "must surely do so," and, together with his student, Reb Shlomo of Radomsk, author of the *Tiferes Shlomo*, he personally traveled across the Polish countryside collecting the funds for his journey.

In those days, the Torah-true Jews of the Old Yishuv in Eretz Yisrael were forced to rely on regular donations from the larger communities of Europe. The Jews of Eretz Yisrael dedicated their lives to Torah study and prayer, while their brothers in exile shared in both their support and reward. In his journeys, Reb Moshe solicited donations not only for his own traveling expenses, but also for solid commitments to the future of the Yishuv.

The Polish journey was also a mystical preparation for the Israeli one, with many enigmatic encounters. In Warsaw, Reb Moshe and Reb Shlomo visited the home of a wealthy Jew. The man offered a token donation towards the trip, but Reb Moshe refused the meager offer. "If a rich man brought a poor man's sacrifice to the Temple, it was not accepted," he said.

"The Rebbe is not my *kohen*, nor am I his rich man," the rich man retorted.

"Very well," Reb Moshe said, "but this much I can tell you. If you manage to reach me with a proper donation before I cross the Polish border, I will accept it. If not, it will be too late."

Not long afterward, the rich man described this strange conversation to his relative, a well-known Chassidic Rebbe. The Rebbe immediately understood Reb Moshe's warning and urged his relative to placate Reb Moshe at once. The rich man hitched up his carriage and raced from town to town chasing after Reb Moshe, who had, by then, begun his final journey. He caught up to him only after he had crossed the Polish border. There he offered Reb Moshe a very large sum; but Reb Moshe refused to take it. From that day on, the man's fortune declined until, eventually, he was destitute.

Another time, Reb Moshe approached a wealthy man for a donation and got a question instead. "I am puzzled by this *midrash*," the man said. "If the Rebbe can explain it to me, I will gladly give him what he requests. The *Midrash Peliah* says, 'Why did Adam sin? Because he saw two, but not three.' What does this mean?"

Reb Moshe answered immediately. "The Mishnah in *Pirkei Avos* (3:1) says, 'Consider three things, and you will not come to sin. Know where you come from — from a putrid drop. Where you are going — to a place of dust and worms. And before Whom you must eventually give an accounting — before the King of kings, the Holy One, Blessed be He.' But Adam was the direct work of Hashem's hands, so he was not able to contemplate the first of these three things; therefore, he came to sin." The rich man was delighted and gave Reb Moshe the large sum he had promised.

Reb Moshe continued on his journey. When he reached Lupshneh, near Keltz, the entire city came out to greet him. Their respect for Torah scholars was tremendous and even the town's two butchers, Torah scholars in their own right, humbly brought Reb Moshe their slaughtering knives for his examination. Reb Moshe handed them to Reb Shlomo to check.

"Rebbe," replied Reb Shlomo in amazement, "I've never seen such beautifully sharpened knives. It's not imaginable that such knives should produce a *treifah*!" Reb Moshe examined them himself. "You're right," he replied. "It would not be fitting for them to ever cause problems." And so it was; thereafter, not one *treif* cow ever came from the hands of these two butchers!

The Two Rebbetzins

A large number of Reb Moshe's followers were to accompany him on his journey, and he tried to collect the funds for their expenses as well. The financial situation in the Old Yishuv was desperate. There was no work, almost all processed products were imported, and extended droughts raised prices even higher. As the Talmud warned, "Eretz Yisrael is acquired through suffering" (*Berachos* 5a). Not surprisingly, many of Reb Moshe's Chassidim were reluctant to leave everything behind in Poland. Even his wife, the daughter of the Yehudi haKodesh, refused to go. How could Reb Moshe leave his Chassidim, and his position as the Rav of Pshadburz, she demanded, to face the rigors of Eretz Yisrael?

The leading tzaddikim of Poland eventually arranged an assembly to try to resolve this problem. Rebbetzin Rivkah Rachel stood by the door, but when one of the tzaddikim asked her, "Riva (her nickname), how long will you foment controversy?" she replied sharply: "Speak with respect to the daughter of the Yehudi haKodesh!" She then slammed the door. The meeting disbanded.

For his part, Reb Moshe was committed to his holy vision — hastening the Redemption — and personal considerations could not stand in the way. Still, it was not easy for Reb Moshe to part from his Rebbetzin. She had stood by him for years, throughout the most difficult times, with the greatest dedication. Despite their disagreement, he continued to show her the greatest respect, and insisted that others do the same.

A certain wagon driver in Pshadburz was upset by the Rebbetzin's attitude and he treated her rudely. The Rebbetzin held her peace, even as the insults mounted daily. Finally, she could bear it no longer, and she told her husband. Reb Moshe did not say a word. He simply stood up and knocked his chair over onto the floor. Outside of the town, the wagon driver was thrown to the ground when his wagon suddenly overturned. From then on, he treated the Rebbetzin with respect.

When Reb Moshe took his leave, his Rebbetzin said to him, "Before my wedding, your holy father, Reb Dovid of Lelov, warned me, 'My son is like a beautiful *mezuzah*. I'm turning him over to you. Make sure you keep him kosher.' Until today, I have done so, and my father-in-law would not be ashamed of me. You certainly will not be spoiled now."

Only many years later, after Reb Moshe had long since passed away, did their oldest son, Reb Yitzchok Dovid, return to Poland to bring his mother to Eretz Yisrael.

In contrast, Reb Moshe did insist that his younger son, Reb Elazar Menachem Mendel, and his young wife, Rebbetzin Matil Feigeh, accompany him to Eretz Yisrael. Rebbetzin Matil Feigeh, a granddaughter of the Seer of Lublin, was only eighteen years old at the time, and her parents were concerned for her health and safety. They begged Reb Moshe to allow the young couple to remain in Poland. "Either she accompanies my son, or she receives a *get*," he flatly declared. Since neither side would concede, they sought the opinion of Reb Sar Shalom, the Belzer Rav.

The Belzer Rav heard the arguments of both families. It saddened him that the connection between the families of the Seer and Reb Dovid Lelover might be broken. He declared that the decision was not the parents', but Rebbetzin Matil Feigeh's alone. She was summoned.

"Do you want to travel with your husband and father-in-law to Eretz Yisrael?" the Belzer Rav asked her. Rebbetzin Matil Feigeh said yes, yes she did. The Belzer Rav then emphasized the great difficulties she would face on the journey and in Eretz Yisrael, but she was unmoved.

"The roads of Poland are also difficult and dangerous," she answered, "and yet Chassidim willingly travel them to visit their Rebbe. Is traveling to Eretz Yisrael any less important?" The Belzer Rav smiled and ruled that she should go.

Farewell to the Chassidim

As preparations for the trip continued, countless Rabbis and tzaddikim came to Pshadburz to bid Reb Moshe farewell. Many longed to hear Reb Moshe's secret reasons for traveling. Reb Moshe shared this secret with his nephew, Reb Yaakil of Opte, who left the room sighing, "What a pity! What a pity! I never knew my uncle was so great, and now he is leaving us!"

Reb Moshe then traveled across the Polish countryside, bidding a final farewell to his Chassidim. About two weeks before his journey, he spent Shabbos in Chentshin, a small town between Opte and Lelov. Tens of thousands of people joined him that Shabbos, including most of the great tzaddikim and Chassidim of Poland.

"My children," Reb Moshe said after Shabbos, "look at me well, engrave me in your minds. It will be good for you." He repeated this four times, once in each direction. Then he entered his carriage and left.

Reb Moshe continued on his journey and spent the following Shabbos in Horbishov. So many people came to say farewell that not everyone could get into the shul for the Friday night *tisch*; but even those who stood outside could hear Reb Moshe's powerful voice: "These are the words which Moshe spoke to all Israel" (*Devarim* 1:1). Moshe represents the tzaddik of the generation, and the words of the tzaddik apply to all Israel! Even when the tzaddik speaks to a large crowd, each individual Jew hears him speaking to himself alone."

The Journey to the Holy Land

Days Will Speak

On the day Reb Moshe left Poland, one of his followers asked him, "Why must the Rebbe leave us?"

"Days will speak," Reb Moshe answered mysteriously.

"And who will lead the flock?"

"I leave you my student, Reb Shlomo of Radomsk. Follow him well. He will lead you and deliver you."

Then the entourage set out. A huge number of Chassidim accompanied it as far as the Polish border. As Reb Moshe took his final leave, he turned to Reb Shlomo and said, "You are a *kohen*. Give me your blessing." Tears streamed down Reb Shlomo's face as he blessed his beloved Rebbe. The Chassidim wept, and Reb Moshe cried as well. Reb Moshe crossed the border from Poland to Galicia, which was then in Austrian hands, and his Chassidim returned home, thoughtful.

Reb Shlomo's frank comments did little to comfort them: "Do you see the Rebbe's burning desire for the Holy Land? His *mesiras nefesh*? He said that he will bring the Messiah, but I doubt it. Rather, since he is a perfect tzaddik, like Yosef haTzaddik, he has merited to move to Eretz Yisrael and to be buried there."

With Reb Sar Shalom of Belz

On his journey through eastern Galicia, Reb Moshe stopped to take leave of Reb Sar Shalom of Belz. He deposited his belongings in a local inn and headed straight for the tzaddik's house. Entering the door, he gasped in amazement. "To feel such holiness in a shul is not a wonder," he said, "but to feel it in a private home is amazing!" Reb Moshe requested an audience, but the attendant told him that the tzaddik was sleeping. Not wanting to disturb him, Reb Moshe returned to the inn and prepared to leave.

When Reb Sar Shalom awoke, he asked the attendant who had stopped by. "No one I recognized," the attendant replied. "Some rabbi from Poland." The Rebbe immediately knew who it was. "Quick!" he declared. "Take a bottle of wine and some glasses and let us go to his inn."

Reb Sar Shalom arrived just as Reb Moshe was preparing to leave.

"I had very much wanted to sit with the Rebbe over a meal," said Reb Sar Shalom.

"But I've already packed," replied Reb Moshe.

"I expected as much, so I brought this bottle of wine."

"But I've packed away the glasses as well."

"I expected that too, so I brought my own."

The two tzaddikim sat together and made a *l'chaim*. Reb Sar Shalom tried to dissuade Reb Moshe from his trip, but Reb Moshe would not be swayed. He wished the Belzer Rav well, and continued on his journey. Reb Sar Shalom accompanied him to the outskirts of the town, an exceptional honor, for the Belzer Rav rarely accompanied anyone beyond the front door.

After Reb Moshe left, Reb Sar Shalom told his son and successor, Reb Yehoshua (Shia) Belzer, "Just see how much love the Lelover Rebbe has for Eretz Yisrael. He continues on his journey even though he knows he probably won't find an *esrog* for Sukkos on his ship."

With the Rebbe of Ruzhin

From Belz, Reb Moshe traveled to Sadigura to visit the Ruzhiner Rebbe, Reb Yisroel of Ruzhin, arriving on *Rosh Chodesh Elul* 5610 (1850). He entered with his two sons, Reb Yitzchok Dovid and Reb Elazar Menachem Mendel, and the latter's six-year-old son, Dovid Tzvi Shlomo (Reb Dovid'l Biderman). The Ruzhiner Rebbe welcomed Reb Moshe with

The Journey to the Holy Land

great honor and held Dovid Tzvi on his lap, showering the future tzaddik special affection. At the end of the visit, he gave Reb Moshe a silver breastplate for a *sefer Torah* to use in his synagogue in Jerusalem.

The Ruzhiner asked Reb Moshe to delay his trip, so the two of them could travel to Eretz Yisrael together, but Reb Moshe pointed to the gray in his beard: "These white hairs tell me not to wait any longer." The Ruzhiner then bid Reb Moshe farewell. "I will give you a blessing: Rabbi Menachem Mendel of Vitebsk and Rabbi Avraham of Kalisk also moved to Eretz Yisrael, but they did not leave behind children to continue their work. I bless you that your light will never be extinguished." The Ruzhiner passed away some two months later, but his blessing was fulfilled; Reb Moshe's numerous holy descendants still head flourishing Lelover and Bostoner dynasties in Israel and America.

After Reb Moshe left, the Ruzhiner commented, "The Polish Jews are fools! They had such a great light among them and they let him go?" Shortly thereafter, the Ruzhiner asked Reb Shlomo of Radomsk why Reb Moshe's Chassidim let him go. "We were sure that he would never raise the money he needed for his journey," he replied.

The Ruzhiner's oldest son, Reb Sholom Yosef, was away from Sadigura during Reb Moshe's visit. When he returned, his father told him, "What a pity you didn't meet Reb Moshe; I have never seen such a humble Jew in my entire life!"

Before leaving Sadigura, Reb Moshe sent a farewell letter to his Chassidim in Poland.

> As you see, I have left my land, the place of my birth, and the house of my holy forefathers. Although the separation is painful, my great love of the Holy Land, and certain secrets known only to me, have strengthened me to throw all this away. May Hashem lead me in the path of truth, and help me accomplish my vision.

G-d forbid that I should cease praying for your welfare. May you be blessed with all good things by the Most High. May we come together to Zion in joy. As your friend and admirer, I wish all your desires to be fulfilled, for all Israel is precious in my eyes. The words of one who waits for the deliverance of Israel.

> Moshe,
> the son of our master and teacher,
> Reb Dovid, *zt"l*

Napoleon's Cloak

Reb Moshe carried to Eretz Yisrael with him the glass *Kiddush* cup of the Seer of Lublin, the silver Torah breastplate of the Ruzhiner Rebbe, and several special objects he inherited from his father. Among them was a red velvet cloak that he planned to use as a *paroches* (ark curtain) in Jerusalem. It was the cloak of Napoleon Bonaparte, Emperor of France.

Almost fifty years earlier, during the Napoleonic wars, the great French general had conquered country after country, until his empire stretched from the shores of the Atlantic to the borders of Russia. Moving eastward through Poland, Napoleon passed through Tchenstekov. There, word reached him of a holy, prescient Rabbi in an adjacent town, Reb Dovid of Lelov. Disguising himself as a simple foot soldier, he went to visit the tzaddik. Once alone with Reb Dovid, Napoleon raised the corner of his uniform to reveal the royal crimson cloak below.

"I am Napoleon Bonaparte, the Emperor of France," he announced. "Tell me, holy man, I am about to wage war on Russia. Will I be victorious?"

"I cannot answer his Highness unless he promises to do me no harm, even if he is displeased with my answer." Napoleon promised.

The Journey to the Holy Land

Reb Dovid stated, "You must know that you will not succeed. In the end, you will suffer a crushing defeat."

"Hear me well, Rabbi!" Napoleon cried. "If your words prove true, then you are indeed a holy man, and I will keep my promise. But if your words are false, and you have upset me without cause, you will suffer a bitter end."

Reb Dovid was, of course, correct. Napoleon's armies suffered a crushing defeat on the frozen plains of Russia, although Napoleon himself managed to escape. Returning to France through Poland, he once again passed through Lelov. "You were all too right, holy man," he told Reb Dovid, and, as a gesture of acknowledgment, he presented Reb Dovid his crimson cloak. The cloak remained in Lelov until Reb Moshe immersed it in a *mikveh* and brought it with him to Eretz Yisrael.

In Constantinople In early Elul 5610 (1851), Reb Moshe and his party boarded a ship in Romania and sailed to Constantinople, the capital of Turkey. (Eretz Yisrael was then under Turkish rule.) When they arrived, Reb Moshe forbade his family to reveal his true identity; and they found lodgings in the home of a simple but goodhearted Jew. After observing Reb Moshe's special behavior, his host soon understood that he was no simple wayfarer, but a tzaddik. He came to Reb Moshe and begged him, "Please, Rabbi, I have a kind and handsome son who cannot speak. Please bless him."

Reb Moshe tried to dissuade him. "What are you talking about? I'm a simple Jew like yourself!" But the man would not give up. Finally Reb Moshe told him, "In a few days I will leave for Eretz Yisrael. Three days later, give the boy a piece of bread and tell him, in my name, that I order him to make the appropriate blessing." Three days after

Reb Moshe left, the man gave his son a piece of bread and related the tzaddik's words. The boy immediately took the bread and made the blessing in a loud, clear voice!

Reb Moshe spent several days in Turkey waiting for a ship to Eretz Yisrael. The local merchants suspected that he had money, and they did everything they could to prolong his stay. "There are not many caravans traveling overland," they told him, "and the ships are not sailing." Reb Moshe then approached a local travel agent who answered slyly, "They say there is a children's plague in Eretz Yisrael. Traveling there could be dangerous. Why not stay in Constantinople for a while?"

Reb Moshe became angry. "Perhaps there is a children's plague in Eretz Yisrael, but here in Constantinople there is likely to be a plague on the adults!" Just then, the agent's wife ran into the room crying. Their oldest son had suddenly become sick and fainted. Then she too collapsed on the floor. The agent fell on his knees and pleaded for Reb Moshe's forgiveness, and begged him to pray for his family.

"If you get us on a ship today then, as I board the ship, your family will recover."

The agent ran and, within the hour, returned to report that Reb Moshe and his family were booked on a ship already waiting in the port. The agent himself helped carry Reb Moshe's bag and accompanied him up the gangplank. Once more, he pleaded for his family. Reb Moshe blessed them and, when the agent returned home, he found them all well.

One Day, One Year Reb Moshe and his party spent the High Holidays on board ship. Shortly after Rosh Hashanah, Reb Moshe asked the captain to stop at a nearby island where *aravos* and *hadasim* could be found (he had already bought a *lulav* and *esrog* in Constantinople). He

The Journey to the Holy Land

also offered the captain a bag of gold coins for permission to build a *sukkah* on the deck of the ship. The captain agreed to both requests; and there was no end to the tzaddik's joy as he sat in his *sukkah* on the first night of the festival. The next morning, a heavy wind blew the *sukkah* into the sea; but Reb Moshe remained happy, for he had successfully fulfilled the main mitzvah, as commanded in the Torah (see *Sukkah* 27).

On the eve of *Rosh Chodesh Cheshvan*, the ship arrived in Akko; and Reb Moshe descended the gangplank onto the holy soil of Eretz Yisrael with tremendous joy. As he walked he muttered mysteriously, "One day, one year," but no one understood what he meant.

The family traveled by mule train to the holy city of Tzefas where they were welcomed with great honor. The sages of the city begged Reb Moshe to remain with them — Rabbi Shmuel Heller, the Rav of the city, even offered his post to Reb Moshe — but Reb Moshe declined. "It is written, 'For Hashem has chosen Zion; He has desired it for His dwelling place' (*Tehillim* 132:13). I, too, wish to follow His ways." Reb Moshe's eyes remained set on the Western Wall, where his prayers would hasten the Redemption.

On the third of Cheshvan, as Reb Moshe sat with a group of Chassidim, he suddenly felt dizzy and short of breath. He went up on the roof for air. When he returned, he said, "A great darkness has descended upon the world. It seems that the tzaddik of our generation, Reb Yisroel of Ruzhin, has passed away."

That Shabbos evening, Reb Moshe held a *tisch* in the Ruzhiner/Sadigura shul. He was overflowing with praise for the Holy Land. When one Chassid expressed a reservation, Reb Moshe responded, "The Torah says, 'The land is *exceedingly* good' (*Bemidbar* 14:9) and the Mishnah says, 'Be *exceedingly* humble' (*Avos* 4:4). Only a person who achieves the latter can see the former."

The Gates of Jerusalem

After Shabbos, Reb Moshe left Tzefas for Tiberias, for a short visit. Then he headed towards Jerusalem. The pleas of his family could not convince him to slow down, or even to rest. His vision drove him on. "As soon as I get to Jerusalem, I will run to the Western Wall. I will raise my voice in prayer. The Heavenly Assembly will shake, and the Messiah will come!"

Yet, the strain of the journey was beginning to take its toll. Reb Moshe became increasingly weak and tired. When, at last, he saw the walls of the Holy City, his strength was temporarily renewed. Jerusalem, the joy of all the earth! But, as he stood outside Jaffa Gate, the glass *Kiddush* cup given to him by the Seer of Lublin slipped out of his baggage and shattered, an ominous omen indeed.

The leaders of the city came out to welcome Reb Moshe. At their head were the two holy brothers. Reb Nachum of Shadik and Reb Yaakov Leib of Beis Levi. The entire city knew that a tzaddik had entered their midst.

Reb Moshe rented a small apartment in the Jewish Quarter, where he decided to rest a little to regain his strength before visiting the Western Wall. His assault on the Heavens would require his every ounce of strength. Instead, however, every day, he became weaker and weaker. Soon he could barely get out of bed. Finally, he told his sons that he must get to the Wall immediately, on that very day, no matter what!

His sons carried Reb Moshe, still lying on his bed, through the narrow streets of Jerusalem. They suddenly encountered bands of Arab youths standing on the rooftops, hurling stones and cursing. The powers of evil were obviously rising up against Reb Moshe to prevent his reaching his destination and praying for the arrival of the Messiah!

Reb Moshe's sons pressed on despite the deadly barrage of stones, but after a few moments, it became obvious that they had no choice but to turn back and run to the Jewish Quarter.

That very day Reb Moshe passed away, at age seventy-four, without ever having reached the Western Wall — exactly seventy-four days after he had arrived in the Holy Land. Now his mysterious words were all too clear: "One day, one year." He was allowed by Heaven one day in Eretz Yisrael for each year of his life. So too, he had told his Chassidim in Poland: "Days will speak."

The Sage's Dream

Reb Moshe's two sons laid their father's body on the floor of his room and lit candles around his head, as was the custom. They sat beside him, crying bitterly. Reb Moshe had not succeeded in bringing the Redemption down to earth; instead, he had been taken up to Heaven.

Reb Elazar Menachem Mendel sat with his head bowed towards his father. He suddenly raised his eyes to his brother, Reb Yitzchok Dovid, and said simply, "Our father has just appeared to me. He wishes to be buried next to the grave of the prophet Zechariah." They were still mulling over this strange, impossible request, when an unknown Sefardi *chacham* entered the room. He was shocked to see Reb Moshe dead, and his children sitting on the ground in mourning.

He explained that he owned a burial plot next to the grave of the prophet Zechariah. Just a few minutes earlier, he had fallen asleep. Reb Moshe of Lelov had come to him

Zechariah's tomb in the valley adjacent to the Old City of Jerusalem, next to which Reb Moshe Lelover, zt"l, is buried

in a dream and had asked him for his very special burial plot. He had come to investigate and, now that he saw that his dream was true, he agreed to the tzaddik's last request. So Reb Moshe of Lelov was buried on the Mount of Olives beside the grave of the prophet Zechariah; and the entire city accompanied his bier and mourned.

Jewish communities across Europe were also shocked by the bitter news. His pupil, Reb Shlomo of Radomsk, sent a letter of condolence to Reb Moshe's sons in Jerusalem: "As the human heart trembles at the roar of thunder, so was I gripped with dread on reading of your bitter mourning on the twenty-eighth of Teves. Where has the Prince of Hashem gone? I sigh mountains of grief over the soul of the tzaddik who has ascended on high and left us.... May Hashem comfort you among the other mourners of Zion and Jerusalem. May we soon hear the voice of good tidings, going to the right of Moshe and his sons to the mountain of Ariel."

EIGHT
Reb Elazar Menachem Mendel

The Dynasty Continues

The Ruzhiner Rebbe had blessed Reb Moshe that his light would never be extinguished. This blessing was fulfilled in Reb Moshe's son, Reb Elazar Menachem Mendel, who continued the Lelover dynasty in Eretz Yisrael, becoming the Rebbe of all the Chassidim of Jerusalem.

Reb Elazar Menachem Mendel was born in Lelov in 1827. He resembled his father, Reb Moshe, and his grandfather, Reb Dovid, both physically and spiritually. Once, as a child of six, he entered his father's study and found a large pile of *kvitlach* (requests) on the table. He gathered them together, stuffed them into his little hat, and put it back on his head. Reb Moshe soon returned and began searching for the missing *kvitlach*. When he finally found their hiding place, he smiled and said, "Elazar Mendel already knows how to bear the needs of hundreds of Jews on his head!"

When Reb Elazar Mendel's own son, Reb Dovid'l Biderman, was a small boy, he once brought his father a pot, and asked him if it still required purification through immersion in a *mikveh*. His father was surprised. "My son, can't you tell by yourself? When I was a boy of six or seven, I could already look at a vessel and tell if it had been immersed."

Like Reb Moshe, Reb Elazar Mendel was an incredibly diligent student. More than once, he secretly moved back the clock's hands in order to snatch a few more minutes from his tutor! Each morning, he would literally run to school; and his parents had to constantly convince him to rest and eat. His devotion to Torah was matched by his good *midos*. "Elazar Mendel never gets angry," his friends conceded.

As a youth, Reb Elazar Mendel married Matil Feigeh, the daughter of Reb Tzvi, the son of the Seer of Lublin. She was named after the Seer's mother, the daughter of Rabbi Yaakov Kopel of Lelov and a great *tzadekes*. The Seer once told Reb Simcha Bunim of Pshischah, "I have searched through all the Heavenly chambers in Gan Eden and cannot find my mother, Matil Feigeh. Where can she be?" "Have you looked in the chamber of our Matriarchs, Sarah, Rivkah, Rachel and Leah?" "You're right!" replied the Seer. "That's where she is."

The First Chassidic Court in Jerusalem Reb Elazar Mendel's decision to remain in Jerusalem was a bold one, since most Chassidim lived up north in Tzefas or Tiberias. Most Yerushalmi Jews were either Sefardim or *Perushim*, followers of the Vilna Gaon, who were among the first Europeans to move to Eretz Yisrael in the early 19th century. Thus Reb Elazar Mendel of Lelov became Jerusalem's first Chassidic Rebbe and, for several generations, the Lelover court was the only well-established Chassidic group in the Holy City.

Despite the hardships, Reb Elazar Mendel was following "family tradition." Most Lelover Rebbes – including Reb

Dovid and Reb Moshe — had to build their followings from scratch. The same was true of their descendants, Reb Pinchas Dovid Horowitz, *zt"l*, the first Bostoner Rebbe, and his son, Reb Levi Yitzchok Horowitz, *shlita* (who, like Reb Elazar Mendel, also became a Rebbe at age twenty-three).

The Tale of the Teacher

Reb Elazar Mendel first had to find a teacher for his six-year-old son, Dovid Tzvi Shlomo (later Reb Dovid'l Biderman). He finally found an excellent tutor among the *Perushim*, a man outstanding in Torah, fear of Hashem and good *midos*. Several days later, Reb Elazar Mendel asked Reb Dovid'l about his new tutor. His son mentioned how every day, before beginning to study, his tutor would gaze out the window and cry. When Reb Elazar Mendel asked the teacher about this, he told the following story:

> Many years ago, in Europe, I visited the home of the Saba Kaddisha of Radoshitz. There I saw the most amazing miracle. A poor woman had been abandoned by her husband many years earlier, and she had not received a *get* from him. She had no idea where her husband was, and without the bill of divorce it was impossible for her to remarry.
>
> The Rebbe told his attendant to go out into the street and bring him the first non-Jew that passed by. After a few minutes, the attendant returned with a *goy*, who appeared confused by the whole odd affair. The Rebbe suddenly became furious and ordered the man to reveal his true identity. Eventually, the man admitted that he was indeed Jewish, and that he was the husband of the very woman who was sitting there! The Rebbe immediately ordered him to give his wife a *get*, which he did on the spot.

I was so astonished by the Rebbe's *ruach hakodesh* that I decided to sneak into his private chamber and hide under his bed, so I could observe his nightly Torah study and prayers. But as soon as he entered the room, the Rebbe felt my presence and ordered me to leave. Trembling with fear, I crawled out from under the tzaddik's bed. The Rebbe turned to me kindly and asked, "Young man, what do you want?"

I answered him, "Rebbe, I only want to fear Hashem."

The Rebbe blessed me, "May it be His Will that whenever you sit down to learn Torah, you will do *teshuvah* in your heart."

"It has been many years since then, but still, whenever I sit down to study Torah, I have such intense thoughts of *teshuvah* that I cry."

Reb Elazar Mendel was amazed. "After experiencing such incredible miracles, why didn't you become a Chassid? Why are you still a *Misnaged* (opponent)?"

The teacher answered, "Rebbe, is there any doubt that what the Saba Kaddisha did was sorcery?"

Reb Elazar Mendel dismissed the tutor that very day. "A person who does not believe in the power of the sages is not going to teach my son."

The Test of Poverty

Reb Elazar Mendel's family had, perhaps, the only strictly Chassidic home in Jerusalem, and lived amidst great poverty. The Chassidic fundraisers of Europe sent all their money to the Chassidic *yishuv* in Tzefas, while Jerusalem was under the care of the *Perushim*. As a result, Reb Elazar Mendel and his family received no financial aid at all.

Their hunger was terrible. Reb Elazar Mendel's wife would travel to the Jerusalem market each night and collect the scattered handfuls of grain that had fallen during the previous day's business. She cooked the grain into a porridge and poured it into the family's one bowl for their hungry children. The children often fought over who got a bigger share of their meager meal. During one such argument Reb Elazar Mendel came out of his study with tears in his eyes. "Can it be that a Lelover family are fighting over material things and crying over food?"

The Problem Is Revealed

Reb Elazar Mendel and his wife never complained, and hid their difficulties from others. Every Friday afternoon, when other families prepared hot food for Shabbos, Rebbetzin Matil Feigeh put a pot of boiling water on the stove to make it seem that they were also cooking.

The Talmud (*Ta'anis* 25a) relates how the poor wife of Rabbi Chanina ben Dosa would burn wood in her empty oven every *erev Shabbos* and pretend to bake bread. Once, a suspicious neighbor peeked into the oven, and Hashem performed a miracle and filled it with hot fresh bread. No such miracle, however, occurred for Rebbetzin Matil Feigeh. One day, a neighbor entered her house and looked in her pot; and all she saw was boiling water!

The neighbor ran straight to the head of Jerusalem's Jewish community, Rav Moshe Leib of Kotnah, author of *Tiferes Yerushalayim*, and told him what she had seen. "This *talmid chacham* and his family are destitute. Will you let them die of hunger?" The Tiferes Yerushalayim already knew of Reb Moshe Lelover's greatness from Europe, and he immediately included Reb Elazar Mendel in the community's distribution list.

Not everyone was happy with this arrangement. Some *Perushim* on the distribution committee were against helping establish a Chassidic court in their midst. During one food distribution, they refused to give a portion to Reb Elazar Mendel's family. The Tiferes Yerushalayim sent them a warning: If they didn't change their ways, he would return his own food parcel and never take one from them again!

Once, during a year of drought, the community lacked coal, which was essential for heating, cooking and baking. The distribution committee was able to acquire only a small amount of this precious substance. Once again, they overlooked Reb Elazar Mendel. That night, Reb Moshe Lelover appeared in a dream to the Rav of Kalish, the head of the committee, and complained. The matter was corrected the very next morning.

Visions of the Night

The situation continued to be difficult. One night Reb Moshe Lelover appeared to the tzaddik, Reb Noson Dovid of Shidlovtzah, in a dream. "I have a son in Jerusalem whom I love dearly. Your life here in Poland is blessed with good things. Why don't you look after the welfare of my son?"

Reb Noson Dovid awoke from his sleep. He immediately wrote a letter to Reb Elazar Mendel, promising to send him several hundred rubles, as Reb Moshe Lelover had insisted. Reb Elazar Mendel wrote back, asking him to use some of the money to buy him a complete set of the Talmud, and Reb Noson Dovid complied.

At the same time, Reb Shlomo of Radomsk made efforts to collect the various pledges originally made to Reb Moshe Lelover before his journey. The Rebbe of Zichlin also began to send money to Reb Elazar Mendel and his family, to lighten their load.

Some time later, the Rav of Kalish sent the Rebbe of Zichlin a letter asking why he had singled out a particular family, that of Reb Elazar Mendel, for financial assistance. There were so many other needy families in Jerusalem struggling to lead lives of Torah and prayer. "Soon, the Rav of Kalish will know," the Rebbe of Zichlin said.

A short time later, Reb Leib Kushmark, a Zichliner Chassid, visited the Rav of Kalish during a trip to Jerusalem. The Kalisher handed him a letter for the Zichliner Rebbe retracting his earlier statements. When Reb Leib expressed surprise, the Kalisher explained his change of heart.

"After I sent the first letter, I saw a dignified old man in a dream. He was furious with me. 'How dare you speak against my holy son,' he demanded.

"'But I do not agree with his way,' I answered.

"'If you were truly humble, you would only see the good in him. Only those who are truly humble can appreciate the good in Eretz Yisrael and its inhabitants!'

"When I awoke, I decided to work on developing more humility. Since then, I have come to see how truly great and holy Reb Elazar Mendel is."

Sufferings of Love

The Zohar (3:272b) says, "the only true poverty is the lack of Torah," and in Torah, Reb Elazar Mendel was rich indeed. Material poverty and suffering he willingly accepted. Although on Yom Kippur we pray, "Erase my sins, but not through severe suffering or sickness," Reb Elazar Mendel prayed "...even through suffering or sickness." He was not healthy and, at night, the lice and bed-bugs bit him until he bled. However, when his wife tried to remove them, he stopped her. "Leave them alone," he said. "I summoned them myself" (as penance, see *Bava Metzia* 84b).

None of this interfered with Reb Elazar Mendel's *avodas Hashem*. He recited his daily prayers with such fiery intensity that the entire congregation trembled. Even inanimate objects in the room would shake. He would be drenched in sweat, and it could take him several hours just to recite the blessings before the *Krias Shema*. On Rosh Hashanah, it took him five hours to recite the *Shemoneh Esreh*.

One of his followers told the following story. "A group of us once traveled with the Rebbe to Chevron. We journeyed by mule team over mountains and valleys, hard rocks and arid plains. It was an arduous journey which took the entire day. We arrived in Chevron after nightfall, exhausted to the point of collapse. Every bone in our bodies was sore. After such torture, we assumed that the Rebbe would not extend his evening prayers; but he spent three hours praying *Shemoneh Esreh*. When he stepped back, as he finished, he muttered to himself, 'Was that a prayer? Better to pray again as a free-will offering' (*Orech Chaim* 106:1). Without a moment's pause, he re-entered *Shemoneh Esreh* and stood there until dawn."

Whenever Reb Elazar Mendel visited Chevron, he would pray at the *Me'aras haMachpelah* (the graves of the Patriarchs), except on Shabbos. He used to say: "All week long the souls of the Patriarchs are here; but on Shabbos they are at the Western Wall (in Jerusalem)."

Greatness in Nistar

Reb Elazar Mendel slowly gathered around himself a circle of Chassidim, true seekers of Hashem. His fame began to spread and even the great Rebbes of Radomsk and Alexander sent him their *kvitlach*. One Pesach night, the Divrei Chaim of Sanz commented,

"The Pesach Seder that Reb Elazar Mendel, the son of Reb Moshe Lelover, is now celebrating in Jerusalem is more beautiful than that of any other tzaddikim!"

When one of Reb Moshe's Chassidim traveled from Jerusalem to Poland, Reb Elazar Mendel gave him a *kvitel* to deliver to the Rebbe of Cherkas, the son of Reb Mordechai of Chernobyl. He also gave him 160 coins for *pidyon nefesh* and showed him how to arrange the coins in a special pattern on the table. The Chassid delivered the *kvitel* and arranged the coins before the Rebbe, without revealing who sent them. The Rebbe took one look and exclaimed, "This must be from Reb Elazar Mendel in Jerusalem. Only he knows the deep Kabbalistic significance of such patterns!"

In 1870, the Shinover Rebbe, the son of the Divrei Chaim of Sanz, visited Eretz Yisrael. He decided to stop in Chevron before traveling on to Jerusalem; and Reb Elazar Mendel quickly sent him a letter. As the letter-carrier traveled to Chevron, his curiosity overwhelmed him, and he peeked into the letter. To his amazement, all he saw were letters of the Hebrew alphabet strewn haphazardly across the page, without forming a single word! The messenger located the Shinover in Chevron and handed him the note. The Shinover opened it and gasped. "If there is a tzaddik in Jerusalem who knows how to write such a letter, I must visit him at once!" By the next day, the Shinover had already visited Reb Elazar Mendel, and a deep bond formed between the two tzaddikim.

Reb Elazar Mendel also designed the famous Jerusalem hanging candelabrum based on Kabbalistic principles. It consists of ten lights arranged in three tiers: the uppermost with three lights, the middle with six and the lowest with one, corresponding to the ten *sefiros* (Divine Attributes) of Kabbalah.

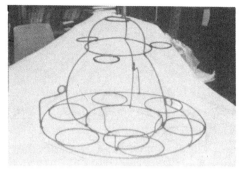

Reb Elazar Mendel's special holder for Shabbos lamps was designed according to Kabbalistic principles. There were three wicks in each of the six middle holders and two each in the lowest one and upper three, making 26 in all (the numerical value of Hashem's name).

Every *erev Shabbos*, Reb Elazar Mendel lit twenty-six lights, the numerical equivalent of Hashem's four-letter name. He was careful to use only olive oil, the choicest of all. Once, on the eve of *Shabbos haGadol*, his family was so busy with preparations that they didn't have time to buy olive oil and had to use kerosene instead. When Reb Elazar Mendel returned from shul and realized what had happened, his face became white. He sat in his chair and put his head in his hands. One by one, the lights went out, in deference to the will of the tzaddik.

Revealing the Hidden

The residents of the Holy City constantly turned to Reb Elazar Mendel for advice. Reb Yaakov Yosef of Polynoye once wrote: "Were it not for the opaqueness of the physical, the eye could see from one end of the earth to the other, and the ear could hear messages from Above." Reb Elazar Mendel had purified his body through fasting and mitzvos to the point that his vision and hearing were totally unobstructed.

Once, a large group of Chassidim fled to Reb Elazar Mendel's house, seeking shelter. "Why are you so afraid?" he asked them.

"Today is a Muslim holiday," they replied. "Every year there are pogroms, riots and beatings."

Reb Elazar Menachem Mendel

Rebbe Elazar Mendel stepped to the window. "I will hear what Hashem will speak..." (*Tehillim* 85:9). He stood silently for a moment, as if listening. "He will speak peace to his people, and to his Chassidim," he said, finishing the verse. "You can return home," he told them. "Nothing will happen to you today."

One night, Rebbetzin Matil Feigeh set the table for supper, but Reb Elazar Mendel refused to sit down and eat. He paced back and forth in his room. "Who baked the bread?" he asked his wife. She told him that it was from one of their pious neighbors. "Still, I would be amazed if she had separated the *challah*," he replied. The next morning, his wife spoke to her neighbor. "You're right," she said. "I was so busy on *erev Shabbos* that I forgot to take *challah*!"

Similarly, Reb Elazar Mendel's grandson, Rav Nota Horowitz (and brother of the first Bostoner Rebbe), told how, one day, Reb Elazar Mendel called in the local Jewish milkman. "Are you sure this milk is from your flock?" he asked. "Of course!" the man replied. "Would I give the Rebbe non-Jewish milk?" Reb Elazar Mendel said nothing, but refused to drink the milk. The next day, Reb Elazar Mendel asked his question again, and again received the same reply.

On the third day, Reb Elazar Mendel summoned the milkman into his private study. "If you do not confess the truth," he warned, "you will suffer dearly." The milkman became frightened and admitted that he had been selling non-Jewish milk for the past few days. "No one in the world knew this but the Rebbe," he said. "An angel from Heaven must have told him!"

One Shabbos night, Reb Elazar Mendel picked up his *Kiddush* cup, and then put it down again. Picked it up, put it down, picked it up, put it down. "Tell me, Dovid'l," he said to his young son. "You bought the wine. Are you sure nothing happened to it?"

"Nothing, Father. I bought it at the usual store, and I held it tightly until I got home. Even though an Arab boy followed me, I never let the bottle out of my hand."

Reb Elazar Mendel asked a few more questions, and finally discovered that the Arab boy had moved the bottle, rendering its contents unfit.

On another Shabbos night, Reb Elazar Mendel refused to eat his bowl of chicken soup. When his wife brought him a plate of the chicken boiled in the soup, they discovered that it had a broken thighbone. They sent the chicken to Rabbi Shmuel Salant, the Rav of Jerusalem, who declared it *treif*, and ordered them to *kasher* their pot and bowls.

There was only one Levi in Reb Elazar Mendel's shul. Whenever the Torah was read in public, he received the second *aliyah*. Each time he was called up, Reb Elazar Mendel would smile slightly; but no one knew why. Many years later the Levi became deathly ill. Reb Elazar Mendel came to his bedside and told him, "Now you can tell the truth. Are you really a Levi?"

"No," the man admitted. "In Europe I had heard that the Jews here look badly upon new immigrants and refuse to call them up to the Torah. By calling myself a Levi, I guaranteed that I would always get an *aliyah*!"

The Cure before the Disease

Reb Elazar Mendel's *ruach hakodesh* often saved the residents of Jerusalem from danger. The following two stories were related by Rabbi Dovid Weingarten, founder of Jerusalem's General Children's Orphanage.

There is a Jewish custom, especially among Chassidim, not to cut a young boy's hair until he reaches the age of three. It is customary to bring the child, usually on Lag b'Omer, to tzaddikim and *talmidei chachamim* to take the first snips (*chalukah*). On the Lag b'Omer after Dovid Weingarten's third birthday, his father, Reb Aharon Yosef, took him to the *beis midrash* of Reb Elazar Mendel. Many other Yerushalmi Jews were also there with their children. However, unlike in previous years, Reb Elazar Mendel suddenly demanded a large sum of money from every father who wanted his child's hair cut. No one could understand why. Many Chassidim paid unquestioningly, while others quietly slipped out of the *beis midrash* unnoticed.

Several weeks later, a plague broke out in Jerusalem that killed many children; but every single child whose father had paid the *chalukah* money was saved. Obviously, the money had been accepted as a *pidyon*, a spiritual substitute that redeemed their lives.

Similarly, one Purim, Reb Aharon Yosef brought a *mishloach manos* package to Reb Elazar Mendel. The tzaddik refused to accept it unless Reb Aharon Yosef gave him a *Napoleon zahavah*, a gold coin of considerable value. Two other Chassidim arrived with their packages, and the Rebbe made the same demand. Reb Aharon Yosef ran home to bring the money, but the two other men left, taking their Purim packages with them.

Not long afterwards, the sons of all three men contracted a terrible disease. As his son's condition worsened, Reb Aharon Yosef ran to Reb Elazar Mendel. "Don't worry," the Rebbe reassured him. "Your son's life has already been redeemed." Eventually Reb Aharon Yosef's son regained his health, while the other two boys passed away.

Not all attempts at redeeming others were, however, successful. A father and his young son were once praying in Reb Elazar Mendel's *beis midrash*. Suddenly, the Rebbe walked over to the boy and slapped him across the face. The child started crying, and the father complained bitterly. The Rebbe said nothing.

Two weeks later the child became sick and died. The father came sobbing to Reb Elazar Mendel. "You should know that I never hit anyone needlessly," the Rebbe explained. "I saw that harsh judgments were hovering over the boy and I sought to annul them. You should have accepted my efforts with love; instead you rejected them."

Annulling Decrees

Rabbi Yosef Praeger, the author of *Minchas Yosef*, lived in Brisk, and served as a *shochet* under the guidance of Rabbi Yehoshua Leib Diskin. Towards the end of his life, he moved to Tzefas, where he wrote the following:

> I spent a great deal of time with the Rebbe [Reb Elazar Mendel] on his many visits to Tzefas. What can I say about him? He was as humble as Hillel the Elder. He was literally nothing in his own eyes. He was holy and pure, kind, compassionate, honest and just — a holy man.... Once a person came to him to ask for his advice and help. The Rebbe sighed and commented, "That which the Rebbe Reb Elimelech of Lyzhansk said is correct — the tzaddik is the cause of the world's problems. The Talmud (*Kiddushin* 40b) says that a person hangs always in the balance; one good deed can push the entire world to merit, and one sin can tip the scales to deficit. It is my own sins that have brought suffering to all of these people. They are right when they ask me to pray for them. You caused us this problem, they say. At least pray for our deliverance!"

Once, when Reb Elazar Mendel visited Tzefas, he told Rabbi Shmuel Heller, the Rav of the community, "This year, dreadful negative judgments were building up in Heaven against Tzefas. It's a miracle that I am here to annul them." Words like these were not spoken out of pride or vanity. A truly humble person knows what level he is on, but takes no credit for having reached that point on his own. All of his achievements he attributes to Hashem's compassion and to the greatness of the Jewish People. Reb Elazar Mendel once commented: "I was born in a small town to a great father. Why should it be a surprise that I am a good Jew? Had I been born in a big city to a bad father, then my *avodas Hashem* would have been truly special."

NINE
Reb Dovid'l Biderman

A Mind of His Own

Reb Elazar Mendel Lelover's son and eventual successor was Reb Dovid Tzvi Shlomo, "Reb Dovid'l Biderman" (not to be confused with Reb Dovid of Lelov, the dynasty's founder). As a young man, Reb Dovid'l married the daughter of Reb Pinchas haLevi Horowitz from Brod (see Chapter 11), one of the prominent tzaddikim of his generation. He was a descendant of the two holy brothers, Reb Shmuel Shmelke Horowitz of Nikolsburg and Reb Pinchas Horowitz, the Ba'al Hafla'ah.

Every Lelover Rebbe was a unique individual and, although Reb Dovid'l was born into an established Chassidic court, he too chose to go his own way. He decided to return to Europe, the major center of Chassidic life, and find himself a teacher among the great Rebbes of the time. His father, Reb Elazar Mendel, opposed the trip. "Why do you need to travel so far for a Rebbe?" he asked. "You have the *Kosel* (Western Wall) here in Jerusalem. Let that be your Rebbe."

"But I need a Rebbe who can answer my questions."

"When one is worthy, the *Kosel* answers his questions. Believe me, when I say *'Gut Shabbos'* to the *Kosel*, I get an answer!"

Reb Dovid'l, however, was not satisfied. If his father was not going to give him his blessing, he would leave without it. He traveled to Akko and found a passenger ship traveling to Europe. Before boarding, he went down to the shore to immerse himself in the ocean. Suddenly, a snake started swimming towards him. He ran towards the shore, but the snake followed him. Reb Dovid'l immediately understood that his father was involved in all this, and that he was being pursued by what the Talmud calls "the serpent of the Rabbis." He decided to cancel his trip; and the snake immediately turned around and disappeared in the high grass.

When he complained to his father, Reb Elazar Mendel replied, "What did you expect? If you don't listen to my gentle opinion, you have to listen to a biting one."

With Leaders of the Generation

Time passed, but Reb Dovid'l still longed to travel to Europe. Finally, his father agreed and, in 1865, Reb Dovid'l left Jerusalem for Vienna. There he met Reb Aharon of Karlin, the Beis Aharon, who was visiting that city for health reasons. From their very first *Shalom Aleichem*, Reb Dovid'l knew that he had found his teacher and guide.

He decided to visit Reb Aharon in Karlin, but the journey from Vienna to Russia proved a long, if instructive, one — with stops to visit the many great Chassidic masters of his day.

From Vienna, Reb Dovid'l first traveled to the Sanzer Rav, the Divrei Chaim, a giant in both Torah and good deeds. He gave everything he had to the poor and, when nothing remained, he would walk around the *beis midrash* trying to borrow money from the congregants. They would rarely give, however, for they knew that this was a never-ending cycle. Reb Dovid'l voluntarily offered the Sanzer Rav several coins from his meager funds. The Sanzer Rav thanked him deeply, and told him: "In *Tehillim* (146:3) it says, 'Do not trust in the wealthy, [but] in men who cannot help.' It is precisely those men who cannot help, that one can trust in."

Reb Dovid'l spent Shabbos in Sanz, and joined the Rebbe for the morning prayers. However, after a while, Reb Dovid'l abruptly left the shul. When asked why, he replied, "When the Rebbe recited *Nishmas*, he started stamping his feet with great strength. I felt him pulling me to become his Chassid. However, I have already made a commitment to Reb Aharon of Karlin. Since I didn't want to insult the Sanzer Rav by refusing, I left the shul."

Next Reb Dovid'l traveled throughout Poland to meet other great Rebbes of his day. He visited Reb Shlomo of Radomsk, his grandfather's disciple; Reb Menachem Mendel of Vorki, "the Silent Rebbe"; Reb Yaakov Aryeh of Radzimin, a leading disciple of Reb Simcha Bunim of Pshischah; and Reb Elimelech of Grodjisk, a grandson of the Kozhnitzer Maggid.

Reb Dovid'l also visited his relative, Reb Yaakov Tzvi of Porisov, who received him with open arms. "Why didn't you tell me you were coming?" Reb Yaakov asked. "I loved your grandfather, Reb Moshe, so much that I accompanied him all the way to Odessa." Reb Dovid'l spent several days in Porisov. Reb Yaakov showed him the *kvitlach* he had received from his Chassidim and, together, the two men prayed on behalf of the needy. One evening, Reb Yaakov showed Reb Dovid'l a *kvitel* from a young woman whose baby refused to nurse. Reb Dovid'l burst into tears. "This is the problem of the *Shechinah* Herself!" he said. "She wants to bestow upon us goodness and blessing. It is we who do not want to receive!"

A CHASSIDIC JOURNEY

In Karlin
Reb Dovid'l continued his travels towards the court of Reb Aharon of Karlin in Russia. Along the way he visited Reb Yaakov of Sadigura, the son of the Reb Yisroel of Ruzhin, and the five sons of Reb Mordechai (the Maggid) of Chernobyl: The Trisker Maggid, Reb Aharon of Chernobyl, Reb Yitzchok of Squer, Reb Yaakov Yisroel of Cherkas, and Reb Dovid of Tolna.

In Karlin, Reb Dovid'l had hoped to go unnoticed as merely another student; but Reb Aharon immediately recognized his potential and spent many hours with him in private conversation, plumbing the depths of Chassidus. Once, as Reb Dovid'l left Reb Aharon's study, he met the Rebbe's son, Reb Asher of Stolin. "Last night, my father spoke to me about you for four and a half hours," said Reb Asher. "He said that, if you want, you can become a truly good Jew."

Once, Reb Aharon visited Reb Dovid'l's lodgings, only to find him napping. He quickly called his son, Reb Asher. "Come and see how a Jew from Eretz Yisrael sleeps!"

A deep love existed between the Rebbe and his disciple. "I am with you, and you are with me, in this world and in the next," Reb Aharon told Reb Dovid'l. However, the more honor his Rebbe showed him, the humbler he became. Reb Dovid'l's love was so intense that, once, he cut his finger while slicing bread and didn't even notice, because he was so absorbed in looking at his teacher.

In 1866, after returning to Jerusalem, Reb Dovid'l established the first Karliner shul in the city. At first, he didn't even have a *minyan*, and was forced to ask two local Sefardim to join in the prayers. Reb Dovid'l was close to all of the Karliner Rebbes of his time: Reb Aharon, Reb Asher and Reb Yisroel. Through Reb Dovid'l many Karliner customs were incorporated into Lelover and, later, Bostoner Chassidus; and his descendants served as the first Rebbes of Pinsk-Karlin.

Reb Dovid'l Biderman

A Pillar of Avodah

When Reb Elazar Mendel passed away, his son, Reb Dovid'l Biderman became the fourth Lelover Rebbe. His name spread throughout the Holy City of Jerusalem, and his powerful prayers attracted scores of Chassidim. One left this description:

> How sweetly and how pleasantly the words left his mouth, like shining pearls, Heavenly grace poured upon them. The dullest heart would burst at hearing them.... He would shout like one wrestling with troops of enemy forces. Then he would lower his voice in gentle entreaty, as though begging forgiveness. Then, in a moment, this would change to a voice of exuberance and assuredness, a voice proclaiming deliverance and hope.

The *nusach* of his prayers was from Lelov, but the force of his prayers was from Karlin. As Reb Yisroel of Karlin used to say: "When a fire is burning, one yells!"

Reb Dovid'l served Hashem with all his heart, all his life. He once said, "From the days of my youth, I have never once removed my thoughts from the verse 'I have set Hashem before me always'" (*Tehillim* 16:8). Towards the end of his life, Reb Dovid'l became sick and was confined to bed but, even in his sleep, he would gesture as if in prayer, and a deep sigh would escape his lips, like a child beseeching his father.

One Yom Kippur night, after the congregation had finished their prayers and *Tehillim*, a number of young men sat together in the Lelov *beis midrash* on floor mats and rested in preparation for the next day's service. As they relaxed, they began joking together and discussing secular matters. They forgot that Reb Dovid'l was sitting near them. Suddenly, they heard him sigh deeply and say: "Rejoice with trembling." A holy silence enveloped the group, as they re-entered the great sanctity of the day.

The Three Pillars

The Mishnah (*Avos*) says that the world rests on three pillars: Torah, Divine service and deeds of kindness. Even as a young child in Pshadburz, Reb Dovid'l was already recognized as exceptionally adept at learning the Gemara with Rashi, Tosafos and the Maharsha. Upon his arrival in Eretz Yisrael, however, he mysteriously forgot everything he had learned in Poland, and had to start all over again from the *aleph-beis*! He used to joke about it: "The Talmud states that Rav Zeira fasted a hundred days, so that he could forget his studies in Babylonia, and learn only the higher Torah of Eretz Yisrael (*Bava Metzia* 85a). I saved myself one hundred fasts; for now I know only the Torah of Eretz Yisrael."

As an adult, Reb Dovid'l's daily schedule of study was so intense that he rarely went to bed. Usually, he would sleep for a short period at his desk and then, at midnight, go to the *mikveh* and walk to Rechovot haNahar, a yeshiva of Sefardic Kabbalists. There he would study Kabbalah until just before dawn, and then pray with them using the *siddur* of the Rashash, which includes the Kabbalistic intentions of the Arizal. His concentration in prayer was so intense that he was oblivious to this world. Once, while praying alone at the Western Wall, an Arab youth beat him cruelly; yet he felt nothing. When he returned home, his family had to show him the bruises.

Each morning, after prayers, Reb Dovid'l would study eighteen chapters of *mishnayos*, finishing the entire Mishnah once a month. Then he would turn to his other Torah studies, concluding them close to midnight. As for deeds of loving kindness, even when there was barely enough food for himself, Reb Dovid'l refused to eat until a beggar or some other poor soul joined him. All the *pidyonos* (donations) he received from his Chassidim he gave away to the poor, refusing to derive any personal benefit from them.

Reb Dovid'l Biderman

Once, Reb Dovid'l's wife noticed that their daughter's shoes were so torn that the rain and mud were seeping in. She took some money from her husband's *pidyon* box and when Reb Dovid'l came home, she told him, "Today, I saw a poor girl from a good family, who had no shoes. So I took some money from your charity box and gave it to her."

"Good," he replied. "That's precisely what it is for."

"And that girl," the Rebbetzin continued, "was your own daughter."

Reb Dovid'l's face turned pale. "What's done is done," he said to her, "but you must never do that again. That money has been designated for the poor, and not for our family."

When the Rebbe Refused to Give

Once, however, Reb Dovid'l refused to give! Reb Nechemia Yosef Wilhelm was a charity-collector in Jerusalem. One day, a poor acquaintance of his asked for help. He had just arranged his daughter's marriage but didn't have the money for the dowry. He begged Reb Nechemia to collect funds for him at once. Despite the stormy weather, Reb Nechemia set out for Reb Dovid'l, a sure donor indeed. "Why are you asking money for him?" Reb Dovid'l asked in amazement. "He's a rich man!"

Reb Nechemia was shocked. He had witnessed the man's poverty for years but, if Reb Dovid'l said that the pauper was rich, then surely he must be. "If that fellow wants to feign poverty that's his business," he thought angrily. "But what a *chutzpah* to send me out on a such a stormy day!"

That evening, he knocked on the "pauper's" door and his friend opened it with a broad smile. "Come in, come in," he said. "I was hoping someone would come, so I could tell him my good news!"

Earlier that day, a local priest, one of the biggest Jew-haters in the city, had gone to the Arab market. He constantly extorted money from the Jews under various pretexts. He stopped at a store that was open to the street, under an awning that protected customers from the rain. The priest chose what he wanted and took out his wallet to pay. Suddenly, a powerful wind blew the wallet out of his hand. It fell into a narrow rain gutter that ran down the side of the steeply sloping street, and it was soon swept away by the strong downpour. The priest ran after his wallet tripping and stumbling over his long wet frock. Arabs and other passersby also started running after the wallet, but it quickly disappeared down the narrow, winding streets of the Old City.

The wallet ended up behind a pile of rubbish, where the priest and his Arab cronies did not notice it. They ran past it down the street. A short time later, Reb Nechemia's friend began walking to *Minchah*, his mind preoccupied with his financial problems. Suddenly, he noticed an abandoned object lying in the gutter. He picked it up and discovered that it was a wallet full of money! Later, when he heard the whole story, he regarded it as an act of Divine retribution. The priest had lost what had never truly belonged to him, and a Jew had been delivered from poverty. Although Reb Nechemia was the first to hear the story, Reb Dovid'l had already known all about it through his *ruach hakodesh*.

True Charity

Reb Dovid'l of Lelov sought to help other Jews, not just financially, but also with his time, intelligence and effort. The current Bostoner Rebbe of Boston, *shlita*, relates in the name of his father how, on public fast days, Reb Dovid'l would visit the homes of sickly widows and pour them coffee from a flask he carried with him. "These poor women really should not be fasting," he explained. "Unfortunately, they have no husbands to make them stop. So I visit them and make sure that they break their fasts."

In addition to his many other responsibilities, Reb Dovid'l was also the director of the Rebbe Meir Ba'al haNess Charity Fund for families from the Poland-Warsaw area. He oversaw the distribution of large sums of money to Jerusalem's needy families, yet never took a penny for himself, although he was certainly as needy as the rest.

Seals and signatures of the kollelim of Jerusalem on a letter explaining that all receipts were signed by Reb Dovid'l Biderman, zt"l, on behalf of the Toras Chessed of Lublin.

One year, when Reb Dovid'l and his family were suffering acute poverty, messengers brought him 1300 gold coins for public distribution. His wife asked him for some money to buy, at least, some bread.

"I don't have any," he replied. She looked at the large pile of coins on the table and Reb Dovid'l read her thoughts.

"This money is fire!" he declared. "Fire! It is forbidden to touch funds of the poor. It's a great danger!"

Another time, when the family's money had run out, Reb Dovid'l's wife started crying. "Can't we borrow a small amount from the Kollel just to see us through this hard time?"

"My dear," Reb Dovid'l replied, "it isn't my money. Using it for ourselves is like deriving benefit from *hekdesh* (sanctified funds). Trust in Hashem and He will provide you with all that you need for the house." The Rebbetzin left the house for the Western Wall, where she could pour out her heart to Hashem. Along the way, on one of the side streets, she found a gold coin in the gutter. She returned home, happy and relieved. She immediately dedicated part of the coin to charity, and spent the rest on their household needs.

Entrance to the Battei Warsaw section of Old Jerusalem

Reb Dovid'l constantly sought to alleviate the poverty of the Torah scholars of the Old City and was among the founders of the Battei Warsaw development, in the center of the "New City," near Me'ah She'arim (next to Kikar Shabbos). Even today, the neighborhood is known as "Hekdesh Biderman." He also helped found the famous Chayei Olom Talmud Torah and Yeshiva for Chassidic children. The school's first principal was Rabbi Meir Adler, Reb Dovid'l's brother-in-law. He saw the yeshiva through its difficult years, until it finally settled in its present location, overlooking Kikar Shabbos.

Reb Dovid'l was beloved by the entire Orthodox community of Jerusalem, and he never distinguished between its many factions. He rose above such details when distributing funds; his signature was never questioned; and his word was as good as gold.

Opposition to America

Reb Dovid'l cared deeply about both the physical and the spiritual welfare of his followers; but there was no question which took precedence. Thus, whenever his Chassidim wanted to go to America, he adamantly refused. America, at that time, was a spiritual wasteland; without yeshivas, day schools, or *shomer-Shabbos* employment. The very air seemed filled with avarice and spiritual insensitivity.

Once, Reb Velvel of Zlatipoli, a well-known Yerushalmi, came to Reb Dovid'l for a parting blessing. He was leaving for America.

"No," Reb Dovid'l replied with conviction. "You are not going to America."

Reb Velvel continued making his arrangements, received his passport and visa, and set off for the port in Haifa. World War I had just broken out, and the ports would soon be closed to outgoing vessels, but Reb Velvel was scheduled to sail on the last ship leaving Eretz Yisrael. Reb Velvel was just about to board the ship, when the captain stopped him.

"You're not getting on board," the captain announced, for no apparent reason. Reb Velvel pleaded, but to no avail; the ship set sail without him. He turned around and returned, wiser, to Jerusalem.

There was only one person whom Reb Dovid'l considered sending to America, his saintly nephew, Reb Pinchas Dovid Horowitz, later the first Bostoner Rebbe. "I'm not worried about him," Reb Dovid'l would say. "He is a pillar of iron, a stone wall. America won't touch him!"

Indeed, in 1910, Reb Dovid'l actually commanded his nephew to travel to America. Someone must tend to our American brothers, he explained, and lift them up spiritually. However, Reb Pinchas Dovid could not even imagine leaving Jerusalem, its holy streets and saintly scholars. "Reb Dovid'l is my teacher and guide," he said, "and I listen to him in everything — except this, that I travel to America." Reb Pinchas Dovid hoped that his Rebbe was mistaken, and Reb Dovid'l heard out his nephew's complaints in silence, knowing full well, through his *ruach hakodesh*, how matters would develop.

Reb Pinchas Dovid did, indeed, eventually end up in America (Chapter 12), but even there he remained true to his heritage. "I may be here, but my every step is directed to Jerusalem," he said. The marriage contracts of Reb Pinchas Dovid's male descendants all stipulate that the groom always has the option of moving to Eretz Yisrael, and that his wife must agree. Reb Dovid'l had been right; America couldn't touch him.

TEN
The Family Horowitz

The Family Horowitz

Reb Dovid'l Biderman's saintly nephew, Reb Pinchas Dovid Horowitz, the founder of the Bostoner dynasty, was the sixth-generation descendant, son after son, of the tzaddik Reb Shmuel Shmelke Horowitz of Nikolsburg.

The Ba'al Shem Tov once said that three Jewish families — Shapiro, Margolios and Horowitz — could be traced back to ancient days, and he stated that "if a Horowitz cries in prayer, from the depth of his heart, he will be answered immediately." The Horowitz family tree went back to Shmuel haNavi, and from there to Rabbi Zerachia haLevi, the Ba'al haMe'or. For generations, members of the Horowitz family filled the posts of Rabbis and leaders in major Jewish settlements.

It was Rabbi Yeshaya haLevi, who dates back to the Spanish expulsion (1492), who purchased the "Horowitz Forests" in Bohemia, which gave the family its "modern" name. His son was Rabbi Shabtai Shaftil; and his son was Rabbi Avraham haLevi, the author of *Bris Avraham*. His son was the holy Shlah, called after the acronym formed by the title of his work *Shnei Luchos haBris*.

Rabbi Yehoshua "The Tall"

Rabbi Yehoshua Horowitz "The Tall," was Chief Rabbi of Premeshla. His father was Rabbi Pinchas haLevi Horowitz, whom the Tosafos Yom Tov described as, "wise in Torah and worldly matters" and "Head of the Four Lands in Poland." Every Friday afternoon, when donning his Shabbos finery, he seemed to grow a foot taller, only returning to his regular height at the end of Shabbos.

His son was Reb Shmuel Shmelke "The Tall," not to be confused with his descendant and namesake Reb Shmuel Shmelke of Nikolsburg. He was first the Rav of Shendishov and then, from 1673 until his death in 1713, the Rav of Tornah. Before his passing, he promised to help his descendants who prayed at his grave. Once, his descendant, Reb Naftali Ropshitzer, came to Tornah to pray at Reb Shmelke's grave. There was no sign of it in the cemetery, and none of the locals could remember where it was. Reb Naftali fasted for a day, and then entered the cemetery, his eyes scanning the field. Suddenly he said, "There is his grave!" They dug slightly below the surface of the ground, and indeed found Reb Shmelke's gravestone.

Reb Meir of Tiktin

Reb Shmuel Shmelke's son was Reb Meir, Rabbi of Belchov, Zlotchov and Tiktin. He was widely known as a holy man, great in Torah and good deeds, immersed in Torah study day and night. One *motza'ei Yom Kippur*, Reb Meir and his *beis din* went out to sanctify the new moon. The sky was cloudy, and Reb Meir cried out, "How brazen is the sky! Meir and his *beis din* are waiting!" Immediately the wind blew the clouds apart and they could see the moon.

Reb Meir was actually exceedingly humble. Once, a traveling preacher delivered a fiery sermon to the residents of

Tiktin, berating them for their sins. Reb Meir broke down in tears. "Why embarrass me in public?" he complained. "If you have to rebuke me, why not do it in private?" The preacher was shocked. He explained that his words had been meant only for the ordinary townspeople, but Reb Meir was unappeased.

"All of our townspeople are tzaddikim. You couldn't mean them. Who could have sinned except me?"

Reb Meir's love of the Jewish People was so great that he would reportedly never eat unless he had first done some act of kindness for a fellow Jew; and every day Hashem would send him an opportunity. Once, however, the entire day passed without Reb Meir finding someone in need, so he didn't eat. Late that night, he heard a loud noise in the street; a wagon loaded with wood was passing by. He ran out and bargained with the driver over the price of the wood. Then he ran to the home of a Jewish carpenter to ask if he was interested. The man agreed it was a bargain, but he didn't have the money on hand, so Reb Meir lent him the required sum. The carpenter bought the wood, and only then did Reb Meir sit down to eat.

In his will Reb Meir ordered: "I forbid any person to eulogize me or show me any respect, for in my heart I know my worthlessness and that I have nothing to be praised for. Years ago, Heaven revealed that the *Shechinah* would have rested on me had the generation been worthy, but my sins may have brought me down."

Reb Meir did not mix the study of Talmud with the study of Kabbalah. He first immersed himself in Talmudic studies for seven years; and his son Reb Yukel, born during that time, was renowned for his Torah knowledge. Reb Yukel became the Chief Rabbi of Gelona and the father of Reb Yitzchok haLevi Hamburger, the grandfather of Reb Naftali Ropshitzer. Reb Meir then immersed himself in Kabbalistic studies for seven years; and his son Reb Tzvi Hirsh, born during that time, was renowned for his holiness and purity.

Reb Meir had twelve sons in all, all giants in Torah. The Seer of Lublin once commented to his student, Reb Moshe of Opte, a descendant of Reb Meir, "Heaven does not give note to *yichus* (lineage), except for the family of Reb Shmuel Shmelke of Nikolsburg, for they are descendants of Reb Meir of Tiktin."

Reb Tzvi Hirsh

Reb Tzvi Hirsh Tiktiner became the Rav of Tshortkov. The Noda b'Yehudah once ended a responsa: "But do not rely on my words without the consensus of the three pillars of the world: the great and famous light, Rabbi Tzvi Hirsh haLevi, Rabbi of Tshortkov [and two others]...if they approve my words, I shall follow their lead, for their decisions are made with pure and holy intent."

Reb Tzvi Hirsh often fasted from Shabbos to Shabbos, both day and night, and was known as a miracle worker, blessed with *ruach hakodesh*. Walking through Tshortkov, shortly after his appointment, he sensed a unique holiness emanating from the far end of town. When he learned that a tzaddik, Reb Itzik the Poor, lived there, he invited Reb Itzik to speak with him. "Behold, the my son's scent is like the fragrance of a field which Hashem has blessed" (*Bereshis* 27:27), he quoted when Reb Itzik entered; and Reb Itzik soon became his closest disciple.

On that same first walk through town, Reb Tzvi Hirsh sensed the various sins and mitzvos emanating from all the different houses. When he came to the main synagogue, he cried out, "What did that *rasha* (wicked person) do?" The congregation made inquiries and discovered that when the building was first erected, the local duke had allowed a priest

The Family Horowitz

to lay the foundation stone, with the explicit intention of ruining the Jews' prayers. Reb Tzvi Hirsh ordered the entire wall destroyed and the stone removed. Only afterwards was he able to pray there.

The Ba'al Shem Tov once passed through Tshortkov. Reb Tzvi Hirsh sent a message with Reb Itzik inviting the Ba'al Shem Tov to remain with him in town. However, the Ba'al Shem Tov continued on his journey. Reb Itzik escorted him a short distance in a carriage. They had barely left town, when the wagon wheel broke. They fixed it and continued; but, it broke again. They fixed it, and it broke again! "That poor Jew is not letting me leave," the Ba'al Shem Tov said. They returned to Tshortkov, and the Ba'al Shem Tov remained there several days. When he and Reb Tzvi Hirsh first met, they closeted themselves in a room and spoke for twelve hours! What they spoke about, no one ever knew.

Several years after Reb Tzvi Hirsh's passing, Reb Levi Yitzchok of Berditchev visited Tshortkov. He prayed as the *shaliach tzibur* in Reb Tzvi Hirsh's shul, using the *nusach Sefard* prayerbook customary among Chassidim. Reb Levi Yitzchok's prayers usually roared like thunder and flashed like lightning. This time, however, in the middle of *davening*, he fell asleep! Reb Tzvi Hirsh appeared to him in a dream and asked "Why are you praying *nusach Sefard* in my shul? Do you know how many years I worked to open the spiritual pathways based on *nusach Ashkenaz*?" Reb Levi Yitzchok woke up, and immediately continued praying... in *nusach Ashkenaz*!

"From here we can see my father's greatness," commented Reb Tzvi Hirsh's son, Reb Yisroel of Tshortkov. "His efforts were so spiritually powerful that they justified interrupting the prayers of the holy Reb Levi Yitzchok, just to change the *nusach*."

Reb Tzvi Hirsh's Children

Reb Tzvi Hirsh left behind several exceptional sons including the two holy brothers, Reb Shmuel Shmelke Horowitz of Nikolsburg, and Reb Pinchas Horowitz of Frankfurt, the Ba'al Hafla'ah. Their mother said of them: "I have two sons; one never says *Birkas haMazon* because he hardly eats, and the other never recites the bedside *Krias Shema* because he doesn't sleep."

The Ba'al Hafla'ah referred to another brother, Reb Nachum haLevi, the *Av Beis Din* of Preskrov, as his Rebbe and to a fourth brother, Rabbi Avraham, as "the Great Light." A fifth brother, Reb Yehoshua Heshel, died at the tender age of fifteen, after it was revealed to him that he was needed by the Heavenly Academy. He passed away suddenly, as if by the "Kiss."

Once, when the Berditchever Rav was visiting Preskrov, he saw a great light shining from the grave of Reb Nachum. On another occasion, when a plague was threatening Preskrov, the townspeople begged Reb Mordechai of Chernobyl to pray for them. Instead, he sent them to the grave of Reb Nachum. They prayed there, and the plague soon ended.

Brothers Dwelling Together

In his youth, Reb Shmuel Shmelke studied with his father in the *beis midrash* of the Vilna Gaon, and with Rav Avraham Abish, the *Av Beis Din* of Frankfurt and the author of *Birkas Avraham*. Afterwards, he studied for many years with his brother, the Ba'al Hafla'ah. About this period the Hafla'ah writes: "My soul became bound to my brother's soul with thick cords of love. We consulted each other in halachah, studied the Talmud and its commentaries together, and examined the roots of our faith and the true foundations of the Torah, all with such amazing love, like the love between Dovid and Yehonasan." Towards the end of his life, the Hafla'ah reviewed their joint insights from this period and printed them in *Sheves Achim*.

The two brothers put every ounce of their strength into their studies. They once struggled over a difficult topic for more than a day. The Hafla'ah, about to collapse from exhaustion, grabbed a pillow and lay down.

"Why are you sleeping?" his brother called to him. "Get up and learn!"

"I am too tired," replied the Hafla'ah. "I have no more strength."

"You had enough strength to reach for a pillow. You should have used that strength to learn a few more lines!"

Another time, they learned together for two and a half days straight, without sleep, in the attic of the *beis midrash*. The Hafla'ah went downstairs to get a certain book they needed. After a long delay, Reb Shmelke went to look for him, and found him collapsed on the stairs from exhaustion. Reb Shmelke woke him up saying, "My dear brother, if we sleep now, what will we do in the grave?"

The Yeshiva of Reb Shmelke

Upon Rav Avraham Abish's recommendation, Reb Shmelke was appointed the Rav of Reitshval. There, he established his famous yeshiva, attracting some of the greatest minds of Europe, including Reb Yisroel, later the Kozhnitzer Maggid; Reb Levi Yitzchok of Berditchev; Reb Menachem Mendel of Rimanov, and Reb Mordechai Banet. The daily schedule included fourteen hours for study, four hours for prayer, a half hour for rest (during which Reb Shmelke would teach *Chovos haLevavos*), a half hour for meals, four hours for sleeping, and one hour open to the public. Even with such a strenuous schedule, the study periods often extended beyond their allotted time.

The intensity of their study was amazing. The Hafla'ah wrote, "When I visited my brother's yeshiva in Reitshval, I saw young men tie their *peyos* to the rafters with strings. If they started to fall over in sleep, the pain would jerk them awake."

Yeshiva Requirements

One scholar of that generation, Rav Meir Karinsnofler, *Av Beis Din* of Brodt, and author of *Yad haMeir*, once wrote of his attempts as a youth, to enter Reb Shmelke's yeshiva. He traveled to Reitshval, where Reb Shmelke warned him, "The main condition for studying here is that you never willingly go to sleep during the week." Meir agreed, and for two full days he sat and studied. By the third day, he could barely keep his eyes open. Reb Shmelke began to deliver a complicated lesson in the Gemara. Suddenly he needed a certain book from his private study and sent Meir to get it. As Meir wearily searched through the bookshelf, he noticed the Rebbe's bed right beside it. Sleep overpowered him. He grabbed a pillow and sank to the floor.

After a while, Reb Shmelke sent another student to look for the book and for Meir. The student returned and reported that Meir was sleeping on the floor.

"Does he have a pillow?" Reb Shmelke asked. "Yes," the student replied.

"Too bad. If he didn't have a pillow, I would let him sleep, because he had no other choice. But if he had time to put a pillow under his head, he went to sleep willingly. Go wake him up."

Meir awoke, realized what had happened, asked the Reb Shmelke for his blessing and returned home.

The Intensity of Reb Shmelke's Study

When Reb Shmelke had to sleep, he would rest his head on a jar of cold water and wedge a lit candle between his fingers. If he overslept, the candle would burn down and wake him up. In this way, he would learn throughout the night. He used to say, "If a person holds the precious diamond of Torah in his hand, should he willingly throw it away?"

One night, as Reb Shmelke napped, the wind blew out his candle. When he awoke, he immediately ran out to the porch to try and get a light from a passerby. Suddenly, a hand appeared out of the darkness and relit the candle, and Reb Shmelke quickly returned to his studies. In the morning, he realized that his study was on the second floor, beyond all human reach! He fasted for several days afterwards to atone for having troubled Eliyahu haNavi to come to his aid.

When Reb Yehoshua Heshel, the Opter Rav, heard this story, he sighed. "Those are the sins Reb Shmelke has to repent for: having troubled Eliyahu haNavi to help him learn Torah. Where does that leave us!"

Reb Shmelke's close friend, the Rebbe Reb Elimelech of Lyzhansk, once paid him a visit. "Prepare a bed for our guest," Reb Shmelke told his wife. Since they almost never slept, his yeshiva students were amazed. "Is the Rebbe Reb Elimelech so sick that he needs to lie down?"

Later that night, the two tzaddikim were discussing deep mysteries of Torah when the Rebbetzin came in and announced, "Our guest's bed is ready." Rebbe Elimelech gave Reb Shmelke a puzzled look. "A tzaddik comes to stay at my home," explained Reb Shmelke. "Is it right that he leave without sleeping a bit?" Rebbe Elimelech agreed, but only if Reb Shmelke also lay down.

It took considerable effort; but Rebbe Elimelech was finally able to persuade Reb Shmelke to deliberately sleep.

The next morning Reb Shmelke awoke with so much energy that, when he reached *Shiras haYam* (Song of the Sea), the entire congregation felt as if they were actually crossing the Red Sea and lifted up their trousers to keep them from getting wet! "Sleep is important," Reb Shmelke had to admit. "But, still, who has time for it?"

In the Shadow of the Maggid

When word reached Reitshval about Reb Dov Baer, the great Maggid of Mezritch, Reb Shmelke and his brother, the Hafla'ah, decided to visit him. "Why do tzaddikim like yourselves have to travel so far to see me?" the Maggid asked them on their first meeting. When they remained silent, he continued, "So I will tell you. A person can rise at midnight to pray, and learn until dawn with great concentration. Then he can recite the morning prayers with such holiness that he ascends through all the supernal worlds. But, if after his prayers, he feels the slightest bit of pride, Heaven takes all of his prayers and Torah, crumbles them up into a ball and throws them into the abyss!"

The two brothers, stirred to their depths, replied, "The Rebbe is right, we did not need to travel to meet him, we needed to crawl to him on our hands and knees!"

"What did you learn in Mezritch?" men asked Reb Shmelke upon his return to Reitshval. "Before I met the Maggid," he said, "I fasted so my body could bear my soul. In Mezritch, I learned how the soul can bear the body!"

ELEVEN
Reb Shmuel Shmelke of Nikolsburg

The Invitation

Ten years later Reb Shmelke left Reitshval to become the Rav of Shinov, where he expanded his yeshiva. Among his new students was the young Yaakov Yitzchok, the future Seer of Lublin. Shortly thereafter, Reb Shmelke and his brother, the Ba'al Hafla'ah, were invited to head the congregations of Frankfurt and Nikolsburg, but they were allowed to decide for themselves which city each would lead.

They decided to ask the Maggid of Mezritch his opinion. As they reached his study, each sought to give precedence to the other. Suddenly, from behind the closed door, the Maggid called out, "Let the Rabbi of Nikolsburg enter first, for he [Reb Shmelke] is the elder."

Reb Shmelke traveled to Nikolsburg with his disciple, Reb Moshe Leib of Sasov. Along the way, he prepared a brilliant sermon to deliver to his new congregation. The two tzaddikim spent Shabbos in Krakow, where Reb Shmelke tried out his new sermon on the Krakow community. They were so impressed that they begged Reb Shmelke to become their Rav, but he continued on to Nikolsburg. There he was met with a reception fit for a king. Both scholars and laymen crowded the Nikolsburg shul to hear his first sermon. Several community leaders, however, had already heard Reb Shmelke's sermon in Krakow, but he didn't have time to prepare a new one. He stepped up to the *bimah* and opened a Gemara at random. He read a few lines and asked several questions. The scholars in the audience joined the discussion, adding questions and comments of their own. The Rebbe repeated his questions, and the questions of the audience — 130 in all — which he rearranged into 72 main topics. Without hesitation, he delivered a brilliant lecture on the topics at hand, answering all 130 questions in the process. He concluded with a comment on the verse, "Behold, Hashem rides on a swift cloud" (*av kal*), since *av* has the numerical value of 72, and *kal* of 130. The audience was stunned by Reb Shmelke's knowledge and oratorical ability.

A Pillar of Torah

The Opter Rav, once wrote: "In his Torah knowledge, Reb Shmelke is as great as Rabbeinu Tam, and, in his fear of Hashem, perhaps even greater." Rabbi Yaakov Orenshtein, author of the *Yeshuos Yaakov*, considered Reb Shmelke to be on the level of the *Tanna'im*. Rabbi Yosef Shaul Natenson, *Av Beis Din* of Lemberg, wrote, "We have heard many stories about his holiness and his amazing ability to transcend physical needs, and about how he has raised many great students, tzaddikim and Chassidim." Even the Vilna Gaon, who opposed the Chassidic movement, when he heard that his student Reb Shmelke had joined the ranks of the Maggid of Mezritch, commented, "I have questions on all of them [the Chassidim], but not on Shmuel."

Reb Shmuel Shmelke of Nikolsburg

Once while spending Shabbos in the town of Sambor, Reb Shmelke invited questions from the congregation on any topic. A local young genius replied, "I have a question which I have asked many great men, but have never received a satisfactory reply." He then presented his question; and Reb Shmelke covered his eyes with his hand and bowed his head in thought.

After several moments, he opened his eyes and offered a brilliant response. The young man jumped out of his chair and cried, "I swear, this is not human!"

Afterwards, Reb Shmelke spoke privately to the young man. "They say you are learned. How many times is Rava's name mentioned in the Talmud?" The young genius immediately named all of the occasions where Rava expressed an opinion in the entire *Shas*!

Unimpressed, Reb Shmelke responded, "You forgot one."

"Oh," the young man replied, "you probably mean that unnamed statement that some commentators attribute to Rava."

Reb Shmelke was so delighted, he kissed the young man on the forehead.

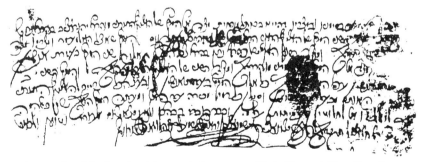

A sample of the handwriting and signature of Reb Shmuel Shmelke of Nikolsburg, zt"l

Torah and Prayer

The Ba'al Shem Tov once opened the door of a yeshiva but refused to enter. "What's wrong?" his Chassidim asked. "I cannot enter because the room is full of Torah." "Isn't that a good thing?" they inquired. "No," he said. "It is full because the Torah learned here lacked the fear and love needed to ascend to Heaven, and it lies lifeless on the ground."

Reb Shmelke's Torah study was different. "The Torah was written in black fire on white fire," he commented, "for just as the darkest part of a flame is at its base, burning the oil, while its lightest part is at its tip, so it is with the Torah. First it burns away the evil inclination below, then it uplifts the pure soul to Hashem." He absorbed the teachings of the Maggid, who insisted that "Whenever a person studies Torah, he must remember before Whom he studies. Otherwise, even Torah study might cause a person to forget Hashem!"

While in Mezritch, Reb Shmelke kept a small diary in which he wrote: "The Torah should be studied selflessly, with fear and love; for when studied without them, 'Hashem heard and became angry'" (*Bemidbar* 11:1).

Reb Shmelke taught that a person must constantly remind himself of Hashem; even during his studies. Only a tzaddik need not do so, since his very study binds him to Hashem "like oil drawn after the wick." Elsewhere he taught, "The Torah is like oil, for it draws down the light of Hashem. The wick is prayer; and, together, the oil and wick can create light. But just as the wick must be clean and fresh to draw the oil, so too, a person must rid himself of all earthly desires and fears, and love and fear only Hashem."

Thus, although Reb Shmelke regarded Torah study as higher than prayer, he still spent four hours a day praying. "Prayer must be said in a loud voice, with all of one's strength," he wrote. "One should pray amidst study, and devote time before the prayers for private contemplation, imagining that the King of the world stands before him, for true Torah understanding is not possible without prayer. Without reciting *Birkas haTorah* with intensity, one cannot have an original Torah thought all day." When one of his students, who had recited his *berachos* hastily, claimed otherwise, Reb Shmelke quickly disproved the boy's "insights."

Reb Shmelke's prayer involved complete attachment (*deveikus*) to Hashem. When he led the congregation in Shabbos or High Holiday prayers, he would concentrate on various Kabbalistic meditations between the words. During that time, he would sing the most inspiring *niggunim*, melodies which had never been heard before. Yet he was unaware of his own singing, for his mind was focused on the supernal worlds. One year, when his choir was about to sing a previously rehearsed melody, Reb Shmelke suddenly broke out into an amazing song they had never heard. The Kalever Rebbe, known for his musical talents, was inspired by Reb Shmelke's singing; and it is said that Eliyahu haNavi once told Reb Shmelke, "My son, when you pray, even the angels and seraphim cannot equal you."

Several generations later, Reb Moshe Teitelbaum of Satmar, the Yismach Moshe, prayed in Reb Shmelke's study in Shinov. The following Shabbos night, he experienced intense fear and awe, followed by a tremendous burning love for Hashem. "I realized that such feelings did not originate from within me," he explained. "Rather, they were the remnants of the prayers that Reb Shmelke offered in that very room."

Horse and Rider Reb Shmelke moved in a world of holiness and purity, detached from physical desires. "A person who wants to cling to Hashem must shun all physical cravings," he taught.

Just as a person running a business does not forget to eat and drink, so a person must never forget his thirst for Hashem.

Reb Shmelke indeed treated his body as something apart from him. He never once scratched an itch, saying, "If my body itches, what do I gain from scratching it?" Similarly, he taught: "In general, we see that each higher form of life rules over that which is below it. Plants grow from the earth, and man rules over the animals.... likewise, the body has no direct business with the soul."

One can serve Hashem through Torah, mitzvos and prayer; but, Reb Shmelke taught, it is still higher to serve Hashem through all of one's actions, including eating, drinking and working. We say, "Who forms light and creates darkness, Who makes peace and creates all." That is, there is a path that is light, which is Torah and mitzvos, and a path that is dark, which is the pursuit of worldly desires. Yet the highest path is one that makes peace between them, in which all of one's actions are united in the service of Hashem.

The Missing Milk

Things existed for Reb Shmelke only by their relationship to his *avodas Hashem*. Once a wealthy local philanthropist invited Reb Shmelke to his home. As they sat and talked, a maid brought them a pot of coffee. Reb Shmelke asked for the milk; and his host pointed to a small pitcher on the table. A few moments later, Reb Shmelke again asked for the milk. His host realized that something was wrong and went into the kitchen to investigate. He discovered that the gentile maid had milked the cow without Jewish supervision, thus the milk was not *chalav Yisrael*.

"The Rebbe is correct," he said returning to Reb Shmelke. "This milk is forbidden. But why didn't the Rebbe just say so? Why did he have to ask where it was?"

Reb Shmuel Shmelke of Nikolsburg

"I honestly did not see it," Reb Shmelke replied. "The *Shulchan Aruch* states that "Milk milked by a gentile, which a Jew does not see, is forbidden." This implies that milk milked by a gentile, a Jew does not even see, and I didn't!"

The Fight Against the Haskalah

Nikolsburg was a great modern city, filled with both devout Jewish scholars and members of the growing Haskalah ("Enlightenment") movement, which denied Torah values in order to better assimilate those of the non-Jewish world. At that time, Moses Mendelsohn and his followers, the main instigators of the movement, were living in Nikolsburg. When the entire town came to welcome Reb Shmelke, Mendelsohn was among them. Reb Shmelke never wasted a minute from study, so even as the congregation filed passed him to shake his hand, his eyes remained focused on the book before him. When the future Reb Mordechai of Neschiz, then a young boy, walked by, Reb Shmelke immediately felt the boy's holiness and looked up to greet him. However, when Moses Mendelsohn shook the Rebbe's hand, Reb Shmelke immediately cried out, "Get away from me, impure one!" and Mendelsohn fled the room in embarrassment.

In order to stop the spread of the Haskalah in Nikolsburg, Reb Shmelke used the weapons of the *maskilim* themselves. Every Shabbos, for seven weeks after his arrival, he lectured his puzzled congregation on another branch of secular wisdom: science, astronomy, mathematics, music, etc. On the eighth Shabbos, he spoke about Torah and *mussar*. Then he quoted the verse, "It is better to hear the rebuke of the wise, than to hear the song of fools" (*Koheles* 7:5). All the wisdom of the world is foolish compared to Torah, he said, and a person who understands secular wisdom thoroughly, and still chooses Torah, must be believed when he makes the comparison.

In general, the Nikolsburg Jewish community maintained a high level of observance; even such practices as the fast of the *shovavim tat* (the seven weeks of fasting, every Monday and Thursday, from *Parashas Shemos* through *Parashas Tetzaveh*) was observed by the entire community. But the *maskilim* did not abandon their plans. Once they boasted to Reb Shmelke, "Surely, the Rabbi will admit that we are true to our word, and that our clothes are always neat and clean, whereas Polish Jews go back on their word within minutes, and their clothing is a mess. Doesn't the Talmud say, 'A Torah scholar who has a spot on his garments deserves death?'"

"One thing depends on the other," Reb Shmelke answered. "We learn in the *baraysa* of Rav Pinchas ben Yair that cleanliness leads to separation, separation to purity, purity to piety, piety to humility, humility to fear of sin and then to holiness, then to *ruach hakodesh* and, finally, to the revival of the dead. Now, when a Polish Jew strives for cleanliness, the evil inclination throws its full weight against him, for if he succeeds, he may continue on to separation, purity and so on. Even if he promises to stop at cleanliness, the evil inclination won't listen, because he can't trust a Polish Jew in such matters. However, when *you* promise not to go beyond cleanliness, the evil inclination believes you and leaves you alone. In that you are indeed reliable."

Reb Shmelke once saw some young *maskilim* walking down the street, decked out in the latest modern fashion. They were clean-shaven, with little round spectacles perched on their noses and walking sticks clasped proudly in their hands. Reb Shmelke commented, "When a person becomes old, his beard turns gray, his eyes need glasses, and he walks with a cane. Then he knows that his end is near and he must do *teshuvah*. But the evil inclination has convinced these young men to shave off their beards, walk with a stick and wear glasses. How will they know they are getting old? When will they remember to do *teshuvah*?"

Victory of the Righteous

Reb Shmuel Shmelke defeated the *maskilim* in Nikolsburg on many occasions and strengthened Torah observance throughout the city. Finally, the *maskilim* decided to denounce him to the government, on the charge that he was an outdated, religious fanatic who did not know the national language, a requirement for every official Rabbi. This, they were sure, would lead to his dismissal.

Reb Shmelke was summoned to Vienna, the capital of the Hapsburg Empire. He and Reb Moshe Leib Sasover traveled there in the middle of the winter, when the Danube River, on the outskirts of Vienna, was frozen. None of the ferrymen would take them across for fear of the large blocks of ice floating downstream. One ferryman finally agreed, after Reb Shmelke paid him well and promised that he would cross safely. Reb Shmelke stood at the prow of the boat and sang the *Shiras haYam* while Reb Moshe Leib sang the bass accompaniment. The large masses of ice immediately parted and allowed the small boat to pass through.

On the other bank of the river, crowds of people gathered to see the amazing sight. Reports soon reached the authorities, who received Reb Shmelke warmly. They asked him if he could speak the national language, and he answered them in fluent German, and even proved his proficiency in writing. According to one version, the Kaiser himself handed Reb Shmelke a Certificate of Rabbinate written in German. Reb Shmelke read it fluently, and the Kaiser placed the official stamp on it with his own hands. After they left, Reb Moshe Leib asked Reb Shmelke where he learned to speak German. "Don't you remember?" Reb Shmelke replied. "Yesterday, we learned a chapter from the *Etz Chaim* which states a person can grasp foreign languages by tapping into their spiritual source. That's how I mastered their language."

The Kaiser and his officials were impressed by Reb Shmelke's extensive knowledge and believed that his position in Nikolsburg enhanced the prestige of the monarchy. They thus gave him full authority to do as he pleased with the *maskilim*. Reb Shmelke decided to expel them from Nikolsburg; and Mendelsohn and his group moved to Berlin, where they continued to spread their poisonous teachings.

In 1775, Reb Shmelke was appointed Chief Rabbi over the entire country of Moravia. This gave him tremendous power to help the Jews. His religious decrees were also enforced, and the remaining *maskilim* were silenced.

The Chain Continues

Reb Shmelke of Nikolsburg passed away three years later, in 1778. He left behind a worthy successor in his son, Reb Tzvi Yehoshua, a distinguished Torah scholar, who first served as *Av Beis Din* in Yemnitz and then in Tivitsch. He married the daughter of his uncle, Reb Pinchas of Frankfurt (the Hafla'ah). Reb Naftali Ropshitzer went to Reb Tzvi Yehoshua for inspiration early in his career. After serving as the Rav of Prusnitz for fifteen years, Reb Tzvi became the *Av Beis Din* of Tarnov, where he passed away three years later, in 1816. He was the author of *Chidushei haRivash*, a Torah commentary, and *Smichas Moshe*. Reb Tzvi Yehoshua's son, Reb Yaakov

Reb Shmuel Shmelke of Nikolsburg

Dovid MiBrod, was the grandson of the Hafla'ah on his mother's side. His saintly son, Reb Pinchas MiBrod, served for many years as the Rav of Magrov, where he succeeded his father-in-law, Reb Yosef haCohen of Magrov.

The kever of Reb Shmuel Shmelke, zt"l, of Nikolsburg. Reb Levi Yitzchok Horowitz, shlita, the Bostoner Rebbe, shown in prayer, is his direct (son-after-son) seventh-generation descendant.

Reb Pinchas MiBrod

Reb Pinchas' greatness as a tzaddik soon became well-known. Once, a Sadigura Chassid asked his Rebbe, a son of Reb Yisroel of Ruzhin, to bless his childless daughter. "There is only one person in our generation who can help you," the Sadigura Rebbe said. "Reb Pinchas haLevi MiBrod." The Chassid's daughter immediately set out to visit Reb Pinchas.

"I can give you a blessing," Reb Pinchas said, "but I cannot promise more than that." The desperate young woman continued to insist on a firm promise, and even followed him into the kitchen. "I'm not letting the Rebbe leave until he promises me," she said. Finally he agreed and, that year, she had a child.

Word of the miracle spread throughout Poland and, after the death of the Sadigura Rebbe, his Chassidim wanted to appoint Reb Pinchas as their leader. In his modesty, Reb Pinchas refused and, to escape their demands, he moved to Eretz Yisrael in 1861. There he made his home in Tzefas, where, free of worldly distractions, he devoted his days to study and prayer.

Shortly after his arrival, he went to visit Reb Elazar Menachem Mendel Lelover in Jerusalem. Upon their first handshake he felt a "strong love" passing from Reb Elazar Mendel to him. Reb Pinchas' daughter Miriam later married Reb Elazar Mendel's son, Reb Dovid Tzvi Shlomo (Reb Dovid'l Biderman).

Shortly before his daughter's marriage to Reb Dovid'l, Reb Pinchas MiBrod and his family moved to Jerusalem. Reb Elazar Mendel's wife, Rebbetzin Matil Feigeh, went to visit her future daughter-in-law but, due to her great poverty, she was unable to bring the girl a gift, as was customary. Reb Pinchas' wife was indignant. "She couldn't bring anything?" she complained. "Not even a trinket? How can our daughter show her face in public?"

The incident happened several days before Shavuos; and two days before the festival, Reb Pinchas, Reb Elazar Mendel and a large group of Chassidim went to pray together at the grave of King David on Mount Zion. Reb Pinchas began to think over his wife's complaint. "If they don't have money, it's understandable. But nothing? Not even a cheap bracelet?" Reb Elazar Mendel suddenly touched Reb Pinchas' arm. "Reb Pinchas," he said, "it's two days before Shavuos, and you're thinking about bracelets?"

When Reb Pinchas returned home, he told his wife, "Listen, my dear. Isn't it enough that the groom's father has *ruach hakodesh*; do we also need trinkets?"

Reb Shmuel Shmelke of Nikolsburg

Reb Pinchas MiBrod's Shabbos

Reb Dovid'l's father-in-law dedicated his entire Shabbos to Hashem. He would not sleep at all, from the beginning of Shabbos until its end. As soon as his Friday night meal was over, he retired to his study and began a long agenda of study. He learned the weekly *parashah* with all its commentaries. He studied the Zohar and other Kabbalistic works. He examined books from all four levels of Torah study: *pshat, remez, drush* and *sod*. All night he bent over his books, studying by the light of a small lantern. His voice would echo in the stillness of the house. A coffee urn stood at arm's length on the burner, and next to him on the table was a small box of snuff. Every so often, he would pour himself a cup a coffee and, with his other hand, take a pinch of snuff...never taking his eyes off the book in front of him. In the course of a Shabbos night, he could drink twenty-four cups of coffee, and inhale an entire box of snuff!

Reb Pinchas bought the coffee and snuff himself from the same spice merchant, every *erev Shabbos*. As soon as the Rabbi entered his store, the merchant would pour a scoop of roasted coffee beans into a small hand-grinder and, from there, into a paper bag. Into another paper bag, he would pour freshly ground snuff. "*L'chovod Shabbos Kodesh,*" Reb Pinchas would say, as he paid for them.

"Once, when my father-in-law was too old and weak to walk to the spice shop, I went for him," Reb Dovid'l said. "The merchant gave me the two small bags but, when I returned home, I accidentally poured the snuff into the coffee urn and the coffee into the snuff box. Since their colors were similar, I didn't notice my mistake.

"That night, after the meal, my father-in-law spent the entire night learning, as usual, drinking his coffee and smelling his snuff, without noticing anything. After Shabbos he asked me, 'What happened to the snuff this week? It had a funny smell.'

"I ran to his study and examined the remnant of the snuff; it smelled like coffee! I opened the coffee urn; it reeked of tobacco!

"That my father-in-law drank the tobacco without noticing a difference did not surprise me. Sometimes a person becomes so involved in his studies that he doesn't notice anything, as the Talmud says [about Rabbi Yehoshua ben Levi and Rava]...I believe that my father-in-law was on that level. But if he was completely immersed in his studies, why did he notice the change in the snuff?

"Finally, the answer came to me. Coffee is something you drink; it is a physical pleasure. My father-in-law was completely above the physical. However, smell is [also] a spiritual experience."

Reb Pinchas MiBrod passed away in Tiberias, a major stronghold of the Chassidic movement in Eretz Yisrael, in 1875.

Reb Shmuel Shmelke of Jerusalem and His Family Reb Pinchas MiBrod's son, Reb Alexander Yitzchok, continued the Nikolsburg line in Eretz Yisrael. His wife, Rebbetzin Tobeh, was a descendant of Reb Yissachar of Zlotchov, the Chacham Tzvi and the Tvuos Shor.

His son, Reb Shmuel Shmelke Horowitz of Jerusalem, married Shayna Elka, a daughter of Reb Elazar Mendel Lelover, and moved to Jerusalem. There Reb Shmuel Shmelke became known for his incredible diligence in Torah study (*hasmadah*) and his fiery prayers, often davening for hours at the Western Wall.

Rebbetzin Shayna Elka bore Reb Shmuel Shmelke five outstanding sons and two daughters. Reb Shmuel Shmelke's oldest son, Reb Pinchas Dovid Horowitz, the first Bostoner Rebbe, is the subject of Chapters 12–16. Reb Yehoshua ("Shia"), the next oldest son, was a respected member of Jerusalem's Chevrah Kaddisha and a popular *gabbai tzedakah*. A walking, one-man charity organization, he would stand at the gate of Me'ah She'arim every Thursday night and Friday morning collecting money for the Shabbos needs of the many needy families in Jerusalem's Old Yishuv.

A rare picture of the saintly Reb Yehoshua Horowitz, zt"l, at a family wedding

Reb Reuven Noson Nota, the next son, was a well-known Kabbalist and tzaddik. The son-in-law of Reb Moshe Eisenbach (Pester), he also had a beautiful voice and innate sense of melody. His sons, all *talmidei chachamim*, inherited his gift and even formed their own singing group, Shiras haLevi'im (the Horowitz family are all Levi'im), whose spiritual melodies are popular within Israel's tight-knit Chassidic community.

Reb Avraham, the next brother, was a great tzaddik whose fervent prayers and *kavanos* had a great impact on Reb Pinchas Dovid, who respected him greatly. During the terrible years of deprivation that accompanied World War I, Reb Avraham almost starved to death (as did so many others). When the British reached Jerusalem they tried to save as much of the population as they could by distributing large amounts of food. Unfortunately, the sudden change was too much for Reb Avraham. His weakened digestive system failed and he passed away, leaving behind several children. Reb Shmuel Shmelke's fifth and youngest son, Reb Moshe, later moved to America.

Reb Shmuel Shmelke's oldest daughter, Rebbetzin Tobeh Chaya Brandwein, was the mother of Reb Yosef Shmelke Brandwein, who later married his first cousin, Freida Gitel (Reb Pinchas Dovid's oldest daughter). Her other son was Reb Zusha Brandwein, known as "the Gabbai of Reb Shimon" because of his many trips to the tomb of the *Tanna* Rabbi Shimon bar Yochai in Meron, on behalf of the Belzer Rav and others. Tobeh's family and Reb Yehoshua's family both lived in the same Old City courtyard as their mother, Rebbetzin Shayna Elka, until 1940. Then the pressures of World War II and the hostility of the local Arabs forced them to move to safer quarters.

Reb Shmuel Shmelke's younger daughter, Rebbetzin Esther Malka, married her cousin Reb Dovid Leib Brandwein. She

The Kosel, the Western Wall of the Temple Mount, at the time of Reb Shmuel Shmelke Horowitz, zt"l, of Jerusalem

was known for her *chessed* and strict observance of Jewish law. Her nephew, Reb Levi Yitzchok Horowitz, *shlita*, the present Bostoner Rebbe, remembers visiting her home in Jerusalem one evening in 1963. Although they had not met for fifteen or so years, his aunt silently motioned him inside, mumbling "Mm...Mm...Mm," and seated him comfortably while she brought him some tea. She had already said the *berachah* of *haMapil*, which immediately precedes sleep, and she refused to speak, no matter what!

TWELVE
Rabbi Pinchas Dovid haLevi Horowitz

His Youth

Reb Pinchas Dovid haLevi Horowitz was born on a Friday afternoon in early Elul 1876, the first child of Reb Shmuel Shmelke Horowitz of Jerusalem, a fifth-generation descendant, son after son, of Reb Shmuel Shmelke of Nikolsburg. His mother, Rebbetzin Shayna Elka, was the daughter of Reb Elazar Mendel Lelover.

That *motza'ei Shabbos*, a dove flew into the newborn baby's bedroom and settled on the rafters. Try as they might, the family was unable to chase it away. Concerned that this might be a bad omen, they asked Reb Elazar Mendel for his advice. "Catch the dove," he said, "and serve it for *melave malka*; for there is a special connection between a dove and King David (*Sanhedrin* 95a) and the *melave malka*."

Even as a young child, Pinchas Dovid's special *midos* were manifest, and his grandfather Reb Elazar Mendel spent many hours directing his spiritual growth. Young Pinchas Dovid visited his grandfather often, and even slept in his bed!

After Reb Elazar Mendel's passing, his son, Reb Dovid'l (Biderman) Lelover, inherited the leadership of the Lelover

Shabbos in the Old Yishuv was ushered in by a lone trumpeter in a horse-drawn carriage.

dynasty and his nephew, Reb Pinchas Dovid, became his chief disciple. He soon joined a small group of students learning *mishnayos* in depth with Reb Shneur Zalman of Lublin, the Toras Chessed, who attempted to demonstrate how Rabbi Yehudah haNasi's words alluded to all the various opinions later found in the Gemara. In the Old Yishuv, the lives of Jerusalem's residents revolved around study halls (*battei midrashim*), and Reb Pinchas Dovid soon gained a reputation for his broad knowledge and sharp mind. Other young men would often test him by reading him only a few lines from a book, challenging him to identify the author. "That is the language of the Ramban," he would say, or "That must be the Rashba." He was always correct.

Rabbi Aharon and Rabbi Tzvi Aryeh of Feltshin Reb Pinchas Dovid was still a boy when the matchmakers of Jerusalem started suggesting offers from the most prestigious families in Eretz Yisrael. Finally, a match was made with Rivkah, the pious daughter of Rabbi Aharon Feltshiner of Tzefas, who had left his Chassidim in Feltshin, Galicia, to move to the Holy Land. His father, Reb Tzvi Aryeh of Feltshin, who also moved to Tzefas, was the son of Reb Yosef Dovid of Alik, son of Reb Tzvi Aryeh of Alik, a leading disciple of the Maggid of Zlotchov.

Reb Tzvi Aryeh of Feltshin was known for his sharp wit. He once went to visit the famous Reb Boruch of Mezhibuzh, a grandson of the Ba'al Shem Tov. Reb Boruch, who insisted on his due respect, had his attendant remove all the chairs from his study, so Reb Tzvi Aryeh would have to stand before him. However, Reb Tzvi Aryeh had clearly anticipated this and brought his own chair!

"What's this?" Reb Boruch asked. "Don't you know that I am the leader of the generation?"

"Yes, of course. But I am also the leader of the generation."

"Can a generation have two leaders?"

"Why not? We have two *chad gadya*s (a refrain sung twice at the Pesach Seder)!"

Reb Boruch thought deeply for a couple of minutes. "You are right. I am the leader of the generation in Torah, you are the leader in wisdom, and Reb Shalom of Prohovitch is the leader in children!"

Reb Aharon Feltshiner's wife Esther was the daughter of the tzaddik Reb Avraham'tzi of Stretin, the son of Reb Yehudah Tzvi of Stretin, a disciple of Reb Uri of Strelisk. Reb Yehudah Tzvi Stretiner's grandfather, Reb Mordechai, was one of the Torah giants of his generation. For sixteen consecutive generations, down through Reb Yehudah Tzvi, members of the family had *ruach hakodesh*. For thirteen generations before him, they were completely free of all spiritual blemishes. Their family tree could be traced all the way back to Reb Yochanan haSandlar, who is mentioned in the Gemara, and from him to King David.

The Intensity of His Youth

After the wedding, Reb Pinchas Dovid and his wife moved to Tzefas to live near his father-in-law and, in that city of scholars and Kabbalists, he continued to grow in Torah and in holiness.

Reb Meir Shochet, one of Pinchas Dovid's study partners in Tzefas, described the young tzaddik's day: Reb Pinchas Dovid had six different study partners and learned three hours with each, for a total of eighteen hours a day! In the remaining six hours he would pray and see to his daily needs. However, since his fiery prayers were so long, they took up the better part of the six hours, leaving him almost no time each day to sleep.

Reb Meir, Reb Pinchas Dovid's first study partner, would meet him early each morning, before dawn. Since Reb Pinchas Dovid's schedule lasted late into the night, he asked Reb Meir to please knock on his bedroom window on his way to the *beis midrash*. "But I never once woke him up," Reb Meir reported. "He was always waiting for me!"

Reb Pinchas Dovid also studied with Reb Moshe Liers, later the Rav of Tiberias, and with Reb Mordechai of Slonim, the future Slonimer Rebbe.

At one point Reb Pinchas Dovid learned at Yeshivas Bar Yochai, in Meron, under Rabbi Yaakov Eliezer Fraiser. He would leave Tzefas on Sunday and return home the following Friday. His study partner was Rabbi Meir Yechezkel Holtzberg, the future Rav of Rosh Pinna in the Galil. Together, they would learn for eighteen hours straight, without wasting a single minute.

The Death of His Father

Reb Shmuel Shmelke was only thirty-six years old when he passed away on the seventh of Nisan 1898. Though he had a serious illness, he paid so little attention to physical matters that he said nothing to Dr. Wallach, his physician. As a result, the good doctor failed to detect the real problem, and prescribed only mild medication. "I will remember you after I am gone, Dr. Wallach," Reb Shmuel Shmelke said as he neared his end. The doctor became frightened that Reb Shmuel Shmelke might denounce him before the Heavenly Court for failing to save his life, but that was not the case. Dr. Wallach lived for many more years, serving Jerusalem's sick, passing away on the seventh of Nisan, the same day as Reb Shmuel Shmelke.

Immediately after his father's death, Reb Pinchas Dovid went to the Mount of Olives to find a suitable gravesite. When he saw how few spaces were left in the section belonging to Kollel Galicia, designated for Polish Jews, he purchased two plots, one for his father and one, beside it, for himself.

A view of the Jerusalem of the Old Yishuv

In the Old Yishuv of Jerusalem, kollels not only supported men who studied Torah, they also served many other functions, organizing burial societies, free-loan societies, health care societies, etc. Later, when Reb Pinchas Dovid became head of the Kollel Galicia, he encouraged the formation of a new burial society, and personally served as its director. Years later, when Reb Pinchas Dovid moved to America, his brother Reb Yehoshua became head of the burial society.

Once, Reb Yehoshua joined a funeral procession only to find that the burial society had dug the grave in the place designated for his brother. When he protested, they retorted, "Your brother is in America. When he comes back we will talk about it; who knows if he will ever return. It is an affront to this deceased to not bury him immediately."

Reb Yehoshua jumped into the open grave and lay down. "So go ahead and bury him," he declared, "and bury me as well!" Seeing that they had no other choice, the burial society turned aside and dug another grave.

The Birth of His Daughter

After his father's passing, Reb Pinchas Dovid returned to Jerusalem to support his mother and siblings, the youngest of them only a few months old. Reb Pinchas Dovid's wife would occasionally visit her family in Tzefas, and every Lag b'Omer he traveled to Meron to stay for several weeks with his father-in-law.

Reb Pinchas Dovid and his wife struggled to raise a family, but several of their first children died in infancy. When their daughter Freida Gitel was born, they feared for her life as well. Reb Dovid'l Biderman told his nephew, "They say that a *segulah* (protection) against infant death is to arrange the child's marriage in the crib." Reb Dovid'l suggested a match between Freida Gitel and her first cousin, Yosef Shmelke, the new infant son of Tobeh Chaya, Reb Pinchas Dovid's sister. The match was made and the infants did indeed thrive and later marry each other.

As a child, Freida Gitel's friends would tease her, and she once complained to her father, "Why am I the only bride among all my girlfriends?" "My dear," Reb Pinchas Dovid told her, "*Boruch Hashem* that you are a bride, and that you are still alive."

Rabbi Pinchas Dovid haLevi Horowitz

Master of Kabbalah

Reb Pinchas Dovid had a deep grasp of the secrets of Kabbalah. In his old age, when his eyesight was weak and he could no longer study from books, it became apparent that he knew the entire Zohar by heart, as well as the *Zohar Chadash* and the *Tikunei Zohar*. He was able to quote every paragraph and to give its location on the page.

In 1906, when Reb Motteleh, the Rachmastrivker Rebbe and the grandson of Reb Mordechai of Chernobyl, moved to Jerusalem from Russia, Reb Pinchas Dovid became a frequent visitor. They would spend long hours discussing the secrets of Kabbalah together.

Once, during a gathering, the Rebbe suddenly ordered all of his Chassidim to leave the room so he could speak with Reb Pinchas Dovid privately. Reb Pinchas Dovid's brother, Reb Yehoshua, wanted to stay.

"Nu, Yehoshua," Reb Pinchas Dovid said, "you should also leave."

"Let him stay," said Reb Motteleh. "He won't understand anything anyway." Afterward, Reb Yehoshua related that he had, indeed, not understood a word of their deep conversation.

Every year on Lag b'Omer, the *yahrtzeit* of Rabbi Shimon bar Yochai, Reb Pinchas Dovid would travel to Meron. One year an enraged Arab raised his hand to strike Reb Pinchas Dovid, only to have it freeze in midair. The Arab began trembling in fear because he could not move his arm and begged Reb Pinchas Dovid for forgiveness. Only after Reb Pinchas Dovid forgave him was the assailant able to lower his hand.

On another occasion, an Arab who was terrorizing Jews admitted that he could not hurt Reb Pinchas Dovid because "he has sweet blood."

The Work of His Hands

For five years, Reb Pinchas Dovid devoted every single night to Torah study. Then he decided to take a job to support his family, rather than accept money from charity. (His father-in-law, Reb Aharon Feltshiner, was also self-supporting, having invested his inheritance in several successful businesses.) Possibly Reb Pinchas Dovid also sought to avoid the growing controversy over the distribution of the funds from Kollel Galicia.

Several dissatisfied individuals accused several of the directors of Kollel Galicia of taking bribes and abusing their power. These individuals sought to start their own Kollel, and even published a booklet, *Shimu Harim* (Hear, O Mountains), to publicize their accusations. When Kollel Galicia's directors summoned their opponents to a *din Torah*, the latter published yet another pamphlet, *Kol D'mei Achichem* (The Voice of Your Brothers' Blood), chronicling further alleged abuses. Despite their indignation, however, the authors nevertheless spoke well of Reb Pinchas Dovid, calling him "humble and soft-spoken." Still, the controversy may have convinced Reb Pinchas Dovid not to take Kollel funds, fulfilling the verse, "You shall be guiltless before Hashem and before Israel" (*Bemidbar* 32:22).

Like his great-grandfather, Reb Shmuel Shmelke of Nikolsburg, Reb Pinchas Dovid's Torah knowledge was matched by a profound grasp of the natural sciences. He had a special gift for mathematics, and could solve difficult problems in the blink of an eye. He put these talents to use in his new profession — architecture. Jerusalem had just started to expand beyond the Old City walls, and Me'ah She'arim was only a block of one-story homes. Reb Pinchas Dovid wanted to help enlarge the neighborhood by adding a second floor to each of the buildings. Later in life, he considered himself as one of the rebuilders of Jerusalem.

As a young Torah scholar-architect, Reb Pinchas Dovid added second stories to existing buildings in the overcrowded Jerusalem neighborhood of Me'ah She'arim.

Reb Pinchas Dovid and his brother, Reb Yehoshua, did more than just draw up plans. They worked on the building sites themselves, supervising construction and directing the Arab laborers. It was a strange sight, seeing two of Jerusalem's most brilliant scholars working like laymen. They were often chided by onlookers who called them "The Laborers." However, Reb Pinchas Dovid was a man of conviction, and mockery never deterred him from realizing his vision.

As soon as the day was over, Reb Pinchas Dovid and Reb Yehoshua would sit down together to study, often until five o'clock in the morning. Reb Yehoshua would then lie down a little, leaving Reb Pinchas Dovid to continue learning on his own. He often studied by moonlight, a practice which may have damaged his eyes.

"I Will Not Let Him Go"

Towards the end of 1903, Reb Pinchas Dovid's wife Rivkah traveled from Jerusalem to Tzefas to be with her family when she gave birth. On the 16th of Marcheshvan, she delivered a baby daughter after a difficult birth. That very day, both mother and daughter passed away. Only Freida Gitel remained.

Reb Pinchas Dovid and his father-in-law, Reb Aharon Feltshiner, both deeply mourned Rivkah's death. Unwilling to part with his beloved son-in-law, Reb Aharon suggested a *shidduch* with his granddaughter, Soroh Sashe, then only a child of eight or nine! Reb Aharon spoke to her father, Reb Yechiel Michel of Torka, impressed upon him the greatness of Reb Pinchas Dovid, and offered him a significant portion of his inheritance to agree to the match. The wedding was held about four years later in Tzefas. Reb Pinchas Dovid and his new wife returned to Jerusalem; and his daughter, Freida Gitel, rejoined them about two years later.

Reb Yechiel Michel of Torka (Poland), zt"l, father-in-law of Reb Pinchas Dovid, the first Bostoner Rebbe

Rebbetzin Esther, the wife of Reb Aharon Feltshiner, passed away on the 11th of Marcheshvan 1906, and he followed her shortly thereafter, on the 28th of Kislev. Reb Aharon was buried in the old cemetery of Tzefas, beside the holy Be'er Mayim Chaim.

Three years later, in 1909, Soroh Sashe gave birth to a son. She wanted to name him Aharon, after her deceased grandfather, but Reb Pinchas Dovid decided to ask his uncle, Reb Dovid'l Biderman, to name the child, as was their family's custom. The night before the *bris*, Rebbetzin Soroh Sashe dreamt that she was standing beside the Western Wall. Suddenly, one of the stones of the wall opened, as though it were a window. Someone from inside handed her her son. "Take Moshe'leh," the voice said. She remembered her dream in the morning, but decided not to tell it to anyone. At the *bris*, she still expected Reb Dovid to name their child Aharon after her father. Then she heard him named "Moshe," just as she had dreamt, after Reb Moshe of Lelov.

Controversy

Reb Pinchas Dovid soon became well-known for his broad halachic knowledge and insightful judgments. On numerous occasions, he was invited by Jerusalem's *Beis Din Tzedek* to offer his legal opinion, and it was generally assumed that he would, one day, join the court as a *dayan* (judge).

In those days, a long, bitter feud erupted between the European fundraisers and contributors of Kollel Galicia in Europe, and the Kollel's distribution committee in Jerusalem. Accusations flew back and forth across the continents; and distrust between the two factions widened. The fundraisers eventually demanded photographs of each recipient family to prove how many members they had! They also specified the allotments for each individual family, no longer leaving this to the local distribution committee. Offended, the Kollel's Jerusalem representatives claimed that the European collectors were acting merely as agents of the Jerusalem community, who alone could set policy.

There were other problems as well. Long before, the Kossover Rebbe, the Toras Chaim, had collected donations for Kollel Chibas Yerushalayim as part of the Rebbe Meir Ba'al haNess Charity Fund he administered. However, during the time of his son, Reb Menachem Mendel of Vizhnitz, large donors in the province of Mormorosh insisted that their contributions should go only to families from their district. Since most of the latter lived in Tzefas, this would seriously affect the Kollel's allocations in Jerusalem.

When Reb Menachem Mendel wrote the Sanzer Rav for advice, he replied: "I cannot find even the slightest justification to give precedence to former residents of Mormorosh living in Eretz Yisrael." To satisfy both sides, Reb Menachem Mendel started a separate new distribution committee for his followers from Mormorosh and Bokovina. His son, the Imrei Boruch, continued to head both funds. In the next generation, Reb Chaim of Antania headed the central Rebbe Meir Ba'al haNess Charity of Galicia, and his brother, the Ahavas Yisroel of Vishnitz, headed the Bokovina/Mormorosh fund.

The fortunes of the latter, however, began to wane. When the Bokovina/Mormorosh fund sought to rejoin the broader Galician Kollel, the European directors of Chibas Yerushalayim were in favor, but the Kollel Galicia members in Jerusalem were concerned that the addition of numerous new recipients would overstretch their meager funds. Furthermore, the new union might prove only temporary. If their financial situation improved, might the Bokovina/Mormorosh Kollel not break away again?

The issues were thorny, and the two sides eventually decided to settle the matter via arbitration. Each party would choose a Torah scholar to represent them, and these two representatives would jointly select a third scholar to work with them. Kollel Galicia chose Reb Pinchas Dovid to represent Jerusalem.

The Departure

Before leaving for Europe, Reb Pinchas Dovid went to his uncle Reb Dovid'l for a *berachah*. Afterwards, he visited his dear friend, Reb Motteleh of Rachmastrivka. The two men sat together sharing words of Torah and tales of tzaddikim for hours, as if they had all the time in the world. Reb Pinchas Dovid's brother, Reb Yehoshua, became nervous. It was getting late, and the boat left from Haifa, far away. He kept mentioning this, but the two tzaddikim paid no attention to him.

"Nu, we have to leave already!" Reb Yehoshua protested. Still, no reaction. Finally, several hours later, Reb Motteleh remarked, "Well, dear friend, now you can go."

"Now? Why now? There is no longer reason to go!" Reb Yehoshua retorted, as he accompanied his brother to Haifa. Just as they reached the port, an announcement ordered all the passengers to board; the repairs on the ship were complete and the ship was ready to sail. Reb Yehoshua immediately understood that the ship had been delayed to permit the discussion between the two tzaddikim to continue. Their discussion had been much deeper than he had realized.

"What were you two really talking about?" he asked. But Reb Pinchas Dovid merely smiled.

In Europe   In Galicia, Reb Pinchas Dovid traveled from town to town, meeting with most of the great leaders of his generation. Although he was only about thirty-seven years old, his elders were impressed by his wisdom and arguments. He published the various letters he had brought to support the position of Jerusalem in a small pamphlet, *Teshuvah k'Halachah*, which included his own lengthy and insightful introduction. Although he signed his work only as a "Messenger of the Rabbis of Eretz Yisrael," the newspapers of the time correctly guessed his authorship.

Reb Pinchas Dovid briefly visited Reb Shlomo of Bobov and Reb Yissachar Dov of Tsheshinov, and then spent several months with Reb Yissachar Dov of Belz. During his stay, he studied regularly every day before dawn with the Rebbe's son, Reb Areyleh Belzer, the future Belzer Rav.

To keep up with such a study partner was no small feat, for Reb Areyleh had a lightning-quick mind. The accomplished scholar, Reb Yisroel Rava, once asked Reb Areyleh to learn with him. However, when Reb Yisroel came, he found Reb Areyleh standing at the head of the table, his lips moving, but his words inaudible.

"I see the Rebbe is occupied," he said. "Perhaps I should leave."

Reb Areyleh immediately became attentive. "Let's learn." He opened his Gemara and with amazing speed finished the first four pages with Rashi and Tosafos. Reb Yisroel withdrew; he could not learn at such a pace.

On another occasion, Reb Yisroel tried again. "Fine!" said Reb Areyleh. "What shall we learn?" Reb Yisroel chose a section of *Yoreh Deah* that he had studied over a hundred times and knew by heart. Reb Areyleh quickly scanned the entire chapter with all the main commentaries, and then said, "Now, let's review what we have read." Without looking again, he summed up the entire chapter according to the Taz; then he returned to the beginning and explained it all over again according to the Shach, pointing out all the differences between them. Then he turned to the *Pri Megadim* and explained the *Shulchan Aruch*, Rama, Shach and Taz via this commentary, all within an hour's time! "Now let's start the next chapter," Reb Areyleh said, just warming up. "One such chapter is enough," replied Reb Yisroel. "I can't continue."

Reb Areyleh Belzer, zt"l, a brilliant Torah scholar, was Reb Pinchas Dovid's chavrusa (study partner) in Belz. He later succeeded his father, Reb Yissachar Dov, zt"l, as the head of the Belzer Chassidic dynasty.

That was Reb Pinchas Dovid's early morning study partner during his entire stay in Belz! Eventually the two representatives for Galicia and Jerusalem agreed on Rav Eliyahu Pruzhner, a leading scholar of the generation, as the third arbitrator. Although the Rabbis of Eretz Yisrael had wanted the case to be heard in Jerusalem, Rav Pruzhner disagreed and the arbitration was held in Galicia. Reb Pinchas Dovid expertly defended the position of Kollel Galicia and, *de facto*, won his case. The two *kollelim* could reunite, but allocations to existing members could not thereby be diminished. Once the financial incentives were removed, the idea of reunification was quickly dropped.

Reb Pinchas Dovid now looked forward to returning home to Jerusalem, but on Tishah b'Av 1914, World War I erupted and most European ports were immediately closed. Reb Pinchas Dovid was trapped in Austria.

A Call to Arms

Although Eretz Yisrael was under Turkish (Ottoman) rule, most Ashkenazi Jews held European citizenship, which provided them with additional consular protection. Citizenship was determined by one's postal agency; so Galician Jews, most of whom lived in the Old City of Jerusalem, were generally Austrian citizens, as the Austrian post office was in the Old City. When the Austrian government instituted an emergency draft to send more soldiers to the front, Reb Pinchas Dovid, as an Austrian citizen, was included! Disaster was imminent.

Reb Pinchas Dovid wrote a letter to his wife in Jerusalem: "They have invited me to the great wedding [war]," he wrote cryptically to avoid the censors, "but I do not know if I will attend." This was his last contact with her for many years.

Reb Pinchas Dovid readily passed his physical examination, making enlistment imminent; but, with Hashem's help, he suddenly had a brilliant, if highly unusual, idea. Greece was then still a neutral nation, serving as an active supply base for all sides. The very air was full of secrets, undercover agents and spies. So Reb Pinchas Dovid offered to go to Greece as an Austrian "spy"! He was fluent in German, Turkish and Arabic and, as a Jew, would never be suspected of espionage. He could, he said, make connections with the local Jewish community, and use that as a base for gathering information for Austria.

The Austrian government, surprisingly enough, accepted this bizarre proposal, and even selected two other Jews to join Reb Pinchas Dovid's plan. All three received Austrian papers identifying them as official secret messengers, and money to buy provisions and establish themselves in Greece. They were accompanied as far as the Austrian border. From there, they were on their own.

The Terrifying Journey

Between Austria and Greece lay Serbian enemy territory; however, once in Greece, it would be easy to board a ship back to Eretz Yisrael. To avoid detection, they traveled by night, with Reb Pinchas Dovid leading the way. They first had to cross the deadly minefields on the Austrian-Serbian border. Before setting out, Reb Pinchas Dovid taught his two companions certain verses to repeat while concentrating on certain holy Names, while following him closely, step by step. One man did as Reb Pinchas Dovid commanded and survived. The other, however, went off on his own, stumbled on a landmine, and was killed instantly in the explosion. Reb Pinchas Dovid was extremely upset and, for the rest of his life, recited *kaddish* on his companion's *yahrtzeit*.

The two continued on their way through enemy territory. Carrying documents implicating them as Austrian spies, they could be shot instantly if caught. They were a mere footstep from death. Shabbos came, and the two men hid in the woods. Immediately after Shabbos, they continued onward, to a broad river spanned by a wide bridge. Reb Pinchas Dovid said, "All my life I have been careful to eat *melave malka*. Now that we have reached water, let's wash our hands and make a *ha-motzi* over bread." The two men went down to the riverbank, washed, lit a small fire, and ate their modest meal.

Suddenly, they heard the sound of enemy troops approaching, the soldiers' heavy boots stomping on the bridge above. For several minutes the marching continued, while Reb Pinchas Dovid and his friend crouched frozen beside the river. A single sideways glance from one of the soldiers would uncover two spies, sitting under a strategic bridge, watching troop movements. "We were completely exposed," Reb Pinchas Dovid later recalled. "Without the merit of King David protecting us, we would have been lost. Our *melave malka* (which is associated with King David) saved us."

From then on, Reb Pinchas Dovid was extra careful to observe this fourth Shabbos meal. Even towards the end of his life, when ill health made eating difficult, he would set the table, wash and eat a small slice of bread.

Out of Greece and Back Again

After many difficult days, the two men finally crossed the border into Greece. Reb Pinchas Dovid had become a close friend of Rav Yaakov Meir, the Chief Rabbi of Salonika and the future *Rishon l'Tzion* (Sefardi Chief Rabbi) of Israel, during the latter's earlier visit to Jerusalem. In Salonika, Rav Yaakov Meir was delighted to see Reb Pinchas Dovid and offered to help him.

A letter of recommendation (in French) from Rav Yaakov Meir, zt"l, the Chief Rabbi of Salonika, Greece, to the Rabbis of Izmir, Turkey, on behalf of Reb Pinchas Dovid, who was trying to return from Europe to Eretz Yisrael after the outbreak of World War I

First Rav Yaakov Meir examined Reb Pinchas Dovid's papers. His Austrian citizenship was an important asset; however, his "spy papers" obviously had to be destroyed immediately. His Austrian passport was also problematic. Since there was an entry visa with no matching exit visa, Reb Pinchas Dovid had obviously left that country illegally. This was certain to cause problems at the port, so how could Reb Pinchas Dovid leave Greece?

After much investigation, Rav Yaakov Meir learned of a young man named Isaac Avraham Birech, who had recently passed away. His family willingly gave his Greek citizenship papers to the Rav; and Reb Pinchas Dovid was able to procure a travel visa back to Yaffo, via the Turkish city of Izmir. Rav Yaakov Meir wrote a letter of recommendation to the Izmir community, in which he described Reb Pinchas Dovid as a traveling fundraiser collecting charity for needy families in Eretz Yisrael. Rav Yaakov Meir also encouraged Reb Pinchas Dovid (in vain) to destroy his Austrian passport, for if he were caught with two different sets of foreign papers, he would surely be considered a spy.

Reb Pinchas Dovid's Greek passport was forged. With the help of Heaven, it sufficed, although he spoke no Greek!

On May 14, 1915, Reb Pinchas Dovid set sail for Izmir. However, on that very day, Greece abandoned its neutrality and formally entered the war as an ally of England and Russia against Austria and Turkey. When the ship arrived in Turkey, it was held in port and finally ordered to return to Piraeus in Greece (near Athens). From there, Reb Pinchas Dovid made his way back to Salonika, to consult yet again with Rav Yaakov Meir.

To America! Reb Pinchas Dovid's Austrian passport now made him an enemy of Greece, and his Greek papers could easily be proven a fraud. He had to leave Greece at once, but Eretz Yisrael, then under Turkish control, was out of the question.

A quick investigation revealed that a ship was soon leaving the port of Kalami, in the south of the country, for America. Reb Pinchas Dovid had long refused to consider traveling there; but Rav Yaakov Meir insisted that this was his only hope of escape. With a grieving heart, Reb Pinchas Dovid used his false Greek papers to set sail, on the 18th of May, for the port of New York.

In the middle of the Mediterranean, the ship was stopped by a German warship, and its cargo and passengers were all inspected by soldiers. Having ignored Rabbi Yaakov Meir's advice, Reb Pinchas Dovid had kept his Austrian passport. Miraculously, he managed to keep it hidden. Had the Germans discovered it, he would have immediately been arrested as a spy.

As his uncle, Reb Dovid'l Lelover, had predicted, Reb Pinchas Dovid, willing or not, arrived in America. Once in New York, Reb Pinchas Dovid made his way to the busy, Jewish Brownsville section of Brooklyn. There, Reb Nisan Pilchik arranged for his son-in-law, a prominent Karliner-Stoliner Chassid, to host Reb Pinchas Dovid until he could establish himself in his new home.

"A Yid from Eretz Yisrael"

Reb Pinchas Dovid tried hard to keep his noble lineage secret. "It's bad enough that I have been sentenced to exile," he would say. "I don't have to drag all my holy ancestors with me!" When people asked who he was, he would answer simply, "A *Yid* from Eretz Yisrael." Later, whenever he saw a Jew taking advantage of his *yichus* (lineage), he would say, "This fellow is hitching his ancestors to his own plow and making them drag it." However, Reb Pinchas Dovid's intense prayers, his holy manner, and his sharp mind soon gave him away, as *Chazal* say, "Whoever runs from greatness, greatness follows after him" (*Eruvin* 13b). Soon he had an attendant who accompanied him, to help him in his *avodas Hashem*.

As his uncle had predicted, Reb Pinchas Dovid was not influenced in the least by America. Shortly after arriving in Brownsville, he stopped eating meat from the local butchers. For the rest of his life in America, he ate only chickens that were slaughtered in front of him, with a knife that he had personally inspected. He was also one of the first to deal with the halachic issues concerning the issue of electricity on Shabbos. Drawing on his broad knowledge in engineering, he even designed a special Shabbos clock to control a house's main circuit-board.

Reb Dovid quickly became a respected member of the community. The directors of Re'im Ahuvim, New York's City's largest Orthodox congregation in those days, asked him to become their Rabbi, offering him a salary of 200 dollars a month, a considerable sum in those days — enough to pay for an entire wedding, including the dowry!

The Move to Boston

Reb Pinchas Dovid, however, still lacked the necessary papers to secure a "green card" and the right to employment. His Austrian passport also proved to be of little help, since the Austrian Embassy in New York suspected its validity. They simply could not believe that anyone could have left Austria and traveled to America in the midst of the war. Finally, the American government did not want to extend Reb Pinchas Dovid's visit as a "tourist." Only through the intervention of influential leaders in the Boston Jewish community was the matter finally settled. Thus, when several members of the Boston community subsequently invited Reb Pinchas Dovid to move there, he agreed out of a sense of gratitude. Fortunately, the Boston Jewish community was then large, with many Rabbis and Torah scholars.

Reb Pinchas Dovid found a house on Barton Street in Boston's Jewish West End neighborhood and, like his holy ancestors, he began to establish his Chassidic court from the ground up. He could have legitimately assumed one of the many titles of his forefathers: the Nikolsburger Rebbe, or the Brodter, the Lelover or the Aliker Rebbe, but, in his humility, he decided to call himself the Bostoner Rebbe. "When people give me their *kvitlach* or *pidyonos*," he once joked, "they should know that they are giving them to a Rebbe from Boston. And how much can they expect from a Bostoner Rebbe?" However, expected or not, Reb Pinchas Dovid's commitment to *avodas Hashem*, his charitable works and his fiery enthusiasm for Torah, were all to earn him a very special place in the American Jewry of his day.

THIRTEEN
Boston

The Community

The religious Jews of Boston in 1918 came from diverse backgrounds. Most — Chassidim of the Rebbes of Chernobyl, Karlin, Slonim and Chabad — had emigrated from Russia to escape conscription in the Russian army; but there were also Chassidim from Romania and Hungary and non-Chassidic Lithuanian Jews. Chassidim from Poland were few, for the Polish Rebbes strongly opposed their followers moving to America, and for good reason. America was a melting pot, a *cholent* in which everyone became mixed together. Most slaved laboriously in large factories and sweatshops, twelve hours a day, seven days a week. Even the fortunate few with *shomer-Shabbos* jobs had little time to pursue holiness; their main concern was to work more, buy more and own more. A visiting European Rosh Yeshiva reported, "I knew that there was hardly any Torah in America, but I assumed that people were 'trampling on money.' But that isn't so; there is hardly any money. Instead, people are trampling on their Torah observance!"

Boston still had a large number of observant older Jews who worked by day and attended nightly classes at the local synagogues; one synagogue even had a seventy-man *daf yomi shiur*. But, tellingly, the Boston community had neither a Talmud Torah for its children nor a yeshiva for its adolescents; and it had no determined visionary leader to help them withstand the forces of assimilation.

Reb Pinchas Dovid immediately set to work in the community, dealing with each of its many factions individually. For example, to the Lubavitcher Chassidim, he taught deep Kabbalistic lessons built upon the principles of Chabad (his style resembled that of Reb Tzaddok of Lublin). To the Russian Chassidim, he became a Rebbe who bore the everyday burdens of his flock. To the Hungarian Chassidim, he became a master of prayer and song, who could deliver complex *midrash*-laden sermons and relate inspiring stories about the great tzaddikim of the past. All the Chassidim needed a Rebbe to whom they could turn for advice, guidance and miraculous intervention. Reb Pinchas Dovid understood their problems and gave them counsel in all areas of life.

Rabbinic seals used by Reb Pinchas Dovid in Boston.

Even the local *Misnagdim* (opponents of Chassidism) were impressed with him, since he had the entire Talmud and its commentaries at his fingertips, and he possessed a sharp mind, well-versed in *pilpul* and halachah. Thus, Reb Pinchas Dovid, like Queen Esther, "found grace in the eyes of all." Reb Pinchas Dovid, for his part, reinforced his followers' connections with their own roots, telling them, "Know where you come from."

Boston

Messages from the Upper Worlds

When Reb Pinchas Dovid first arrived in Boston, his financial situation was quite poor. When the fierce New England winter arrived, he still had nothing but his thin jacket to cover him. In the shul where Reb Pinchas Dovid prayed, there was an old European Jew named Rosenblatt, a former Chassid of Reb Moshe of Lelov. One cold winter night, Rosenblatt dreamt that Reb Moshe stood at the foot of his bed, hitting it with his walking stick. "My grandson is cold, and you lie here sleeping!" the Rebbe exclaimed.

The dream repeated itself several times that night and, the next day, Rosenblatt asked Reb Pinchas Dovid his name. Refusing to be put off with his standard answer, "a Jew from Eretz Yisrael," Rosenblatt finally discovered his true identity. That very day, Rosenblatt bought Reb Pinchas Dovid a heavy new winter coat. Reb Pinchas Dovid wore that coat for years, until it was so worn out that it was useless. Even then, he did not throw it away, but hung it lovingly in his closet. "For this coat, my grandfather descended from the Upper Worlds; it is only right that I save it and respect it."

Two other miraculous events helped reveal Reb Pinchas Dovid's greatness to the Jews of Boston. In the nearby town of Cambridge lived a Jew named Reb Yisroel Andler, who was afflicted by a terrible, incurable disease. One day, he saw an unknown tzaddik in a dream and was told that only this tzaddik, who lived in Boston, could help him recover. His family had never heard of any tzaddikim living in Boston, but Reb Yisroel was insistent. After making numerous inquiries, the family finally learned about Reb Pinchas Dovid.

With his last ounce of strength, Reb Yisroel traveled to Boston. When he reached the home of Reb Pinchas Dovid, he was shocked to recognize the very man he had seen in his dream. Reb Pinchas Dovid blessed him, and Reb Yisroel soon recovered from his illness. A similar story is told regarding the Rebbe and Reb Joseph Mael of Millis, Massachusetts.

The War Years in Jerusalem

Meanwhile, Reb Pinchas Dovid's wife, Soroh Sashe, was trapped in Jerusalem with their two young children. The suffering and privation of the Jews of the city during World War I are hard to imagine. Rabbi Moshe Blau provided a firsthand description in his book, *Al Chomosayich Yerushalayim*:

> When Turkey entered the war on the side of Germany and Austria, against Great Britain [and later America], Jerusalem and Eretz Yisrael were cut off from their source of financial support. From the very first day of the conflict, the condition of the Jewish community deteriorated. Prices rose and goods began to vanish from the market.... Hundreds were conscripted into the [Turkish] army, and few ever returned. Hundreds of Jews hid, only to live in constant fear of death.... Most yeshivas stopped operating entirely, and the few that continued did so under tremendous financial constraints.... [These terrible] conditions continued in Jerusalem for three and a half years.
>
> The hunger, the filth — for soap and water were lacking — and the unclean food resulted in a horrible plague of typhus. Thousands of Jews died, with the death toll among infants the highest. The Sefardi Burial Society's records show that the death rate of children jumped from about seven to 120 a month. Hundreds died from famine, especially yeshiva students, who had no income.... Most vulnerable were the elderly and the weak. In the Wittenburg

neighborhood of the Old City, run by Kollel Chabad, every single resident passed away!

The Rebbetzin Goes into Exile

Rebbetzin Soroh Sashe, fearing for the lives of her young children, decided to leave Eretz Yisrael for Poland, where her father was the Chassidic Rebbe of Torka. The family traveled from Eretz Yisrael to Europe overland, by army transport trains. Enemy planes often tried to bomb their railway cars, which they assumed carried guns and ammunition. Passengers ran from the cars and threw themselves to the ground to avoid the flying shrapnel. Sometimes troops would commandeer the entire train for military purposes. The passengers were stranded in foreign towns along the way, relying on the kindness of strangers until the next train came along.

After much travail, the Rebbetzin and her children reached Budapest, Hungary, in time for the High Holidays. There she heard terrible news. The city of Torka had been completely demolished in the war! A near panic gripped the Rebbetzin. What had happened to her father? What would be with herself and her children? Continuing on to Galicia, she went from city to city searching for some word of her father. Finally, she learned that he was alive and well in the city of Gaya. She traveled there and stayed with him until the end of the war.

The Family Reunites

During the war, Reb Pinchas Dovid had been totally out of contact with his family in Jerusalem. Finally, he sent word of his escape to America through the Spanish Embassy in Palestine. His friends and family were relieved; but when Reb

Dovid'l Biderman (Lelover) was told, he merely said "I already knew" — he had predicted it long before.

In the meantime, Reb Pinchas Dovid had become a prominent figure in the Boston Jewish community. People flocked to him for prayers, *tisch*, blessings and advice. His home was open to all: visiting Rabbis, fundraisers from abroad, paupers and the homeless. Within a short time, he had to move from Barton Street to Milton Street to Chambers Street to Poplar Street, where he lived in a twenty-two-room house.

In the winter of 1919, Reb Pinchas Dovid traveled to New York to consult with doctors concerning his deteriorating vision. On December 31, Rebbetzin Soroh Sashe arrived in New York with her son, Moshe, and stepdaughter, Freida Gitel. That same week, Reb Yosef Shmelke Brandwein, Frieda Gitel's childhood *chassan*, also arrived in New York. Now, the entire family was reunited. The Rebbe arranged a huge and elegant wedding for Freida Gitel and Reb Yosef Shmelke, to be held in Boston on February 3, 1920.

Never before had the Jews of Boston — perhaps of all America — seen such a grand Chassidic wedding. Even the secular American newspapers reported it with amazement. Approximately six thousand people attended — giving some indication of the Rebbe's status — yet the strictest standards of modesty were maintained. The women were asked to sit separately and cover their hair... and they did!

The *chuppah* was held in the courtyard of the Great Synagogue on Crawford Street in the Roxbury neighborhood. The *Kabbalas Panim* lasted most of the afternoon. One of Boston's leading Rabbis, Rabbi Zalman Yaakov Friederman, son-in-law of Rabbi Yaakov Lipshitz (author of *Zichron Yaakov*), was the *mesader kiddushin*. The wedding banquet and *sheva berachos* were held at the Rebbe's New England Chassidic Center at 87 Poplar Street.

The young couple at first lived with the Rebbe; but he later sent them back to Eretz Yisrael, with a promise that he would follow them soon. Still feeling that he was a "*Yid* from Eretz Yisrael," he deliberately never learned English. He was from Jerusalem, and wanted nothing to do with America.

And You Shall Teach Your Children When Reb Pinchas Dovid's son, Moshe, reached the age of eight, he firmly refused to send him to public school, no matter what State law required. Instead, he hired a private tutor. Unimpressed, the Board of Education summoned him to court.

"You have your laws of education," Reb Pinchas Dovid told the judge, "and we have ours.... Rabbi Yehoshua ben Gamla started our school system over 2000 years ago but, in our schools, we teach our children only Torah."

Although the judge was unable to agree to that, he allowed Reb Pinchas Dovid to educate his children at home, if private tutors taught them all state-required subjects. Reb Pinchas Dovid did hire such teachers, but he never really allowed them to teach his child secular subjects.

In the following year, on the 27th of Sivan 1921, Reb Pinchas Dovid's second son was born. The Rebbe was extremely happy and, despite his failing vision, he performed the *bris milah* himself. The child was given the exact same name as the Berditchever Rav, Levi Yitzchok ben Soroh Sashe, for the Rebbetzin had been named after her ancestor, the Berditchever's mother. Reb Pinchas Dovid was overjoyed. "From the time of the Berditchever's passing until now," he exclaimed, "there has never been another Jew called by precisely that name!"

Reb Pinchas Dovid also hired a private tutor for Levi Yitzchok but, this time, the Board of Education did not even

A CHASSIDIC JOURNEY

Shortly after his wife's arrival in Boston, Reb Pinchas Dovid was blessed with a second son, Levi Yitzchok. Although born in America, he was raised largely as a European cheder bachur.

bother challenging him. The following year, on the 16th of Elul, his second daughter, Matil Feigeh, was born.

Exiled to a Place of Torah

In 1924, the Moetzes Gedolei haTorah (Council of Torah Sages) in Europe sent a group of five leading Rabbis, headed by Rav Meir Dan Plotzki (the Kli Chemdah) to help strengthen Torah observance in America. With him were Rav Asher Lemil Spitzer, Rav and Rosh Yeshiva of Kurchendorf (Hungary), Rav Meir Hildesheimer of Berlin, Rav Yosef Lev of Warsaw, and Dr. Noson Birnbaum, a famous *ba'al teshuvah*. The Rabbis spoke to all the leading Jewish communities in America, making a tremendous impression wherever they went. In Boston, they visited Reb Pinchas Dovid, who was known for his own efforts to strengthen Torah observance. Reb Pinchas Dovid was particularly impressed by Rav Asher Spitzer of Kurchendorf, and decided to send his oldest son, Moshe, to study with him in Hungary.

It was unheard of to send a young boy from the comfort of America to live, without friends or family, in the poverty of Europe; but Reb Pinchas Dovid was concerned only about the spiritual development of his son.

The Warmth of Mitzvos

Reb Pinchas Dovid was a pillar of fire in the midst of the community, and countless individuals were drawn to his light and warmth. People would travel to his *tisch* from as far as fifty or sixty miles away. On Simchas Torah, he would dance with all his strength for hours. Once, when Reb Moshe Eisman expressed his shock over the tumult, Reb Pinchas Dovid quoted the Rambam concerning Simchas Torah: "The joy a person has in the fulfillment of mitzvos, and in the love of Hashem Who commanded them, is a very great mode of spiritual work."

"And," Reb Pinchas Dovid concluded, "when one works, one sweats."

Concern for Youth

When Reb Pinchas Dovid arrived in Boston, even young men from religious homes did not strictly observe the mitzvos, since they had grown up without a religious education. America had just entered World War I, and there was a large group of young men, waiting to be enlisted, who were neither working nor studying. Reb Pinchas Dovid opened a yeshiva for them, the United Rabbinical Schools of Boston, whose various parts were named in honor of Reb Dovid of Karlin, Reb Chaim of Brisk and Reb Meir Simcha of Dvinsk (the Ohr Same'ach). As Rosh Yeshiva, he chose Reb Shimon Esrog, from Tzefas, who was then living in New York. When the war ended, many men left the *beis midrash* to search for jobs, but their time in yeshiva had made a lasting impression.

He also opened afternoon and evening classes for younger Jewish children enrolled in public schools, and there were

A CHASSIDIC JOURNEY

Reb Pinchas Dovid helped start many new communal organizations in Boston, such as this yeshiva for young men, housed in his shul.

eventually over 150 students; but Reb Pinchas Dovid was not satisfied. How could Jewish children learn half-day in non-Jewish public schools? He would cite the *midrash* concerning Rivkah: Whenever she passed a house of idolatry, Esav responded. Whenever she walked past a yeshiva, Yaakov responded. Assuming that she was carrying only one child, with two radically different inclinations, she was deeply concerned. When she was told that, "two nations are in your womb," she was relieved. Better to have two different individuals, each with their own way, than one confused one.

He thus (reluctantly) suggested opening a Jewish day school in which the children could learn secular studies in the morning and religious subjects in the afternoon, all under the guidance of religious Jewish teachers. This then-novel idea was met with great opposition from the other Rabbis of Boston, who could not accept including secular studies within a *beis midrash* framework (later standard for American day schools). Disappointed, and regarding the current system as unworkable, Reb Pinchas Dovid eventually withdrew from the yeshiva he had worked so hard to build. Enrollment in the yeshiva declined; but a kernel of the most committed students did remain to become a cornerstone of the Boston Orthodox community.

An Open Hand

Reb Pinchas Dovid had inherited both Reb Shmelke of Nikolsburg's fiery commitment to Torah study and Reb Dovid of Lelov's boundless love of Israel. Countless Jews flocked to receive his blessings and advice, but the Rebbe donated almost all their *pidyon* money to charity, including his many relatives in America and Eretz Yisrael. He also gave freely to anyone who knocked on his door, often distributing more than he received and borrowing to cover the difference. The little money that occasionally remained supported his own family.

Once a *talmid chacham* from Poland visited America to raise money for his daughter's wedding. The Rebbe asked: "How much do you need?"

"About two hundred dollars."

The Rebbe opened his *tzedakah* drawer and gave the scholar four hundred dollars, a huge sum, at a time when his family had almost no funds of their own.

When the Rebbe was sick with heart problems, his doctors ordered him to recuperate in a more relaxed setting. The Rebbe borrowed two hundred dollars to cover his expenses but, that same day, a letter from a Jew in Eretz Yisrael asked him for a donation for his daughter's wedding. The Rebbe immediately ordered his family to borrow another two hundred dollars for the man.

"We just borrowed two hundred dollars for our trip," they objected. "How can we borrow another large sum?"

"If we can borrow for ourselves, we can certainly borrow for someone else!"

Another time, a stranger asked the Rebbe for help. He received work through public bids and made such a meager profit that he was barely able to support his wife and eight children. Now he had to finish a job by the end of the month in order to receive payment. The work was almost done, but he needed to borrow two hundred dollars to finish it.

The Rebbe asked his daughter to go to a local businessman and borrow two hundred dollars in his name. "But father," she complained, "you do not even know this man. How can you lend him so much money?"

"What are you saying?" the Rebbe replied. "If a Jew is drowning, he must be saved!" The man took the money, finished his job, and indeed paid the Rebbe back soon thereafter.

One Can Always Help

The Rebbe also gave generously of his time and effort. Once, during Prohibition, a Boston Jew was arrested for illegally manufacturing whiskey in his home. The police evidence weighed heavily against him and a long jail sentence seemed inevitable; but the Rebbe worked hard for his release. His efforts eventually brought him to the regional prosecutor's office.

The prosecutor looked over the man's unenviable file. "I would like to be helpful," he said, "but what can I do?"

"That's why you are sitting on that side of the desk, and I am sitting on this side," said the Rebbe. "If I were in your place, I would surely have found some means of helping him by now!" The prosecutor was so impressed by the Rebbe's answer that he indeed found a way to secure the man's release.

The Open Door

In 1923, Congress passed a law to limit the number of immigrants accepted by the United States. A passenger ship left Europe for America just before the law went into effect and, by the time it reached Boston harbor, the deadline had passed. The local authorities were confused. Did the new law apply to this ship or not? Meanwhile, the passengers, including twenty-three Jewish families, were detained on board.

When the Bostoner Rebbe learned of the situation he began calling senators, congressmen and other public officials to obtain the passengers' release — at least until Congress could pass a new law. Word of their release reached the Rebbe late Friday afternoon, and all twenty-three families became his instant Shabbos guests, sleeping at his home or at the homes of his followers. Congress finally passed a special law allowing the passengers to become American citizens.

As a port city, Boston was a main immigration center and many Jewish families spent their first days in America as guests of the Rebbe. What a relief it was for them to find, in their first taste of the New World, an authentic taste of the old one. At times, the Rebbe's home was so full of guests that there were simply not enough blankets and pillows. Every evening, the Rebbe, despite his infirmity, would quietly climb the stairs and check every guest's bed. If he found a hard pillow, he would take it downstairs and exchange it with his own!

The Rebbe's vision became so bad that, in order to read, he needed two pairs of glasses, a magnifying lens and a special strong reading light. Despite this, he still studied late into the night, only to awaken at four o'clock each morning to continue learning.

His attendant, Reb Leibel Singer, would also rise at four in the morning to fix the Rebbe a thermos of coffee. Then he headed to the kitchen to prepare meals for the coming day. Meanwhile, the Rebbe shared his own coffee with the guests who found the kitchen locked.

A CHASSIDIC JOURNEY

Suitable Greetings

Before each Rosh Hashanah, Chanukah and Purim, the Rebbe sent thousands of greeting cards, full of blessings, to Jews in the surrounding areas. "May you immediately be written and sealed for a good life in the Book of the Righteous.... May blessing and success dwell in your home. And may all of us together merit to return to Zion in joy." Then the Rebbe would always add several personal words encouraging the reader to observe Shabbos, *kashrus* and family purity. Why specifically then? "Before Rosh Hashanah, I make an accounting of all my deeds; and I am always worried that I did not sufficiently admonish my fellow Jews. Therefore, just before the end of the year, I encourage everyone, once again, to observe these essential mitzvos."

On the Chanukah after World War II began, the Rebbe added the words: "May Hashem help us that, just as in days of old, we will see the downfall of our enemies, and the complete deliverance of the Jewish People." The following Purim, the Rebbe sent his followers two special blessings as *mishloach manos*: "The first blessing, deliverance for the entire Jewish People.... And the second blessing, that you

The Rebbe's Purim seudah invitations always included two berachos for the recipient.

and your family should have only health and prosperity, good fortune, blessing and plenitude." He also added his yearly invitation to "a Purim *seudah* of great joy and merriment, like in the Old Country, for when one joyfully fulfills a mitzvah, he draws down deliverance and consolation."

The Calculated Sukkah

The Rebbe readily used his unique insight to help others. Once Rabbi Elchonon Stimler received an order from the Boston municipality to dismantle the *sukkah* on his roof. He asked the Rebbe's advice.

"Give 91 cents to *tzedakah*."

"Then I might as well give a dollar."

"No, exactly 91 cents," the Rebbe insisted. "And don't worry. The laws of the Torah have been around thousands of years longer than those of the city."

When the case came to court, the judge, a non-Jew, ruled in Rabbi Stimler's favor, saying: "The laws of the Torah have been around much longer than those of our city. How can we annul them?"

When Rabbi Stimler later asked the Rebbe why 91 cents, he replied, "That's the *gematria* of *sukkah*."

The Rebbe was particularly fond of the mitzvah of *sukkah*, because, "a person can enter into it totally, with his whole body, his clothes, his possessions...." He would leave it only for the most pressing reasons. Even if he had to go into his house because of rain, he would not sit in a chair, but only lean on the armrest. In 1938, he ordered a special bed with a nylon canopy that rose to a point (not considered an obstruction to the mitzvah) so he could sleep in his *sukkah* even during a thunderstorm!

The Rebbe explained the *midrash* that the mitzvah of *sukkah* is equal to all the other positive mitzvos in this manner:

The minimum length and width of a *sukkah* are each seven *tefachim*; the minimum height, ten *tefachim*. There must be two full walls, and a third wall of at least one *tefach*. Thus, the floor of the sukkah is 7x7 = 49 *tefachim* square. So is the roof. Each of the full walls is 70 *tefachim* square, and the partial wall is 10 *tefachim* square. The sum of these figures (49+49+70+70+10) is 248, the total number of positive commandments!

The Rebbe meticulously kept his Yerushalmi customs in America. Here he conducts tisch in his sukkah surrounded by his guests Reb Gershon Lapidus, a gaon from Yerushalayim, and Reb Asher Werner, later Chief Rabbi of Tiberias.

A Sample of His Teachings

Reb Pinchas Dovid's few surviving teachings show the richness and originality of his thought. For example, the verse states, "I will cut off all the horns of the wicked [plural]; the horn of the tzaddik [singular] will be exalted" (*Tehillim* 75:11), while *Chazal* say, "[Hashem's] Name will not be whole, and His Throne will not be whole until Amalek is destroyed." Now every word has two "horns" (corners) — its first and last letters. The two "horns" of the word "the wicked" spell *ram* (high), which has the same numerical value as Amalek.

The two "horns" of the word "tzaddik" spell *ketz* (end). Thus, the verse hints to us: when an end is made of the haughty Amalek, then the End of Days will come, and with it the Redemption.

೫ ೫ ೫

Reb Aharon of Karlin used to say: "There is nothing worse than the apathy caused by depression.... On the other hand, bitterness and brokenheartedness are good qualities.... Although the line between the two is very fine, there is, nevertheless, a clear sign to distinguish between them. A depressed person goes to sleep, becomes withdrawn, and can barely tolerate himself, much less others. But a person who is brokenhearted, who [realizes he] hasn't begun to serve Hashem, is full of energy and determination."

Reb Pinchas Dovid brought a proof for these words from Chana, who "was bitter in her soul" (I *Shmuel* 1:10), and then "prayed to Hashem and wept bitterly and vowed a vow...." Her bitterness brought her to action. Depression, however, followed Adam's sin: "Cursed be the ground for your sake, in sadness will you eat all the days of your life" (*Bereshis* 3:17). This is a terrible curse, for even if a person must toil for a living, he should at least enjoy the results.

೫ ೫ ೫

Reb Pinchas Dovid would sing songs with special melodies he inherited from the Seer of Lublin. Regarding the words of *Azamer Bishvochin*, the Friday night song written by the Arizal, "To the right and to the left and, between them, the bride," Reb Pinchas Dovid explained: The entire world derives sustenance from the holy Shabbos, the source of blessing. Now the nations of the world are nicknamed "right and left": Avraham represents the attribute of kindness, which is on the right side; and the negative aspect of this quality, lust, characterizes his son, Yishmael (thus the

Ishmaelites would not accept the Torah when they heard that it prohibited adultery). Yitzchok represents self-control, which is on the left. Its negative aspect is brutality, which characterizes Esav (thus the Edomites did not want to accept the Torah when they heard it prohibited murder). According to the Zohar, all seventy nations of the world can be similarly divided between Esav and Yishmael, right and left, lust and brutality.

Yishmael and Esav also want to draw benefit from the holy Shabbos; thus they surround it with their own days of rest: the Arabs on Friday (the right) and the descendants of Edom on Sunday (the left), with the Shabbos bride caught between them. In order to prevent this, we are commanded to start Shabbos early and end it late, claiming the surrounding weekdays as our own. Thus, as we sing, "To the right and to the left you will spread out, and Hashem you will praise," Shabbos (one of the names of Hashem) pours out her blessings onto the holy people who sanctify her.

ෆ ෆ ෆ

In the Shabbos *Shemoneh Esreh*, we pray: "Satisfy us with Your goodness," because, although whatever Hashem does is for the good, we often can't see how a particular occurrence is really for our good. Thus, we pray for *chassadim tovim*, kindness that even we will recognize as good. Similarly, *Chazal* have said that a blind man, or one who sits in a dark room, will never be satisfied from a meal (*Yoma* 75a). Thus, the verse says, "*Show* us Your mercy Hashem" (*Tehillim* 85:8), that is, deal with us in ways that are openly merciful and thus satisfying.

ෆ ෆ ෆ

Chazal say that the 248 positive commandments correspond to the 248 limbs of the body: so a person cannot be complete until he fulfills all of these mitzvos. Yet, *teshuvah*, the repenting of one's sins, is also one of these mitzvos. If a person has fulfilled everything else, how can he fulfill this last mitzvah? What can he repent? He can repent, said Reb Pinchas Dovid, fulfilling the entire Torah to less than its highest standards.

FOURTEEN
A Passion for Mitzvos

The Matzos and Mitzvos of Eretz Yisrael

Reb Pinchas Dovid always longed to return to the Holy City of Jerusalem. Even in Boston he wore the golden Shabbos garments of a Yerushalmi Jew, prayed with the *nusach* of Lelov and Karlin, and recited the fifteen *Shirei haMa'alos* in his *sukkah*, just as he had done in Jerusalem. In the words of the Ba'al Shem Tov, "Wherever a tzaddik lives is called Eretz Yisrael."

Typical was Reb Pinchas Dovid's annual effort to acquire *shemurah matzos* for Pesach. Since there was then no such thing as American *shemurah* flour, flour ground from wheat religiously supervised from the time of harvest, he leased a field not far from his home and personally supervised the planting, harvesting and winnowing of the wheat! He then found proper milling stones, had them hewn to size, ground smooth and mounted together. With these he hand-ground his flour. As Pesach approached, he built a small matzah oven in the basement of his home.

He carefully tried to observe the Yerushalmi customs associated with matzah-baking. For instance, Jerusalem bakers pressed the dough thoroughly with a heavy metal or wooden roller, hinged on one end, before forming it into balls. Although unable to reproduce this exactly, Reb Pinchas Dovid pressed his dough with thick wooden clubs, before rolling out the matzos on a cool, glass-topped table that was easy to clean and check. He did the baking himself; and although the finished matzos were thick and hard, to him there were none tastier or more beautiful. They were truly "the bread of affliction." He shared these matzos with his close friend, Rabbi Zalman Yaakov Friederman, another Torah giant who had not been influenced by America. Although Rabbi Friederman personally considered machine matzos acceptable, he was delighted to receive Reb Pinchas Dovid's annual gift.

Reb Pinchas Dovid also made most of his other Pesach foods, even salt and pepper!

Reb Pinchas Dovid was also among the first to introduce *chalav Yisrael* to American Jewry. He sent a congregant to oversee the milking at a nearby farm and shared the milk with other families who had taken upon themselves this stringency.

On one trip to check the field where he grew his Pesach wheat, Reb Pinchas Dovid decided to visit the nearby office of the local Jewish milk distributor. "What's this on your desk?" asked the Rebbe, who was almost blind, pointing to a nondescript document. His attendant read it out loud; the distributor was also ordering milk from a non-Jewish dairy.

"How can you sell both *chalav Yisrael* and non-Jewish milk in our community?" the Rebbe demanded.

"Rebbe, almost no one in Boston drinks *chalav Yisrael*. If I only sold to those families who did, I would never make a living!"

Reb Pinchas Dovid was furious, and argued until the man finally agreed to sell only *chalav Yisrael* from then on.

Reb Pinchas Dovid would only use his own private utensils and cup, for fear that those of others may not have been immersed in a *mikveh*. Once, the Rebbe was asked to bless the wine at a *bris;* but his attendant had forgotten to bring along his cup. Reb Pinchas Dovid took an apple, hollowed it out, and used that instead!

The Importance of Purity

Reb Pinchas Dovid was never a *tzaddik in pelts* (furs), warmed by his own *avodas Hashem* without sharing it with others. For example, Reb Pinchas Dovid not only had his own private *mikveh* in which to immerse every day, he also tried to establish public *mikvaos* for women throughout New England, where there were almost none. Whenever neighboring Jewish communities invited him to spend Shabbos with them, he would make a large *melave malka* Saturday night to raise money for charity. However, if the town did not have a *mikveh*, all proceeds went towards building one.

American Jews simply didn't understand *taharah*. Reb Pinchas Dovid would tell them, "We all accept the existence of electricity, although we can neither see it nor feel it. So too, with spiritual worlds. We can neither see them nor feel them, yet they exist, and exert great force. But just as an electrical current needs a complete circuit though which to flow, so too spiritual forces flow only though a person who has made himself complete and pure.... With the mitzvah of *mikveh*, one must be careful to observe every smallest detail to make the proper connection with the supernal worlds."

Even in his latter years, when his health was failing and his vision was nearly gone, Reb Pinchas Dovid would travel from town to town to inspect *mikvaos* and question the builders. Once, he ordered a synagogue attendant and several congregants to descend into the *mikveh's bor* and dry it thoroughly, as the halachah requires, before pouring fresh water in. Afterwards, they left the room for a few minutes and, when they returned, the Rebbe was missing! They found him inside the *mikveh*, bent over, wiping the last drops of water from the floor. Once, when he discovered a New York City *mikveh* with serious halachic problems, and the local supervising Rabbi ignored his concerns, he made a public presentation to the congregation, proving that his concerns were justified. The *mikveh* was soon fixed.

The Rebbe's exceptional expertise in the construction of *mikvaos* was constantly sought by various American communities. He even received questions from Havana, Cuba. To defend his stringencies, he often debated the greatest *poskim* in America. One, Rav Avraham Yitzchok Zalmenovitz, z"l, once wrote: "[The Rebbe] insists on stringencies that are not found in any *mikvaos* in the world.... Nevertheless, in order to appease his honor, I will apply these criteria to our *mikvaos* as well, so long as they do not cause significant expense."

Guardian of Shabbos

Reb Pinchas Dovid was also a pioneer in encouraging Shabbos observance. In those days, almost no American business closed on Shabbos and simple, working-class Jews could find no other employment. Thus, every shul had two *minyanim* on Shabbos, and the early one was always packed...with men who prayed quickly and then ran off to work!

The Rebbe organized pro-Shabbos demonstrations on streets where Jewish-owned shops were open. He would enter each shop and speak privately with its owner, trying to convince him to close on Shabbos; and he was often successful. When a deadly influenza epidemic broke out, taking thousands of lives, Reb Pinchas Dovid organized large public sermons in which he guaranteed that those who observed Shabbos would be spared. Unfortunately, once the epidemic ended, many new "Shabbos-keepers" reverted to their old ways.

Reb Pinchas Dovid was also shocked to learn that Boston's timetables for candle-lighting came from New York, where sundown is nineteen minutes later. Boston Jews, relying on those tables, might actually light their candles after sundown! Using his knowledge of astronomy, Reb Pinchas Dovid formulated a timetable for New England, with (following the opinion of the Rama) Shabbos beginning more than 18 minutes before local sunset. Each week he would print his special local Shabbos calendars and distribute them among the public. He also warned that many people "think that Shabbos is over and that work is permitted when the electric streetlights come on. But how often the lights come on before sundown on a cloudy day! Such people could be committing capital offenses!"

Disagreeing with standard American and Western European practice (originating with the Gaonim and popularized by the Vilna Gaon), Reb Pinchas Dovid retained the original conclusion of the Rama and the Shulchan Aruch that Shabbos is not over until 72 minutes after sundown, in accordance with the halachic opinion of Rabbeinu Tam. When Reb Pinchas Dovid later moved to New York, he published a new version of his calendar which recounted the major opinions, and concluded that, "The main opinion is that of Rabbeinu Tam, for most halachic authorities agree with him. The Pri Chodosh in his *Kuntress d'Bei Shimsha*, lists by name 70 major *poskim* who agree with Rabbeinu Tam. Although at present I do not have this book before me, I myself have been able to find 39 such major *poskim* who follow this opinion.... These times have been set according to halachah, and in accordance with the astronomical calculations of Harvard Observatory [which he had consulted!]. Who dares be careless when such serious transgressions [as ending Shabbos early] are at stake?" Nevertheless, standard American practice continued to follow the Gaon.

Shabbos Demands

Whenever someone asked Reb Pinchas Dovid for a blessing, he would make it contingent on their observing Shabbos. His daughter Matil Feigeh, the current Altstadter Rebbetzin, still remembers how Mrs. Tannenbaum, one of the Rebbe's followers in Boston, arrived one day escorting her aging cousin, who had suddenly gone blind. The doctors were unable to find a cure; and his insurance company had even paid him his disability benefits, but what he really wanted was to regain his sight. She begged the Rebbe to pray for him.

The Rebbe sat deep in thought. He crushed some tobacco in a little red snuffbox on the desk before him. Suddenly, he held up the box. "What am I holding in my hand?" he asked the man.

"A red snuffbox!" the man cried out in excitement. "I can see! Rebbe, I can see! Just tell me what you want from me. Anything you ask, I will do."

"You must keep the Shabbos carefully from now on," the Rebbe said. The man agreed, and left.

The following week, however, Mrs. Tannenbaum was back, leading her cousin as he stumbled up the stairs. His blindness had returned! The Rebbe sat silently in his chair. "Rebbe, what can we do?" But the Rebbe only muttered, "A person who fools me, is only fooling himself."

Mrs. Tannenbaum started to cry. "Last Friday afternoon, my cousin, despite his promise, went to get his hair cut as usual. He sat in the barber's chair and glanced at the clock in front of him. The minute Shabbos came in, his blindness returned."

A Passion for Mitzvos

Reb Pinchas Dovid could have asked for large donations in exchange for his miraculous blessings, but he never did. To him, the entire upheaval of World War I was only to bring him to America, to help return its straying flock to Yiddishkeit. His special blessings and prayers were only meant to encourage his fellow Jews to observe the Torah.

Blessings and Insight

The Rebbe never gave blessings without first clearly understanding all the details of the problem at hand. In cases involving illness, he would also inquire about the doctors, their diagnoses, and the patient's medical history. If he refused to give his blessing, it was unusual for the matter to end well.

A mother and daughter once came to ask the Rebbe's blessing for their new business. The Rebbe discussed the details of their enterprise, and then turned to the daughter asking, "Now, tell me something about yourself."

The young woman was startled. "But Rebbe," she said, "we've come for a blessing for a business."

"First," he responded, "tell me about yourself."

The young woman sat silently for a minute. "Rebbe, I see that you know," she said. "But give me a week to think about it." The two women then left the room.

The very next day, the young woman returned to the Rebbe's office alone and told the Rebbe how her first Jewish marriage, an unhappy one, had ended in divorce. Her first husband refused to give her a proper *get* (Jewish divorce). When she later wanted to remarry, she and her brother traveled to New York. There her brother told the *beis din* that he was her husband and gave her a *get*! She then illegally married a second man and had a son by him, while halachically still her first husband's wife. The Rebbe immediately arranged for her to receive a *get* from her first husband;

and then wrote to several leading *poskim*, asking for their opinions. They ruled that the young woman was required to separate from her second husband, and her son was, unfortunately, a *mamzer*.

The Rebbe also tried to help *agunos*, married women whose husbands had abandoned them without giving them a Jewish divorce. The Rebbe would try to comfort them and do everything possible to track down their husbands and convince them to deliver a *get*. For example, one of the Jewish newspapers of that time reported: "Sheindel H. has finally received a *get* from her husband, who abandoned her six years ago, thanks to the help of the Bostoner Rebbe, Rabbi Pinchas Horowitz, *shlita*, who traced her husband to San Francisco." Another time, he helped a young woman perform *chalitzah*, freeing her from her deceased husband's brother.

A Speedy Cure

Early one morning, one of the Rebbe's Chassidim, Reb Gershon Kessler, visited the Rebbe's house, extremely upset. His son was in the hospital, and the doctors were about to perform a difficult ear operation. He begged the Rebbe for a blessing.

"I don't see any need to operate," the Rebbe said.

"I didn't come for the Rebbe's advice," the distraught father responded. "I need his blessing."

"I still don't see any reason to operate. Go tell the doctors, in my name, to wait a little while."

At the hospital, the doctors reexamined the patient and agreed to wait. When they checked the boy again, a short time later, his condition had improved, and soon the problem cleared up entirely, without any need for an operation!

When women were in difficult labor or faced a Caesarean section, the Rebbe would sometimes ask the doctors to wait a certain period of time — ten minutes or half an hour — and, when the time passed, the baby would be born naturally and safely.

Once, a young man from Hartford, Connecticut, came to the Rebbe. A short time before, for unknown reasons, he had lost his power of speech. The Rebbe suggested certain remedies and, when the young man took them, he immediately began to speak again. Such miracles were not uncommon, but the Rebbe also had an amazingly expert grasp of normal medical details. One of Boston's leading surgeons, Dr. M.P. Smithwick, would often seek the Rebbe's opinion before performing a difficult operation.

"Beware of Their Coals"

Just as people gained from the Rebbe's blessings, they often lost from ignoring his words. For example, one wealthy Boston philanthropist left a large portion of his estate to charities in Eretz Yisrael. His son-in-law, however, sought to invalidate the will and inherit the money himself. Reb Pinchas Dovid tried to convince the young man to honor his father-in-law's last request, warning him, "The money belongs to charity. Don't touch it! If you do, you yourself will eventually require charity!" The young man ignored the warning, lost all his money in faulty business deals, and was indeed forced to seek charity.

Defender of the Tradition

Seeing himself as an emissary from Jerusalem, carrying laws and customs that American Jewry had forgotten, the Rebbe allowed nothing to be changed.

The Jewish community of Hartford, Connecticut, once invited him to spend a Shabbos with them. When he arrived on Friday morning, he saw that the *bimah* (reader's desk) had been moved from the center of the synagogue to the front, near the *aron kodesh*, a change first instituted by the Reform movement to imitate American churches. Reb Pinchas Dovid immediately returned to Boston. The synagogue had already printed announcements and had arranged a large fundraising dinner for *motza'ei Shabbos*; and nothing was ready for the Rebbe's Shabbos at home. No matter. He ate sparsely that Shabbos, but nothing could make him abandon even the slightest tradition. Several weeks later, the Hartford synagogue returned the *bimah* to its central position, and the Rebbe returned to give them a memorable Shabbos.

When the Rebbe visited Chelsea, Massachusetts, he again found the *bimah* in front of the *aron*. "It's not our fault," the shul's directors explained. "The shul is too small to put it elsewhere." The Rebbe immediately removed his long *gartel*, measured the synagogue, and determined its exact center. He showed them where to put the *bimah* — if they cared to — and only after they moved it did he agree to stay.

Defender of Kashrus
According to the Ba'al Shem Tov, Shabbos, *mikveh* and *kashrus* are the three fundamentals of Judaism. The Rebbe's fight to raise the standards of American *kashrus* were legendary. When a new *shochet* arrived in Providence, Rhode Island, who not only infringed on the livelihood of the established *shochetim* but also used unfit (nicked) slaughtering knives, the local Rabbis prohibited his meat. When he continued to slaughter and sell it, Reb Pinchas Dovid wrote an official public letter (*Kol Koreh*) to the Providence community, in both English and Yiddish:

Beloved Brethren and Dear Friends:

I am astonished to hear of what has happened in your city, the city of Providence, a city known for its respect for Torah, for its strict observance of *kashrus*, and for its charity and shelter of the poor.... My heart bleeds when I am aware that innocent people are led to desecrate their homes with *treifah* and *neveilah* and the dangerous sin of *massig gvul* (*Devarim* 27:17). "Can a man take a fire in his bosom and his clothes not be burned?" (*Mishlei* 6:27).

Dear friends, for the past twenty-five years I have led you in the paths of righteousness.... Save yourself and your dearly beloved while there is yet time.... Go hand in hand with the recognized Rabbis of your city and help them keep Providence a traditionally kosher city. Keep away from the destroyers and do not help them. Those who will obey and listen to my words of warning and advice shall be blessed with peace and happiness.

Always your friend,
Grand Rabbi P.D. Horowitz of Boston
Known as the "Bostoner Rebbe"

The War Over Lebanon

Although Reb Pinchas Dovid usually fought quietly, he once publicly took on, almost single-handedly, one of the largest and most influential meat packing plants of his time.

One day his friend, Rav Zalman Yaakov Friederman, mentioned that he was retracting his *kashrus* certification from the Lebanon Kosher Sausage Factory, a new kosher affiliate of Swift Premium Meats, a well-known non-kosher meat processor. The Lebanon plant appeared to be producing more "kosher" sausages than possible from their cattle, presumably by using *treif* meat purchased through their sister plant.

"Quitting is not enough," the Bostoner Rebbe insisted. "You must publicly announce your resignation." Rav Friederman did so in various Jewish newspapers, but the plant's owner simply found a less troublesome Rabbinic figurehead. In the face of such indifference, Reb Pinchas Dovid convoked a Rabbinic assembly which asked the certifying Rabbi to prove that Lebanon's meat was kosher; but he refused to appear.

The Rebbe fought to maintain kashrus standards throughout New England. This letter was sent at the request of the Orthodox Rabbinate of Providence, Rhode Island.

Reb Pinchas Dovid then quietly questioned the factory's *shochetim* to determine precisely how much kosher meat was slaughtered each week, and then asked to see the company's output figures. He soon realized that major discrepancies did indeed exist, and he hired a private detective to monitor the plant's operations. Late one night, the detective knocked on the Rebbe's door. At that very moment, large trucks were unloading *treif* meat at the

Lebanon sausage plant! Conclusive evidence in hand, the Rebbe and Rav Friederman placed large advertisements in the Jewish newspapers declaring all Lebanon meat products *treif*.

When the plant's owner summoned Rav Friederman to a *din Torah*, the latter asked Reb Pinchas Dovid and Rav Dovid Meir Rabinowitz to represent him. They presented their proofs; and the owner could offer no direct refutation. The *beis din* asked the two Rebbeim to investigate further and to return with validated proofs, which they did. They next called an assembly of Rabbis from the Boston area, although many Rabbis were afraid to attend. They too agreed that the meat was *treif*, and Reb Pinchas Dovid and Rav Rabinowitz then printed a booklet called, "To Separate Oneself from the Forbidden," relating the whole story and concluding that "no *kashrus* certificate is of value, for they (Lebanon Sausages) employ various deceitful means which would make it impossible for any *mashgiach* to oversee the meat."

The Rebbe's psak, "To Separate Oneself from the Forbidden," refuted the fraudulent claims of a local meat factory. Insert: A letter from Rav Moshe Zevulun Margolios of the Union of Orthodox Rabbis, declaring the meat b'chezkas treifah (presumably non-kosher).

Threats and Enticements

Unfortunately, Lebanon, like many other American slaughterhouses, was under the control of the Mafia, who were used to silencing their opposition. After intense pressure, Rabbi Rabinowitz left the fray; but Reb Pinchas Dovid pressed on.

Lebanon's representatives first attempted bribery. No doubt, they said, Reb Pinchas Dovid, who was no longer young, was wearied by his intense efforts in *avodas Hashem*. Perhaps he should take a vacation of about a year at some luxurious spot where he could relax and revive himself. Lebanon would be more than happy to cover his expenses and support his family during the entire time, at a cost of tens of thousands of dollars (a tremendous sum in those days). The Rebbe rejected the offer without a second thought. They then tried a different strategy. Let the Rebbe appoint a *mashgiach* of his own choice; for instance, his son-in-law, Reb Yosef Shmelke Brandwein. Since this seemed merely another form of bribery, he rejected that as well.

Lebanon's messengers then became more direct. "This is America, Rebbe, and in America there are unorthodox ways to remove obstacles." When the Rebbe ignored their veiled threat, they repeated it more bluntly: "Rebbe, they will not hesitate to shoot you." The Rebbe showed them the door.

Forgery After Forgery

Lebanon then mounted a counterattack. In advertisements and fliers, they bitterly attacked both Reb Pinchas Dovid and Rav Rabinowitz, accusing them of lies and slander. The proclamations were signed by two leading New England Rabbis. Reb Pinchas Dovid immediately contacted the Rabbis, who insisted that the entire statement was a forgery! Next Lebanon published a second announcement, signed by Rabbi Moshe Zevulun Margolios, head of Agudas haRabbanim of

America and two other noted Rabbis, stating Lebanon's meat was kosher. In fact, the Agudas haRabbanim had sent representatives to Boston for only one day to look into the matter. Their quick visit to the packinghouse was followed by an unannounced visit to Reb Pinchas Dovid, whose proofs had convinced them that the Lebanon meat was, on the contrary, *treif.*

Finally, Rabbi Eliezer Silver, President of the Agudas haRabbanim, convened a special *beis din* to decide the matter. Reb Pinchas Dovid presented his evidence, and Lebanon denied it all. The Rebbe tried to summon witnesses, but they were all too afraid of the Mafia to publicly testify.

Reb Pinchas Dovid eventually met a local Rabbi who mentioned that, years before, Lebanon's owner had owned a wagon from which he sold kerosene and ice on Shabbos, calling his religious credibility into question! Although this Rabbi was also too afraid to testify, Reb Pinchas Dovid convinced him to simply come to the *beis din* and attend the session. The next day, Reb Pinchas Dovid rose to his feet and shouted the words of the Rambam: "A witness must testify in a *beis din*, presenting all the evidence he knows... to incriminate his friend or to acquit him, as the Torah says, 'If a person...does not testify, he must bear his guilt' (*Vayikra* 5:1)!" Reb Pinchas Dovid shouted so forcefully that his eyes filled with blood. His companion, trembling in fear, rose and gave testimony. "Now do you understand the true character of Lebanon's owner?" Reb Pinchas Dovid declared. (Two years later, when the Rebbe began to lose his vision, he partially attributed it to the shout he had directed at that witness.)

The *beis din* then started a serious investigation. Many individuals were called and were firmly commanded to give testimony, and Reb Pinchas Dovid's evidence was examined in a new light. The court's final conclusion was that the

Lebanon plant was "suspected" of selling *treif* meat. But Reb Pinchas Dovid was not satisfied with such a weak statement. He printed fliers carrying the *beis din*'s words, but included his own, more forceful "commentary."

No sooner had the *beis din* returned to New York, then Lebanon Sausages published a false letter of acquittal in its name! "Such forgery and insolence are unheard of, even by the decadent standards of America," wrote the Rebbe in frustration.

Reb Moshe Zevulun Margolios then forwarded him a letter entitled "To Remove the Stumbling Block." In it, he established that the *beis din*'s "decision," as publicized by Lebanon, was quite false, and that the products manufactured in the meat plant were of questionable *kashrus*. The Rebbe printed this letter on a large poster, with further explanations, and had it displayed around town. Because of the bad publicity, Swift Premium Meats, which had never represented itself as kosher, tried to break its affiliation with Lebanon, although there were legal difficulties.

Unrepentant, the Lebanon plant still continued producing "kosher" meat under its own rabbinical supervision. In response, Reb Pinchas Dovid remarked that the plant would certainly not continue to operate and deceive the religious public. Suddenly, in the middle of the Swift-Lebanon negotiations, a fire broke out on the plant's premises and destroyed both Lebanon Sausages and the neighboring Swift Premium Meats plant! The Rebbe's prediction had come true.

A Silver Lining

In the course of the *din Torah* Rav Eliezer Silver met Reb Pinchas Dovid and was amazed by his brilliance and Torah knowledge. A Litvak, Rav Silver had assumed that

A Passion for Mitzvos

those Polish Jews who were knowledgeable in Torah became Roshei Yeshivos, whereas those who were unlearned but pious became Chassidic Rebbes. After hearing Reb Pinchas Dovid present his case, Rav Silver exclaimed, "Why is such a man a Chassidic Rebbe? He could easily sit among us as a *dayan*!"

This was not Reb Pinchas Dovid's first contact with a member of the Agudas haRabbanim. Shortly after his arrival in America, the Rebbe wrote to Rav Zev Wolf Margolios concerning a complicated matter of halachah: "I do not feel confident to answer [such] halachic questions, especially since I have no books with me, and am like a sojourner in a foreign land." Yet, even without his books, the Rebbe went on to provide a complex, in-depth analysis of the problem under discussion, quoting from memory the Gemara and *Shulchan Aruch*, answering contradictions between the *Talmud Bavli* and *Yerushalmi*, settling textual discrepancies, and solving the problem of the Maharsha on the subject!

FIFTEEN
Journeys

The First Trip Back to Eretz Yisrael

In 1925, Reb Pinchas Dovid tried to realize his long-standing dream of returning to Eretz Yisrael. Despite his Rebbetzin's descriptions of the harrowing conditions during World War I and the letters he received regularly from Jerusalem, he wanted to see for himself. He also wanted to fulfill the mitzvah of *kibud eim*, since he had not seen his mother for thirteen years. Moreover, during that year, on the first Wednesday of Nisan, the sun would complete its twenty-eight-year cycle, returning to its original place in the firmament, and a special blessing would be said. Springtime in Boston is usually rainy, whereas in Eretz Yisrael the sun would surely be visible. "If I miss this opportunity," he worried, "who knows if I will live to make this blessing again." (He did not.)

He arrived in Eretz Yisrael just before Nisan, and remained there for about two months. The Pesach Seder he led at his mother's house, full of songs and praise, was remembered by Jerusalem residents for decades to come. The Lelover Rebbe, Reb Menachem Mendel, recalled it to his Chassidim some sixty years later!

Jerusalem was then beset by a fierce struggle between the followers of the two great leaders of the generation: Rav Yosef Chaim Sonnenfeld, head of the Eidah Charedis and Agudas Yisroel, and Rav Avraham Yitzchok Kook, the Ashkenazi Chief Rabbi. Although Reb Pinchas Dovid had his own opinions, he kept silent and scrupulously avoided controversy. He wouldn't eat meat during his entire stay, since he did not want to eat meat with the Rabbinate's *hashgachah*, and was afraid that eating only meat with the Eidah's *hashgachah* might indirectly offend Rav Kook. Even his Seder meal consisted only of dairy products and eggs!

The Rebbe had hoped, as an "outsider," to help bring peace between the factions, but his efforts were unsuccessful. Disappointed, he noted that on Shabbos night we pray, "Spread your canopy of peace over us, over all of Israel and over Jerusalem." Jerusalem apparently needs a special blessing for peace, because it can be a rare commodity there!

At the end of Iyar the Rebbe journeyed by rail to Alexandria, Egypt, by boat to Trieste, Italy, and then by rail to Vienna. He spent two weeks in Austria visiting various eye specialists, hoping to cure his failing vision. In Vienna, he bought two beautiful silver candlesticks for his Rebbetzin. Each had twelve cups for oil, arranged in two tiers of six. Added to the two single candlesticks she already had, the Rebbetzin lit twenty-six Shabbos lights in all, corresponding to the numerical value of the four-letter name of Hashem, as was the custom of Reb Pinchas Dovid's uncle and teacher, Reb Dovid'l Biderman.

A Visit to the Tshortkover

Reb Pinchas Dovid's eldest son, Reb Moshe, traveled from his yeshiva in Hungary to meet his father in Vienna. Together they visited the famous tzaddik, Reb Yisroel of

Journeys

Tshortkov, a grandson of Reb Yisroel of Ruzhin. The Tshortkover's study had no seats for guests, only an armchair for the Rebbe. Although Reb Pinchas Dovid tried to conceal his identity, the Tshortkover immediately ordered his attendant to bring a seat for his important guest.

During their discussion, the Tshortkover related a family story about Rabbi Aharon Feltshiner of Tzefas, Reb Pinchas Dovid's father-in-law. In the Ruzhiner Rebbe's home in Sadigura, every child had his own room. When important guests would visit, the Ruzhiner let them sleep in one of the children's rooms. When Reb Aharon Feltshiner visited, he shared a room with Reb Dovid Moshe, the first Tshortkover Rebbe. Not because the Ruzhiner lacked beds; the Ruzhiner lived like a king and his house was a palace. Rather, he wanted his young son to sleep in the same room with such a holy man as Reb Aharon.

The two men spoke about the greatness of the Ruzhiner, his fabled wealth, and his influence. The Tshortkover showed Reb Pinchas Dovid a gold-plated *aron kodesh* he had inherited from his grandfather, a special privilege. He also wrote down Reb Pinchas Dovid's name and promised to pray for his eyesight.

From Vienna, Reb Pinchas Dovid traveled to Liverpool, where he boarded a ship for Boston. Arriving back home, he learned of the passing of his mother-in-law in Torka, Poland. He immediately wrote to his father-in-law, the Torka Rav, Reb Michel Brandwein, and suggested that he come to Boston. He agreed and arrived on the first of Elul 5685 (1925).

The Second Trip

The Rebbe's trip in 1925 only strengthened his determination to return to Eretz Yisrael, since he could see that life was returning to normal and that the religious community there was growing rapidly. His children, Levi Yitzchok and Matil Feigeh, were now school age, and he wanted them to be educated in the holy air of Jerusalem.

By 1928, while only in his fifties, the Rebbe's eyesight deteriorated further and his blood pressure became dangerously high. Although his doctors had warned him not to exert himself, he literally dripped sweat after his fiery morning prayers. His intense Torah study also became increasingly difficult, yet he would not give it up. A large number of people approached him daily, to tell him their problems, and to seek his advice and intervention. Finally, his intense involvement in numerous community and charitable activities further sapped his strength. His return to Eretz Yisrael would allow him to serve his followers by praying for them at the Western Wall, while his daily burdens would be less.

With all these considerations in mind, Reb Pinchas Dovid decided to return with his family to Jerusalem. Many of his followers were prosperous businessmen who pledged to support him there; but the news of his departure created a major stir in the Boston community.

Once the Rebbe's physical condition improved enough to travel, he promptly shipped some of his possessions to Eretz Yisrael and sold the rest. He could not sell his large house on Poplar Street, however, for it was old, and there were no buyers. (This proved to be a blessing in disguise for, when he was eventually forced to return to Boston, his house was waiting for him.)

The Rebbe planned to depart on June 23, 1929. Two ships were sailing from Boston Harbor to the Mediterranean that day: The Cunard Line's ship left at 3:00 p.m., and the *St. Louis* left at 12:30 p.m. The Rebbe chose the former because he anticipated a long, emotional farewell from his Chassidim. But the captain of the *St. Louis* called and offered to set sail at 4:00 p.m., if the Rebbe would sail with him. Hearing about this offer, the Cunard Line's captain also offered to delay his departure until 4:00 p.m. for the Rebbe. Finally, the captain of the *St. Louis* promised the Rebbe a private cabin, where he could study and pray, thus winning the duel.

Hundreds of the Rebbe's followers and admirers accompanied him to the port to see him off, in one hundred taxis supplied by one of the Rebbe's followers, who owned a taxi company. A band of Jewish musicians waited at the pier. The music was joyful, but there were tears on many cheeks, as the Rebbe left his home and community to return to the Holy Land.

Unable to part from him, the crowd followed the Rebbe up the gangplank and on board the ship to shake his hand yet once more, to receive yet one more blessing. The ship's captain was forced to wait until around five o'clock, when he finally convinced the visitors to leave the ship. Then a crowd of new visitors trying to come up the gangplank made it impossible for the earlier ones to descend. It was the first time in memory that the gangplank was removed with people still on it!

The Rebbe (l.) on board ship, before setting out for Eretz Yisrael, speaking with his eldest son, Reb Moshe (center) and his gabbai, Reb Leib Hirsh Baumel (r.).

Turkish rule in Eretz Yisrael ended with World War I and, in 1925, Reb Pinchas Dovid was issued a "Palestinian" passport by the British mandatory authorities.

Bitter News

Reb Pinchas Dovid's ship docked in Germany, and he traveled overland to Vienna to consult with yet more doctors about his weakening eye condition. From there he traveled to Karlsbad, Czechoslovakia, to try its famous mineral hot springs. He planned to rest there several weeks and then leave on August 20; but tensions between the Jews and Arabs in Eretz Yisrael had reached the breaking point.

Ostensibly, the conflict involved the claim of the Wakf (the chief Muslim religious council) that the Western Wall and the Temple Mount were Arab, not Jewish, property, and that Jews should not pray there. The real reason was Arab concern over the rising number of Jewish emigrants entering the Holy Land. The Arabs did everything possible to disturb Jewish worshipers at the *Kosel*. In the middle of Shabbos davening, Arab youths would arrive with drums and tambourines to perform loud Muslim dances. Arab workers would lead their donkeys across the (then) narrow Western Wall courtyard, cursing the Jews in their way. Finally, the Arabs built a small mosque and minaret right in the courtyard, where the muezzin would call out Muslim prayers at all hours of the day.

Journeys

On the 25th of Tammuz, a band of Arabs attacked a small group of Jews walking to the *Kosel* to pray. In response, the British mandatory authorities told the Jews not to gather by the *Kosel* on Tishah b'Av, so as not to "provoke" the Arabs.

In protest, the Young Beitar Zionist Movement appeared in force at the *Kosel* on Tishah b'Av night carrying banners with deliberately provocative slogans, crying out, "*Shema Yisroel*, the *Kosel* is ours, the *Kosel* is one!" Then they deliberately left the Old City through the Armenian Quarter, chanting and shouting as they went.

Two days later, the Arabs took revenge. On Friday afternoon, after an inflammatory sermon in their mosque on the Temple Mount, the Arabs streamed into the *Kosel* courtyard wielding sticks and clubs. Fortunately, the courtyard was almost empty (most Jews were home preparing for Shabbos), but they beat the lone Jewish attendant mercilessly, and rampaged through the courtyard, ripping apart prayerbooks and *sifrei Tehillim*. The following day, they stabbed a Jewish youth on Shmuel haNavi Street. He died three days later. During the large funeral procession that followed, the Jews tried to enter the Old City through the Jaffa Gate, but they were held back by the British police.

Several days later, again provoked by their leaders, thousands of Arabs attacked the Jewish neighborhoods of Talpiot, Jaffa Street, and Me'ah She'arim, wielding knives and clubs, and shouting "Kill the Jews." The British police were then noticeably absent, allowing seventeen Jews to be killed and dozens injured, during the two-hour rampage. That same day, in Hebron, an Arab mob massacred sixty-three Jews, among them twenty-seven students of the Hebron Yeshiva.

The pogroms spread as far north as Tzefas, and continued the following day as well, in Motza, Atarot, Kiryat Anavim and Arzah. The Arabs ran wild, unchecked for an entire week, shouting, "The [British] government is with us!" Indeed, the British turned a blind eye.

The Land of Israel was on fire. The Rebbe, in Karlsbad, received an urgent telegram from his mother, who begged him to change his plans. The Rebbe reluctantly traveled to Lemberg and the Hotel Greenberg, leaving that "modern" city to spend the High Holy Days with the Chassidic congregation of his father-in-law in Torka.

Meanwhile, the British government set up an investigatory commission headed by Sir Walter, the senior judge of Egypt; but the Mufti of Jerusalem, the main instigator of the riots, insisted that they subserviently come to him. The Mufti then arrogantly confronted them with the most outrageous arguments, permitting his lawyer Uni Ibad Il-Hadi to conclude: "The Muslims will not accept any verdict to their disadvantage, even if the decision is made by the entire world." Never courageous, the British commission decided in their favor!

The Talmud teaches us that "A tzaddik protects the city or the country where he lives" (*Sanhedrin* 99b). Coincidence or consequence, shortly after Reb Pinchas Dovid left Boston on the first day of Sukkos, October 19, 1929, the New York stock market crashed and America, the richest country in the world, plunged into the Great Depression. Thousands of people lost their wealth and jobs overnight, including many of the Rebbe's formerly prosperous Chassidim, their promises of support now worthless.

Despite the bad news on both sides of the Atlantic, the Rebbe insisted, "Once a person goes up, he does not go down." He sent his wife and young children back to their now-empty home on Poplar Street (all their furniture had been sold), and around Chanukah time traveled with his oldest son, Reb Moshe, to Tiberias in Eretz Yisrael. There he enrolled his son in the yeshiva of Rav Moshe Kliers, his former study partner. A few months later, Reb Pinchas Dovid left Tiberias to be closer to his mother in Jerusalem.

The Wedding of Reb Moshe

In Israel, Reb Pinchas Dovid also arranged Reb Moshe's marriage to Leah Freidel, the daughter of Reb Avrahamtzi of Zydachov, and the sister of Reb Menachem Mendel of Zydachov. The wedding was set for Chanukah 1931 (it was later delayed until Shavuos time). The Rebbe sailed home soon thereafter, returning to Poland with his whole family in 1931. The father of the bride met them and accompanied them to Zydachov. The wedding was a joyous one, attended by many Chassidic leaders from the vicinity. The Rebbe's uncle, Reb Alter of Sosnovitza, a younger brother of Reb Dovid'l Biderman, was the *mesader kiddushin*. After the wedding, Reb Moshe stayed with his bride's family in Zydachov, while the Rebbe and his family returned to Boston.

The Third Trip

A source of spiritual strength in prosperous times, the Rebbe was even more important to his congregants in the depths of the Depression. Even while his family struggled to survive, he continued sending funds to his relatives in Eretz Yisrael, hosting the needy, and making secret donations to Jews whose fortunes had been lost in the Crash. Meanwhile, he still longed to return to Eretz Yisrael. His younger son, Levi Yitzchok, was now almost thirteen, and the Rebbe wanted to celebrate his bar mitzvah in Jerusalem.

Expecting opposition, he first sent his family on ahead. Remaining in Boston alone, he told them, would help save enough money to support them once he himself returned to Eretz Yisrael. On January 11, 1934, the family set sail from New York to Haifa on the *Aquitainia*. Most of the Chassidim assumed that they had merely gone for a visit; the rest assumed that the Rebbe would never gather sufficient funds to move. All were shocked when the Rebbe, in the middle of his Purim *seudah*, calmly announced that he was leaving for Eretz Yisrael the following day! His family in Jerusalem were just as shocked to receive his telegram: "I have left America, and am on my way to you."

The Rebbe's ship was delayed at sea and arrived in Haifa a day late, on Shabbos. The Rebbe refused to disembark, despite all orders of the captain, the crew, the port police and the British immigration officials. The captain threatened to continue on to Beirut, Lebanon, but the Rebbe was unmoved.

Impressed, the captain asked, "If we hold the ship until sunset, will the Rebbe disembark?"

"No, only 72 minutes after dark (Rebbeinu Tam time)!"

Incredibly the ship waited for seven hours, until full darkness. The port offices were all closed, and the proper officials had to be tracked down and hauled back to their posts to stamp the Rebbe's passport. The following day, Israel's Jewish newspapers were full of the amazing story of the tremendous *kiddush Hashem*. The Bostoner Rebbe had delayed an entire oceanliner to prevent desecrating Shabbos.

In Jerusalem

In Jerusalem, the Rebbe moved into the small apartment his family rented in Kerem Avraham, just north of Kikar Shabbos in Geulah. Their family suffered terribly, lacking food, clothing and kerosene, which was used for both cooking and for heat. Ironically, those Jerusalem families whom the Rebbe had supported with checks, during his years in America, now lived comparatively well. In contrast, his own family now barely had enough to survive. Despite poverty and ill health, the Rebbe's first Pesach in Jerusalem was an extremely joyous one; he only regretted losing the second Seder he had conducted for eighteen years in Boston.

Later, the family moved to a bigger apartment on Chaggai Street, in the heart of Geulah. Once again, the Rebbe attracted followers and conducted a daily *minyan* with all the fiery enthusiasm of his youth. Also that year, on the 27th of Sivan, young Reb Levi Yitzchok became bar mitzvah, with Jerusalem's leading Rabbis in attendance. The Rebbe wrote to his followers in Boston, describing his son's Torah progress and his regret that they could not be there, but "if you gather in the *beis midrash* on Poplar Street and drink a *l'chaim* for the event, it will be as if I were there."

If Only for This

Soon thereafter, the Rebbe oversaw the burial of his uncle, the Sosnovitza Rebbe, who had passed away in Poland a year and a half earlier. The family had sent his casket to Eretz Yisrael for burial in the Lelover family plot on the Mount of Olives, and Reb Pinchas Dovid ordered that the body be removed from the casket for burial. The custom of Eretz Yisrael is to bury the deceased directly into the ground, since "whoever is buried in Eretz Yisrael is as if he is buried under the [Temple] altar" (*Kesubos* 111a). The local burial society warned against it since, after so much time, the slightest contact might cause the body to crumble. Reb Pinchas Dovid devised an ingenious method for disassembling the casket without touching the body, and taught his nephew, Rabbi Zusha Brandwein, a member of the burial society, the technique. But, when the casket was opened — to their amazement — the tzaddik's body was completely intact!

The Rebbe said, "If I had only come to Eretz Yisrael for this, it would have been enough." He later explained his special technique to his whole family, as if it was important for them to remember it. Only years later did they realize that the Rebbe was giving instructions for his own burial, which was held under similar circumstances.

The Beis Midrash When their new apartment became too small, the family and shul moved to the second floor of the Mandelbaum House, at the edge of Me'ah She'arim and Battei Ungarin. Many of Jerusalem's finest scholars came to pray there; and Reb Moshe and his wife came from Poland to join his father there.

Unfortunately, the British governor of Jerusalem, who lived just below them, didn't appreciate their loud prayers and lively Friday night *tisch*. His Honor would storm up the stairs shouting and demanding quiet. The constant interruptions forced the Rebbe to move once again but, in the end, the governor may have regretted his complaints. The next tenant was the brother-in-law of Emir Abdullah, ruler of the Hashemite Kingdom of Trans-Jordan (and the grandfather of King Hussein). The Arabs needed to move in a day early, on Shabbos, and the Rebbe kindly agreed. Over Shabbos, the Rebbetzin mentioned their unpleasant neighbor to her Arab counterpart.

"He will regret your leaving," the Arab woman said, smiling. "We grind our own flour in hand-mills, pound our own spices in mortars, and hold extremely large parties all week long. Your noise will be nothing compared to ours!"

Givat Pinchas When yet another new apartment became too small, the Rebbe decided to build his own new Chassidic neighborhood on the outskirts of Jerusalem, the first in all of Eretz Yisrael. Jerusalem was rapidly expanding. When Reb Moshe of Lelov arrived in Jerusalem in 1851, the city's Jewish population was about 5,000. By 1914, it had jumped to 15,000. New neighborhoods were constantly being built adjacent to the existing ones, but the Rebbe had his eye set on future generations. He decided to purchase land far beyond the city's advancing edge.

The tzaddik Rabbi Amram Blau, the Rebbe's "real estate broker," visited him daily, spreading out maps of various sites in the hills around Jerusalem. Finally, the Rebbe chose a distant location, not far from the tomb of Shmuel haNavi, and a name — Givat Pinchas. The land belonged to several Arab families, and had been further subdivided by inheritance among their numerous children. Rabbi Blau had to negotiate with each of them individually, which was extremely tiring work. Each time one agreement was reached, another Arab would retract from his promise and the bargaining had to begin again. Furthermore, radical Arab groups had issued warnings and death threats to Arabs selling land to Jews.

Once all the obstacles had been overcome, another concern arose: If other real estate dealers learned of the deal, they might try to scoop up the land or sabotage the proceedings. Therefore, the Rebbe invited all forty illiterate Arab landowners to stay overnight in his house. The following morning, they were to "sign" the official contract at the Registrar's Office with their right thumbprints. The group's leader, however, would sign with his left hand, for his right thumb was missing. It was apparently lost when he led one of the Arab massacres of 1929! One can imagine the tension in the house that night: forty Arabs sleeping and, at their head, one of the leading enemies of the Jews.

After the signing, Reb Pinchas Dovid breathed a deep sigh of relief. He rode his donkey to Givat Pinchas and took halachic possession of the land by walking around its borders, not unlike Hashem's command to Avraham, "Rise and walk through the length and breadth of the land, for I have given it to you and your seed" (*Bereshis* 28:13). His joy was intense.

Since land in Jerusalem and the lengthy negotiations were both extremely expensive, and since Reb Pinchas Dovid had almost no money, he needed partners to help cover the payments, while profiting from reselling their shares of the land. He chose Rav Avraham Jungreis and Rav Yonah Zvebner, who together purchased 60 percent of the land. Dr. Shlomo Jammer, a dear friend from Germany, lent the Rebbe 20 percent of the sum, and the Rebbe himself undertook to raise the remaining 20 percent, thus acquiring 40 percent of the land. The three partners soon paid their shares, and the Rebbe, having no other choice, left for America, accompanied by Reb Moshe, to convince his friends to invest in the Givat Pinchas community. The Rebbe planned to return quickly and begin building.

The Return to America

The journey was difficult, and the Rebbe suffered terribly. "I don't think I have the strength to make this trip again," he said. And, indeed, he never returned to Eretz Yisrael alive.

The financial situation in Boston was still bleak. Although his many followers turned to him for advice and helped support him and his family, no one had enough money to invest in land in far-off Jerusalem. Despite his failing health, the Rebbe traveled the eastern seaboard to raise money for his project. The results were the same. International conditions appeared too unstable, and therefore no one wanted to invest.

The Rebbe wrote optimistic letters home: "The project is a success; people...are making commitments. I will return soon." But Reb Moshe, who transcribed these letters, had to add: "Up to here are the holy words of the Rebbe, *shlita*. What follows are the words of his student. You must know that the matter is dark and difficult. There is no progress and no interest. I worry that father is wasting his strength for nothing."

The Rebbe remained in Boston for two whole years, trying to establish Givat Pinchas. Meanwhile, back in Jerusalem, his family's financial situation had become extremely difficult, and Rebbetzin Soroh Sashe finally took matters into her own hands. First she approached a relative whose generous support from the Rebbe had enabled him to open a business and become quite prosperous. He had refused to loan the Rebbe money for Givat Pinchas, and he hadn't given the Rebbetzin a penny during the two years she struggled on alone. The Rebbetzin, swallowing her pride, asked him to lend her enough money to return to Boston; but he turned her away, once again.

She next turned to Reb Nachum Roth, a bookstore owner who regularly davened in the Rebbe's *minyan*. He guaranteed a loan that allowed the Rebbetzin to purchase four tickets to Boston, for herself, her two children and Reb Moshe's wife. Using the Rebbe's own strategy, she sent him a telegram on the day of the trip: "We have left Jerusalem and are on our way to America."

The family sailed to Marseilles, France, and then traveled by rail to Cherbourg, where they boarded the *Washington*. The ship docked in New York Harbor on February 7th, 1936, two years to the day after they had left. In Boston, they were greeted by a crowd of Chassidim, who rejoiced that the Rebbe would now probably remain among them. "But," the present Bostoner Rebbe, *shlita*, said, "I will never forget the look on my father's face.... It was the end of his dream. There would be no community and no future for him in Eretz Yisrael." Reb Pinchas Dovid's own bitter words were, "It seems Uncle still doesn't let." Reb Dovid'l still would not let him leave America.

Postscript The Rebbe's home on Poplar Street once again became a center of hospitality and kindness for the Jews of Boston and beyond. One day, the Rebbe received a letter from the same relative in Jerusalem whose ingratitude had caused his family so much suffering. His fortunes had soured, and he now wanted the Rebbe to get him a visa so he could raise money in America!

The Rebbe immediately went to work and did not rest until the man was assured a visa. When his family questioned his "rush," the Rebbe answered, "I worried that feelings of revenge might creep into my heart, so I had to act particularly fast to make sure that couldn't happen."

SIXTEEN
Boston in New York

The Neighborhood Changes

America has always been a country of rapid change. Boston's Jewish community began to dwindle as a major Orthodox Jewish community began to take shape in New York.

By 1936, Rabbi Shraga Feivel Mendlowitz had opened Yeshivas Torah Vodaath in the Williamsburg section of Brooklyn, and the Rebbe sent his younger son, Levi Yitzchok, there to study (the rise of the Nazi Party in Germany prevented his learning in Eastern Europe; and, in fact, the Rebbe advised all visiting fundraisers not to return to Europe). Soon afterwards, the Rebbe himself decided to move, saying, "The Mishnah tells us to live only in a place of Torah. If I can't live in Eretz Yisrael, at least I can live in Williamsburg, close to the yeshiva." He was one of the first Chassidic leaders to move there.

The Rebbe's followers found him an apartment at 542 Bedford Avenue, at the corner of Wilson Boulevard. The ground floor became the *beis midrash* and the second floor a home for his family. Although ready to leave Boston in the summer of 1939, the Rebbe waited for two unique, but vital, facilities to be built: a matzah oven and a *mikveh*. Private *mikvaos* were a great rarity in America, but the Rebbe went to *mikveh* every day (sometimes several times a day). When he was too sick to immerse, he would send someone else to act as his substitute. Once, during a summer in Sharon, Massachusetts, the Rebbe caught a cold. His wife attributed it to his immersing in the cold waters of a nearby river. "I knew you would blame the river," he said. "That's why I didn't immerse today; just to prove that people can catch a cold without immersing, and to deliver the institution of *mikveh* from false accusations."

The Rebbe's *mikveh* was completed in February 1940, and he left Boston a month later. A crowd of supporters accompanied him to the train station, and the farewell ceremony dragged on and on. Finally, late at night, Reb Pinchas Dovid boarded the train to New York.

Although the trip from Boston to New York takes only a few hours, the Rebbe's frailty, high blood pressure and weak heart made it an extremely difficult one. In the middle of the night, at one of the stops along the way, he had to leave the train and rest for several hours. Arriving in New York early the next morning, he found a group of concerned Chassidim waiting for him. They took him to his new home.

With his last strength he climbed the steep steps to his apartment. At the door, he stopped and stood there for a long moment, trying to regain his strength. Then, reaching into his right pocket, he removed a *mezuzah* in its case. From his left pocket, he took a small hammer and nails. With great intensity, he recited the blessing over the *mezuzah* and nailed it onto the doorpost. Only then did he enter.

Reb Pinchas Dovid named his *beis midrash* and home at 542 Bedford Avenue in Williamsburg "Netzach Yisroel," seeing in its address an allusion to the numerical value (542) of *Mevaser*, the announcement of the ultimate Messianic Redemption.

Boston in New York

Holy Work

A great tzaddik once suddenly began to publicly display tremendous enthusiasm for *avodas Hashem* in his old age. On hearing this, another tzaddik commented, "Alas, he has become old and weak. He no longer has the strength to hide the fire burning inside him." In his last days in New York, the Bostoner Rebbe also publicly exhibited an exceptional passion for *avodas Hashem*, most obvious in his fiery prayers and in his Shabbos night *tisch*. His home on Bedford Avenue turned into a center of Torah; and Rav Mendlowitz sent over students from Torah Vodaath for inspiration. In New York, as in Boston, the Rebbe offered something unique to everyone.

On the seventh night of Pesach, hundreds of Chassidim joined the Rebbe on his midnight walk to the East River, to sing *Shiras haYam*, the "Song of the Sea," as had been his custom in Boston. On Simchas Torah hundreds of Chassidim joined him for *hakafos*.

In 1939, Rav Yaakov Thumim, a recent arrival from Europe, joined the Rebbe for Simchas Torah. Catching the Rebbe's attention, he requested a blessing for his grandfather, Rabbi Chaim Yitzchok Yerucham, the *Av Beis Din* of Altstadt, Poland; but the Rebbe dismissed him with a wave of his hand. Rav Thumim was upset, until he received a letter informing him that his grandfather had passed away four days earlier, on the third day of Sukkos.

Every Shabbos night, after *Ma'ariv*, the Rebbe would climb the stairs to his apartment, wish his wife "*Gut Shabbos*," and then sit down to learn. Someone would read to him (he was virtually blind) sections from the Ba'al Shem Tov on the Torah, the *Ponim Yaffos* and the *Pri Tzaddik*. Then he would descend to the *beis midrash* for his three-hour Shabbos *tisch*, his face radiating light and joy. The Rebbe seemed to be barely in this world, often drifting into deep *deveikus*. He would whisper inaudible words of Torah under his breath, and then sing Shabbos songs with tremendous longing, love and sweetness. On the festivals, his attachment to Hashem became even deeper. From the beginning of Nisan a festival spirit pervaded the house, and he would often remind himself, "It's now one hour closer to Pesach!" On the last day of Sukkos he would hug and kiss the *arba'as haminim* before putting them away, and kiss the four walls of his *sukkah* before leaving.

Once before reciting *Kiddush*, the Rebbe turned to two guests who reportedly played cards, and said, "*Chazal* say that a person who gambles is not fit to testify, and they also say that *Kiddush* is a testimony that G-d created Heaven and earth. Therefore, please forgive each other for any money you lost to the other, so that we should all be fit to testify to the greatness of Hashem."

The Talmud says that in the World to Come, a banquet will be held for tzaddikim. Afterwards, they will ask the seven shepherds — Avraham, Yitzchok, Yaakov, Moshe, Aharon, Yosef and David — to lead the Grace after Meals. All will refuse, for various reasons, except for King David. He will agree, saying, "I will bless, and it is fitting for me to bless."

"Why so?" asked the Rebbe. Because King David wasn't supposed to be born at all, but Adam gave him 70 years as a gift (shortening his own life span from a thousand years to 930 years). King David was thus really a guest in this world, and the halachah is that a guest should lead the *bentching*. The Rebbe was also referring to himself. These were borrowed years, a gift to be used only for the sake of Heaven.

Guardian of Purity "When a Torah scholar comes to a city, all the matters of the city become his responsibility" (*Mo'ed Koton* 6a). When Reb Pinchas Dovid arrived in New York, he found most local *mikvaos* in terrible condition. He reported the problems to the local Rabbi in charge of *mikvaos*, offering his help to correct them. The Rabbi, however, thought that the Rebbe was overstepping his bounds. Despite his weakness, the Rebbe immediately established a Committee for Family Purity, headed by his close Chassid, Reb Moshe Leiber, to inspect local *mikvaos* and oversee their repair.

A follower who lived outside of New York had invited the Rebbe to celebrate his son's bar mitzvah, promising him fifty dollars to make the trip (a large sum at that time). The Rebbe hated traveling, but he agreed on the condition that the fifty dollars would be given to the new Committee for Family Purity — their first donation. He also encouraged Reb Leiber to publish a small digest of laws to help familiarize people with the rules of family purity. The Committee is still active in Williamsburg, and numerous similar committees have since been established elsewhere.

From the Valley of Death

The Rebbe worked desperately to save Jewish families from the European inferno and, thanks to his intervention, hundreds of families escaped the Holocaust. Among them was Rabbi Feivel Zack, *mechutan* of Reb Aharon (Areleh) of Belz, who boarded the last boat from Romania to America. The Rebbe also tried, unsuccessfully, to save the life of the son-in-law and successor of the Sosnovitza Rebbe, Reb Mordechai Biderman, and his son, Reb Moshe Biderman. May Hashem avenge their blood.

His Last Days

Boston's Jews, seeking to maintain their connection with Reb Pinchas Dovid, bought him a house in Dorchester, then a new Jewish neighborhood. Although he never lived there, he did once visit the house. There, he headed straight for the basement to choose a suitable spot for the *mikveh*.

In the fall of 1941, the Rebbe's condition worsened, and he was barely able to leave his bed. His remaining days were few. His doctors ordered him not to fast on Yom Kippur but, of course, he did. All day he lay in bed and, unexpectedly, joined the congregation for *Ne'ilah*, praying with an intensity that shocked all those who knew his true condition.

On *motza'ei Shabbos, Parashas Toldos*, the Rebbe lay upstairs in his sick bed while, in the *beis midrash* below, the shul's Board of Directors met to discuss communal affairs. The Rebbe sent a message asking them to establish a free-loan society (*gemach*) and offered to make the first contribution. The board approved, and today that *gemach* is one of the largest in Williamsburg.

That same *motza'ei Shabbos* his son, Reb Levi Yitzchok, attended an engagement party for a fellow student at Yeshivas Torah Vodaath. He asked his father for an appropriate *dvar Torah*, in case he was asked to speak. Reb Pinchas Dovid replied:

"In *Berachos, daf* 31, there is an appropriate thought. At the wedding of the son of Ravina, they asked Rav Hamnuna to sing for them. So he sang: 'Woe to us that we must die!' 'What [refrain] should we sing after you?' they asked. 'But the Torah and mitzvos will protect us!' he answered. There you have a ready-made *dvar Torah* to say at the engagement."

It was the Rebbe's last *motza'ei Shabbos*.

The Last Day Thursday, November 29, 1941. A cold winter's day. Outside the Rebbe's room, as at his birth, a dove was perched on the windowsill. It refused to move from its place.

Boston in New York

The Rebbe paced back and forth in his room, lost in thought. When his daughter wondered at his actions, he told her, "Last night, I had a dream. My uncle, Reb Dovid'l Biderman, came and told me, 'Prepare yourself to make *Kiddush* for a *Yom Tov*, but pray the weekday *Ma'ariv*.' I argued with him, 'My prayer should also be that of *Yom Tov*'."

In retrospect, Reb Dovid'l had told the Rebbe to prepare to enter into a world that is all good: "Prepare yourself for a *Yom Tov*," but since he would be buried in America, the closing prayers would be those of a regular (non-holy) weekday. The Rebbe had argued with his uncle. He also wanted his burial to be holy; he wanted to be buried in Eretz Yisrael. In the end, both tzaddikim had their way.

The Final Evening

The days are short in the winter. The Rebbe's sons were at an important community meeting at Yeshivas Torah Vodaath. It was a week before America entered World War II, and they were discussing civil defense. Most regular congregants were still at work, and it seemed unlikely that a *minyan* would gather for *Minchah*. "Don't worry," the Rebbe told his daughter, "people will still show up tonight." He then named several Chassidim from Philadelphia, Boston and elsewhere. "They'll all be here," he said, but his words were mysterious at best.

The Rebbe slowly went downstairs to immerse in the *mikveh* in the basement. Meanwhile, a *minyan* gathered. They prayed *Minchah* and *Ma'ariv*, and then stepped outside to sanctify the new moon. Afterwards, the Rebbe returned to his study and spoke quietly with his Chassidim. He expressed his pain at not having seen his mother for so long, and not being able to fulfill the mitzvah of *kibud eim*. "Who knows if I will ever see her again."

At about 8:30 p.m., the Rebbe suddenly complained that he did not feel well. His family saw that his condition was rapidly deteriorating, and they quickly called Dr. Neuberger, who arrived within minutes. The Rebbe had suffered a major heart attack. Another specialist, Dr. Feller, arrived moments later; but both doctors realized that they were powerless to help. A few minutes later, the Rebbe's son, Reb Levi Yitzchok, arrived home from yeshiva. At 8:55 p.m., on the 8th of Kislev, 5702, Reb Pinchas Dovid Horowitz, the first Bostoner Rebbe, *zt"l*, returned his pure soul to his Maker. He was 65 years old.

The Funeral

Word of the Rebbe's death spread quickly throughout the Jewish communities of the eastern seaboard. Large numbers of his followers from Boston, Providence and Philadelphia boarded trains for New York, among them the individuals the Rebbe had specified to his daughter. The Williamsburg Burial Society immersed his body in a *mikveh* before dressing it in its shrouds. They later testified that he seemed to bend his head into the water and smile.

Newspaper notice of the passing of Reb Pinchas Dovid Horowitz, zt"l, the first Bostoner Rebbe

The next day, a Friday, Williamsburg held one of the largest funeral processions in its history. The Rebbe had ordered that no eulogies were to be recited at his funeral;

thus each of the thousands attending bore his pain silently. His oldest son, Reb Moshe, spoke for them all: "We have become orphans, fatherless."

Although the Rebbe had wanted to be buried in the plot he had purchased on the Mount of Olives in Jerusalem, World War II made that impossible. The family therefore buried him in America, but with a condition. Whenever it became possible, they would bring him back to Eretz Yisrael.

Burial in the Holy Land

Three and a half years later, in 1945, the Rebbe's son, Reb Levi Yitzchok, accompanied the casket on one of the very first ships to travel to Eretz Yisrael after the war. At Haifa, a dockworkers' strike stranded the Rebbe's metal casket on deck in full sunlight for two days. At times it was too hot to touch! Later the casket was loaded into an old van which bumped and banged all over the rough, twisty roads from Haifa to Jerusalem.

On the Mount of Olives, Reb Levi Yitzchok asked the members of the Burial Society to disassemble the casket, using the special method his father had devised years earlier. However, even his cousin, Reb Zusha Brandwein, who had assisted in the burial of the Sosnovitza Rebbe, refused to get involved. The Bostoner Rebbe had passed away over three years earlier; and the casket had been tossed at sea, broiled in the sun and jolted all the way to Jerusalem. The body's sad condition could well be imagined.

When Reb Levi Yitzchok remained adamant, Reb Zusha reluctantly called on the Rebbe's brother, Reb Yehoshua Horowitz, and Reb Mordechai Eisenbach to help him. Disassembling the casket, they were shocked to see that the Rebbe's body was still completely intact, as if he had just passed away. All Jerusalem was amazed at the news of this miracle.

From 1948 until 1967, the Mount of Olives remained in Jordanian hands. The Arabs broke tombstones, desecrated graves, and even paved a road through the middle of the cemetery, right over the graves themselves. The Rebbe's grave was the very last one in the road's path but, in the end, the road missed it by just a few feet. His rest was not to be disturbed.

Yahrtzeit seudah for Reb Pinchas Dovid, zt"l, at Beis Midrash Givat Pinchas, the Bostoner shul in Har Nof, Jerusalem

SEVENTEEN
The Chain Continues

Reb Moshe, the Bostoner Rebbe of New York

With the passing of Reb Pinchas Dovid Horowitz, the first Bostoner Rebbe, his Chassidim turned to his two sons. Reb Levi Yitzchok, still unmarried at the time, declined and the full responsibility fell upon Reb Moshe who, during the Rebbe's last years, had often served as his representative. Reb Moshe frequently spent Shabbos with communities around New York City at his father's request. If he felt strong enough, Reb Pinchas Dovid would later join them for a *melave malka* to raise money for charity; if not, Reb Moshe would take *kvitlach* from the congregation back to his father. He became one of the first Rebbes to succeed his father in America, and thus establish a continuing American Chassidic dynasty.

Reb Moshe continued his father's efforts to expand Yeshivas Torah Vodaath and the local *mikveh*. As a young man, Reb Moshe had supervised the dedication ceremony for the new Torah Vodaath building on south Third Street. Reb Pinchas Dovid had helped raise money for the building and had even accompanied Rabbi Shraga Feivel Mendlowitz and Reb Levi Yitzchok Greenwald, the Tzelemer Rav, on a visit to the wealthy philanthropist Rav Naftali (Henry) Feuerstein. When Rav Feuerstein saw how ill the Rebbe was, he made a particularly generous donation and said, "This is for the pain I put the Bostoner Rebbe through."

Reb Pinchas Dovid's sons, Reb Moshe Horowitz (l.), zt"l, and Reb Levi Yitzchok Horowitz, shlita, carried on their father's tradition in New York City and Boston, respectively.

Soon after becoming Rebbe, Reb Moshe was appointed to the Moetzes Gedolei haTorah (Council of Torah Sages) of the Agudas Yisroel of America. He was also deeply involved in establishing relief projects to help meet both the physical and spiritual needs of the many Jewish refugees from Europe. After several years in Williamsburg, which soon became the new home of the rapidly expanding Satmar dynasty, he moved to Crown Heights, which then had a relatively small Chassidic (mostly Chabad and Bobov) community. There he helped expand Yeshivas Darchei Noam, which soon had hundreds of students — and equally spiraling expenses.

With his typical *mesiras nefesh* for Torah education, Reb Moshe poured increasing amounts of his effort and personal savings into this noble but doomed venture, exertions which eventually led to his first heart attack. He then moved to 56th Street in Boro Park, where he hoped there would be less pressure. Soon his sensitivity and astuteness in helping people handle difficult problems led to another flourishing *beis midrash*.

The Chain Continues

A deeply beloved leader of his many Chassidim, Reb Moshe passed away in New York City on the 14th of Sivan 5745 (1985). He was succeeded by his sons, Reb Chaim Avraham Horowitz, *shlita*, and Reb Pinchas Dovid Horowitz, *shlita*, who continued his traditions in New York.

Reb Levi Yitzchok, the Bostoner Rebbe of Boston

Reb Pinchas Dovid's younger son, Reb Levi Yitzchok, an outstanding student at Yeshivas Torah Vodaath, received his rabbinical ordination in 1944, one of the few students to receive "*Yoreh Yoreh, Yoden Yoden*" from the Rosh Yeshiva, Rabbi Shlomo Heiman, *zt"l*.

At the age of 21, he married Raichel Ungar, the daughter of Rabbi Naftali Ungar of Neimark, Poland (who was murdered by the Nazis in 1942) *hy"d*. Reb Naftali was the son of Reb Yehudah Unger, the *Av Beis Din* of Sokolov in Galicia, who was a descendant of the Kozhnitzer Maggid. On her mother's side, Rebbetzin Raichel was a descendent of Reb Naftali of Ropshitz and Reb Shmuel Shmelke of Nikolsburg. Literally thousands of well-wishers attended their wedding.

Soon thereafter, the Jews of Boston asked Reb Levi Yitzchok to re-establish Bostoner Chassidus in Boston, living in the house they had purchased for his father, in the new Jewish neighborhood of Dorchester.

Reb Levi Yitzchok was twenty-three when he moved to Boston, and the remaining disciples of his father were very few and, mostly, very old. Like his predecessors, including his own father, he had to build his own community almost from scratch. He succeeded, nonetheless, and then — again like his father — he reached out beyond his own community to draw Boston's large Jewish student population back to the path of Torah.

Healing Body and Soul

Boston is famous for its colleges: Harvard, MIT, Boston University, Brandeis. Of its 150,000 students, about 20 percent — approximately 30,000 — are Jews, most largely ignorant of their spiritual roots. Reb Levi Yitzchok spoke to them about Judaism in the terms of *Chazal*, but also in terms they understood. Philosophy, psychology and logic all became vessels for conveying the light and fire of Chassidus. Students were drawn to the Rebbe's genuine warmth, sense of humor and uncanny ability to answer their deepest questions. They came to him alone and in groups, in tailored suits and dungarees, with crew cuts and ponytails, with backpacks and briefcases. But beneath it all were pure Jewish souls searching for their Father in Heaven.

The Rebbe arranged special Shabbatons for hundreds of students, six to eight times each year, in addition to the regular flow of guests at his Shabbos table each week. They accepted his invitations, heard his teachings and could "taste and see that it was good." Many changed their entire lives, built true Jewish homes, and became active members of Boston's growing Chassidic community. The Rebbe soon became a pioneer in the nascent *ba'al teshuvah* movement. Even a local Jewish college journal, *Genesis 2*, wrote, "What draws all these young people to a Chassidic synagogue?"

Students came during the week to speak privately with the Rebbe and to ask his advice. A Harvard professor who had fallen into depression found a new zest for life; a Christian minister had told a young woman to be proud of her Judaism and she wanted to know what it was all about; a young man from Long Island came to break his long addiction to drugs — no two cases were alike. The Rebbe was a father to them all.

The Chassidic dynasties of Lelov and Boston were famous for their concern for the physical welfare of the Jewish

The Chain Continues

people, and here too, the Rebbe did his utmost. About forty years ago, the Chazon Ish advised an Israeli patient to contact the Bostoner Rebbe, and many others followed. Patients from around the world come for advanced treatment at Boston's many famous hospitals. Among them are Jews from Israel and Europe, lonely and confused, with no place to stay and, often, without enough money for treatment. The Rebbe advises them, helps arrange their treatment and makes them feel at home. Like his father, the Rebbe has a vast knowledge of medical detail, often advising uncertain doctors how to proceed.

As needs grew, the Rebbe established the ROFEH (Reaching Out Furnishing Emergency Healthcare) organization to help provide counseling and support. He even purchased a special building where patients and their families could recuperate after their operations and, for shorter visits, provided thirteen rooms in the New England Chassidic Center itself.

The success of the Rebbe's ROFEH medical outreach program led to the purchase of ROFEH House, near the New England Chassidic Center in Brookline, Massachusetts.

Boston Spreads

Although Reb Pinchas Dovid's persistent attempts to return to Jerusalem had ended unsuccessfully, Reb Levi Yitzchok realized his father's dream, building a permanent *beis midrash* and Bostoner community in the Har Nof section of Jerusalem. He called his shul Givat Pinchas, after the neighborhood his father had planned so many years before. The community and its related institutions have grown and the

Rebbe now spends part of each year in Jerusalem. There he is a member of the Moetzes Gedolei haTorah of the Agudas Yisroel of Israel. His warm association with all leaders of Orthodox Jewry often allows him to act as a mediator between Israel's differing religious factions.

Besides weekday lectures and Shabbos *tisches*, the *beis midrash* also hosts the Boston Kollel, where *bnei Torah* and those returning to Jewish practice can learn together, without first relegating the latter to special yeshivos. Downstairs a Boston-run Talmud Torah provides the neighborhood's children with a traditional Jewish education. ROFEH also has a branch in Har Nof which serves the Jerusalem community and often works in tandem with the main branch in Boston.

In 1992, the Bostoner Rebbe spoke at the laying of the foundation stone for a new religious neighborhood, Shuafat (Ramat Shlomo), in northern Jerusalem, adjacent to the plot that his father, Reb Pinchas Dovid, had purchased for Givat Pinchas. In emotional tones, he spoke of the fulfillment of his father's dream. Now, finally, thousands of Orthodox Jews would be moving into the community envisioned by his father over fifty years before.

Boston – New York

Bostoner Chassidus continues to spread. Reb Chaim Avraham Horowitz, *shlita*, the elder son of Reb Moshe Horowitz, *zt"l*, the Bostoner Rebbe of New York, expanded the Boro Park *beis midrash*, established Kollel Hafla'ah, and more recently established a Bostoner community in Ramat Beit Shemesh, Israel. He also inherited both his father's gift for music (writing many original Chassidic *niggunim*) and his tradition of showing a warm personal concern for all. Now spending much of his time in Eretz Yisrael, he appointed his oldest son as the

The Chain Continues

Bostoner Rebbe of Lawrence, New York, initiating the fourth generation of Bostoner leadership.

Reb Moshe's younger son, Reb Pinchas Dovid, *shlita*, became the founder and Rosh Yeshiva of the new Darchei Noam Yeshiva in the Flatbush section of Brooklyn, New York. Unlike its unfortunate namesake, the new yeshiva prospered, and its many students and friends soon started families of their own. After years of seeking his guidance in all aspects of life, his followers eventually convinced him to become the Bostoner Rebbe of Flatbush.

The previous Gerer Rebbe, the Beis Yisroel, zt"l, and the current Bostoner Rebbe of Boston, shlita, at the wedding of the latter's nephew, Reb Pinchas Dovid, the Bostoner Rebbe of Flatbush

Reb Yaakov Thumim

Rebbetzin Matil Feigeh, Reb Pinchas Dovid's younger daughter, married Rabbi Yaakov Thumim, *shlita*, the Altstadter Rav. Born in Vienna, Austria, he was raised by his holy grandfather, Chaim Yitzchok Yerucham, the Rav of Alstadt and one of the leading halachic authorities of his day.

When the Germans invaded Austria, Chaim Yitzchok and his family (including Reb Yaakov) fled to Switzerland, where they were sheltered by the Sternbuch family. The

Swiss government eventually placed them in a local refugee camp, where they remained for three years, until the end of the war.

Afterwards, they made their way across Europe and boarded the *Nova Mar*, a cargo ship with accommodations for only twelve individuals. On its infamous 1941 voyage to America, the overloaded ship carried 1200 refugees! Many passengers died from the unspeakably crowded, unsanitary conditions.

Once in Williamsburg, Reb Yaakov entered Yeshivas Torah Vodaath where he eventually became a well-loved rosh yeshivah. He also served as the Rabbi of the Ahavas Yisroel Synagogue in Williamsburg and now he heads the Altstadter congregation in Boro Park.

Never Extinguished

Some 150 years ago, Reb Yisroel of Ruzhin had told Reb Moshe Lelover, "I bless you that your light will never be extinguished." The Ruzhiner's blessing was fulfilled through Reb Elazar Menachem Mendel, Reb Dovid'l Biderman, Reb Pinchas Dovid Horowitz, and their many descendants.

The kever of Reb Dovid'l Biderman, zt"l, on the Mount of Olives in Jerusalem

Reb Dovid'l Biderman, *zt"l*, passed away in 1918, shortly after receiving Reb Pinchas Dovid's report that he had arrived safely in America. He was succeeded by his eldest son, Reb Shimon Noson Nota (Shimeleh) Biderman, who

The Chain Continues

was born in Tzefas in 1870. Since his father's following was more personal than dynastic, Reb Shimeleh felt free to leave Jerusalem for Poland. There he established his own flourishing Lelover court in Krakow, returning to Eretz Yisrael seven years later. Like his father, he also remained very close to the Karliner Rebbe and Chassidim of his day. Their family's history was recorded in *Tiferes Beis Dovid* and Reb Dovid'l's Torah insights were preserved in *Likutei Divrei Dovid*.

Several recent Lelover leaders, each of whom founded his own communities and institutions in Eretz Yisrael

Reb Shimeleh's eldest son, Reb Moshe Mordechai, joined his father in Poland in 1920, and later returned with him to Eretz Yisrael. After his father's passing in 1929, he established a formal Lelover Chassidic court in Jerusalem, Tel Aviv and then Bnei Brak. Known for his holy and often hidden ways, he was the author of the *Kedushas Mordechai*. While continuing to head the Lelover dynasty, he acceded to the requests of a prominent group of Karliner Chassidim to lead them as well, thus founding the Pinsk-Karlin community. He passed away in 1987.

His son, Reb Shimon Noson Nota, continued to lead both Lelov and Pinsk-Karliner communities, while his brothers Reb Avraham Shlomo and Reb Alter Elazar, and other relatives, also established Lelover communities, *battei midrash*, *kollelim*, *chadarim* and other institutions in Jerusalem and Bnei Brak. A respected Torah scholar and author of *Har Bashan*, Reb Shimon established his own *beis midrash* in Bnei Brak. In 1990 he turned over the leadership of Pinsk-Karlin to Reb Aharon Rosenfeld, *zt"l*.

The Unending Chain

The children and grandchildren of Reb Levi Yitzchok Horowitz, the Bostoner Rebbe of Boston, *shlita*, and his recently departed Rebbetzin, Raichel, *a"h*, have become prominent Rebbeim and Rebbetzins. The Rebbe's son, Reb Pinchas Dovid, heads Congregation Kahal Yeraim of Chust; and his son, Reb Moshe Shimon Horowitz, is the Rav of the Bostoner community in Beitar, near Jerusalem.

Reb Levi Yitzchok's second son, Reb Meir Alter, is Rav of the Bostoner community in Har Nof and its associated institutions such as the Boston Cheder, Yeshiva and Kollel.

The *bachurim* and *avreichim* of the community have organized themselves into a particularly active and tight network of *chaburos*, serving members from age ten to twenty, and beyond. The Rebbe's third son, Reb Naftali Yehudah, is the Rav of the Bostoner community in Boston and its associated institutions, such as ROFEH and several Bostoner educational institutions and college outreach programs.

The Chain Continues

Reb Levi Yitzchok's two sons-in-law are Rabbi Yosef Chaim Frankel, the Rebbe of Vielapola and Rav of Congregation Bnei Shlomo Zalman in Brooklyn, and Rabbi Moshe Chaim Geldzahler, a *dayan* and Rav of Congregation Beis Shlomo d'Boston in Har Nof.

So the chain of love, warmth and Chassidic fire continues, from Lyzhansk to Lublin, from Lelov and Nikolsburg to Boston, from Poland to America to Eretz Yisrael to wherever Jews are found. "The house of tzaddikim will stand," says the verse, until the coming of our righteous *Mashiach*, speedily in our days.

The holy light of Chassidus continues to warm and inspire. Here, the Bostoner Rebbe of Boston, Reb Levi Yitzchok Horowitz, shlita, recites Hallel on one of the middle days (Chol haMoed) of Sukkos.

Genealogy

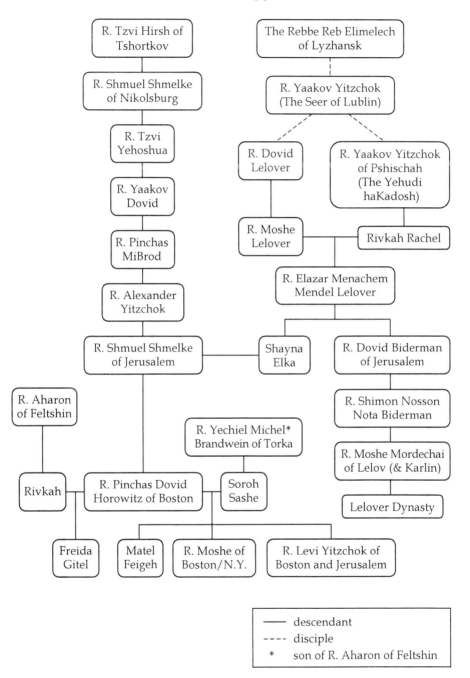

Acknowledgments

THIS BOOK WAS BASED ON *Shalsheles Boston*, researched and written by Meir Valach, and published in Hebrew by Mosdos Boston (Jerusalem, 1994). It was translated into English by Eliezer Shore, and then adapted for publication, with additions, by Dr. I. M. Asher. Thanks are also due to Mr. and Mrs. Moshe Adam for their editorial assistance, and to Mrs. Batsheva Geffen for typing the many subsequent drafts.

Feldheim Publishers' editors and graphic artists have once again displayed the sensitivity and attention to detail that have made them so justly famous. Their devotion to quality and the highest printing standards deserve both our admiration and deepest appreciation. We also wish to thank Ben Gasner and his talented staff for the outstanding cover.

Particular thanks are due to Grand Rabbi Levi Yitzchok Horowitz, the Bostoner Rebbe of Boston and Har Nof, *shlita*, for his unceasing effort, encouragement and support, without which this attempt to capture some of the history, depth and flavor of Polish Chassidus on three continents would not have been possible.

Selected Sources

Chapter One
Divrei Emes
Zos Zicharon
Zicharon Zos
Neta Sha'ashuim

Chapter Two
Migdal Dovid

Chapter Three
Migdal Dovid
Ohel Yitzchok

Chapter Four
Likutei Divrei Dovid
Migdal Dovid
Pri Kodesh Hilulim
Siach Sarfei Kodesh

Chapter Five
Tiferes haYehudi
Sichos Chaim
Migdal Dovid
Pri Kodesh Hilulim

Chapter Six
Pri Kodesh Hilulim
Ohel Yitzchok

Chapter Seven
Pri Kodesh Hilulim

Chapter Nine
Tiferes Beis Dovid
Moshe Eved Hashem

Chapter Ten
Shemen haTov
Beis Pinchas

Chapter Eleven
Shemen haTov
Zos Zicharon
Yetiv Ponim
Divrei Shmuel

Chapters Twelve – Seventeen
Horowitz family oral traditions

Glossary

The following glossary provides a partial explanation of some of the Hebrew, Yiddish (Y.), and Aramaic (A.) words and phrases used in this book. The spellings and explanations reflect the way the specific word is used herein. Often, there are alternative spellings and meanings for the words.

ACHARONIM: classic Torah scholars active from the time of the Shulchan Aruch onwards.

AHAVAS YISRAEL: lit., "love of Israel," that is, of one's fellow Jew.

ALEPH-BEIS: the Hebrew alphabet; the first two letters of the alphabet.

ALIYAH: the honor of being called up for the reading of a Torah portion.

ARBA'AS HAMINIM: lit., the "Four Species": the lulav, citron, myrtle branches, and willow branches bound together and used on Sukkos.

ARIZAL: "the Ari, of blessed memory," R. Yitzchok ben Shlomo Luria, the great sage and kabbalist.

ARON KODESH: the cabinet in the front of the synagogue in which the Torah scrolls are kept.

AVREICH: a young married man (usually in kollel).

BA'AL TESHUVAH: a formerly non-observant Jew who becomes religiously observant.

A CHASSIDIC JOURNEY

BACHUR: an unmarried young man of yeshiva age.

BAR MITZVAH: the celebration of a boy's reaching the age of 13, when he is obligated to fulfill the mitzvos.

BARAYSA: (A.) traditional teachings not included in the Mishnah, but often discussed in the Gemara.

BEIS DIN: court.

BEIS MIDRASH: lit., "house of study," the study hall of a yeshiva or synagogue.

BENTCH: (Y.) to recite the Grace after Meals.

BERACHAH: a blessing.

BIMAH: the reader's desk in the synagogue.

BNEI TORAH: religiously observant men, especially those with a solid yeshiva education.

BOR: the compartment of a mikveh which stores the rainwater.

BRIS: the ceremony of circumcision.

CHALAV YISRAEL: milk supervised by a Jew from the milking onward.

CHALITZAH: the ceremony which breaks the Levirite bond between a childless widow and her brother-in-law (*Devarim* 25: 5-9).

CHALUKAH: a boy's first haircut, at age 3.

CHAS V'SHALOM: "Heaven forbid!"

CHASSID: a follower of a Chassidic Rebbe (pl. Chassidim).

CHASSIDUS: Chassidism, a Jewish religious movement started by Reb Yisroel Ba'al Shem Tov in the late eighteenth century.

CHAVRUSA: (A.) a Torah study partner.

CHAZAL: a Hebrew acronym for "our Sages of blessed memory."

CHEDER: (Y.) a primary school for little boys.

CHESSED: loving-kindness; compassion.

CHEVRAH KADDISHA: (A.) the burial society.

CHOLENT: a savory Sabbath stew kept warm overnight and eaten during the day on Shabbos.

Glossary

CHOZEH: a seer.

CHUPPAH: the marriage canopy.

CHUTZPAH: nerve; arrogance.

DAF YOMI: the program for learning one folio page of Talmud each day.

DAVEN: (Y.) pray.

DAYAN: a judge.

DEVEIKUS: attachment to the Divine.

DVAR TORAH: a short presentation of a Torah thought.

ERETZ YISRAEL: the Land of Israel.

ERUV: an (often minimal) enclosure that converts a large area into a "private domain" for the purpose of carrying on Shabbos.

GABBAI TZEDAKAH: a collector and distributor of charity.

GALUS: exile.

GARTEL: (Y.) a long woven sash worn around the waist during prayer.

GEMACH: a charitable association.

GEMARA: commentary on the Mishnah; together they comprise the Talmud.

GEMATRIA: the numerical value of a Hebrew word (assigning specific numbers to each letter).

GET: a bill of divorce.

GIVAH: a hill.

GOY: a non-Jew (pl. goyim).

GUT SHABBOS: (Y.) "Have a good Sabbath!"

HAKAFOS: joyous circular processions with Torah scrolls on Simchas Torah.

HALACHAH: Jewish law.

HASHEM: lit., "The Name"; circumlocution for "G-d."

HASHGACHAH: religious supervision (especially for kashrus); Divine Providence.

HASKALAH: lit., "Enlightenment"; the European movement that sought to destroy traditional religious Jewish observance and replace it with concepts and behavior more acceptable to non-Jewish society.

HASMADAH: diligence in Torah study.

HEKDESH: something set aside for a holy purpose.

ILUI: a child prodigy; a genius.

KABBALAH: lit., accepted traditions; Jewish mysticism.

KAVANOS: intent; the mystical intentions and secrets hidden in the prayers and mitzvos.

KIBUD EIM: the mitzvah of honoring one's mother.

KIDDUSH: the special benediction said over wine on Shabbos.

KIDDUSH HASHEM: lit., "sanctification of the Name"; behavior that raises public appreciation of Hashem.

KIKAR: a public square.

KODESH: holy.

KOHEN: a man of the priestly caste, descended from Aharon.

KOL KOREH: a proclamation.

KOLLEL: a post-yeshiva academy of advanced Torah study for married men.

KOSEL: the Western Wall of the Temple Mount in Jerusalem.

KOSHER: ritually fit.

KVITEL: (Y.) a small note handed to a Rebbe, containing the petitioner's name, mother's name and request.

L'CHAIM: lit., "To life!"; traditional Jewish toast.

LEVI: a descendant of the tribe of Levi.

LI'SHMAH: for its own sake, without ulterior motives.

LULAV: palm frond used on Sukkos.

MAMZER: offspring of an adulterous or incestuous union.

MASHGIACH: religious supervisor, especially for kashrus.

MASKILIM: proponents and activists of the Haskalah.

Glossary

MASSIG GVUL: lit., "removing the boundary"; improperly infringing on someone else's livelihood.

MATZAH: flat unleavened bread (eaten on Pesach).

MAZAL TOV: Good luck! Congratulations.

MECHUTAN: the father of one's daughter-in-law or son-in-law.

MELAVE MALKA: meal after Shabbos to "escort" the holy day out.

MESADER KIDDUSHIN: officiating Rabbi at a wedding.

MESIRAS NEFESH: lit., "giving over one's life"; complete devotion.

MEZUZAH: a small scroll containing verses from *Devarim* affixed to the doorpost (see *Devarim* 6:9).

MIDOS: character traits.

MIDRASH: nonlegal teachings from the Oral Tradition.

MIKVEH: a pool for ritual immersion.

MINYAN: quorum of ten Jews needed for communal prayer (pl. minyanim).

MISHLOACH MANOS: gifts of food given on Purim.

MISHNAH: classic authoritative compilation of traditional Jewish laws, the foundation of the Talmud.

MISNAGDIM: the religious opponents of Chassidus.

MITZVAH: a Torah commandment; a righteous deed (pl. mitzvos).

MOSDOS: institutions.

NEVEILAH: an animal improperly slaughtered, or which died of natural causes.

NIGGUN: a melody (pl. niggunim).

NUSACH: order of prayer (the two main textual traditions are Nusach Sefard and Nusach Ashkenaz).

PARASHAH: the weekly reading from the Torah.

PIDYON: ransom.

PIDYON NEFESH: lit., "soul-ransom"; charity given by a Chassid to a Rebbe upon making a request.

PILPUL: a complicated, in-depth analysis of Talmudic issues.

POSKIM: Rabbis specializing in deciding issues of Jewish law.

PSHAT: the straightforward explanation.

RASHA: a wicked person.

REBBE: (Y.) a Chassidic rabbi and leader.

REBBETZIN: (Y.) the wife of a Rebbe.

RISHONIM: the classic Torah scholars who lived between the eras of the Talmud and the Shulchan Aruch.

ROSH: head, leader.

RUACH HAKODESH: lit., "the holy spirit"; a lower degree of prophecy.

SHA'ATNEZ: a forbidden mixture of wool and linen (see *Devarim* 22:11).

SHABBOS: the holy Sabbath (Friday night and Saturday).

SHALIACH TZIBUR: one who leads the communal prayers.

SHALOM: peace, a traditional greeting.

SHECHINAH: the Divine Presence.

SHEMURAH: lit., "guarded"; referring to matzos or flour under constant meticulous supervision.

SHEVA BERACHOS: the seven blessings recited at a wedding and at celebrations held throughout the following week.

SHIRAS HAYAM: the Song at the Sea (*Shemos* 15:1-18).

SHIUR: a Torah lecture.

SHLITA: an acronym for *"sh'yichyeh l'orech yamim tovim, amen —* May he live long and good days, amen."

SHEMONEH ESREH: lit., "eighteen"; the eighteen Rabbinically ordained benedictions, which form the core of each prayer service.

SHOCHET: a ritual slaughterer (pl. shochtim).

SHOFAR: a ram's horn (blown on Rosh Hashanah).

SHOMER SHABBOS: one who keeps the laws forbidding work on Shabbos.

SHUL: a synagogue.

Glossary

SHULCHAN ARUCH: the Code of Jewish Law, compiled by Rabbi Yosef Karo (completed 1555 C.E.).

SIMCHAS TORAH: the joyous holiday which immediately follows Sukkos.

SUGYAH: (A.) a topic, particularly give-and-take argumentation in the Gemara.

SUKKAH: a temporary booth which Jews build and live in on the Festival of Sukkos.

TAHARAH: purity.

TALLIS: the fringed garment worn during prayer.

TALMID CHACHAM: a Torah scholar.

TALMUD: the basic corpus of Jewish law (200 B.C.E.–500 C.E.), consisting of the Mishnah and Gemara.

TASHLICH: special prayers recited by a river or other body of water on Rosh Hashanah afternoon.

TEFACH: a handbreath (pl. tefachim).

TEFILLIN: small leather boxes containing Torah passages written on parchment, and worn during weekday prayers.

TEFILLOS: prayers (sing. Tefillah).

TEHILLIM: [the Book of] Psalms.

TESHUVAH: repentance; spiritual return.

TISCH: (Y.) lit., "table"; a Chassidic gathering at the Rebbe's meal.

TISHAH B'AV: the fast on the Ninth of Av commemorating the destruction of both Temples.

TORAH: the Five Books of Moses; more broadly, the whole corpus of authentic Jewish tradition.

TREIF: non-kosher.

TZADDIK: a saintly person (fem. tzadekes; pl. tzaddikim).

TZEDAKAH: charity.

TZITZIS: knotted strings (fringes) attached to the corners of the tallis.

YAHRTZEIT: (Y.) the anniversary of the passing of a loved one.

YERUSHALAYIM: Jerusalem.

YICHUS: lineage, especially distinguished descent.

YID: (Y.) a Jew.

YISHUV: settlement; "the Old Yishuv" was the old European Jewish community of Eretz Yisrael, dating back to the late 1700s and the 1800s.

Z"TL: a Hebrew acronym for *"Zecher tzaddik livrachah* — May the memory of the righteous be blessed."

ZOHAR: the classical Jewish mystical text, written by Rabbi Shimon Bar Yochai.